Numa Gremling

Leaflet Cookbook

Recipes for Creating Dynamic Web Maps

loca✛e
PRESS

Credits & Copyright

Leaflet Cookbook

Recipes for Creating Dynamic Web Maps

by Numa Gremling

Published by Locate Press LLC

Editor   Gary Sherman
Interior Design   Based on Tufte -LATEXdocument class
Publisher Website http://locatepress.com
Book Website http://locatepress.com/lcb

Contents

Foreword

Leaflet is among the leading JavaScript libraries for creating interactive maps. From the beginning, it was not about developing a framework that can do everything. Leaflet focuses on getting the basics to work perfectly and meeting the needs of the vast majority of developers. A wide array of third-party plug-ins provide additional capabilities. Leaflet comes with excellent documentation of the API and easy to read source code.

Easier and leaner than many comparable libraries, Leaflet is a good choice for almost all web mapping requirements.

The author of *Leaflet Cookbook* is a proven expert who has been using Leaflet in numerous projects and has extensive practical experience.

Numa is an active FOSS4G member and open source developer. He has conducted numerous Leaflet training sessions and taught over 500 students in using Leaflet. His background and experience has given him a unique knowledge which is reflected in this book.

The book is primarily aimed at Leaflet beginners, who are quickly able to create their own web mapping solutions based on numerous practical examples.

The later chapters also cover more complex functions of Leaflet, offering new opportunities to active Leaflet users.

All in all, the book is absolutely a rewarding introduction to Leaflet!

Martin Dresen
CEO geoSYS
Germany

1 *Introduction*

Contents

Welcome to the world of Leaflet! This chapter will introduce you to some basics, such as the cookbook concept, how to read this book, and what prerequisites you'll need.

1.1 What You Should Already Know

Leaflet is a web mapping library, and that means that you should at least know how to create simple web pages using HTML and CSS. You don't need to have advanced skills, though. Most applications created in this book actually use very little HTML and CSS and the template created at the very beginning of the next chapter can be used throughout the book.

You should also have at least a basic knowledge of JavaScript, as using Leaflet really means one thing: *writing JavaScript*. Here again, you don't need to be a pro! If you know what strings, floats, variables, loops, and functions are, then you most likely know enough to complete every single recipe in this book.

If you are still insecure about your JavaScript skills, then let me tell you that you will not master JavaScript from tutorials or by reading books, but by using it to reach your goals. Trying to create interesting web maps with Leaflet, for example, is a perfect opportunity to boost your skills and to figure out how JavaScript really works.

1.2   How to Read This Book

Have you ever used a cookbook to cook one of your favorite dishes?
You probably have, and if not, you still know what a cookbook is
and how to use it. A programming cookbook might differ in a few
ways but the general idea is exactly the same: you look at the table
of contents, find a recipe of a dish that looks good to you, and then
you start cooking. If you followed the recipe carefully your result
will be a success—if not, you might end up with something ranging
from "interesting" to "total failure." Maybe you diverged on purpose
and got exactly what you wanted from the beginning, making it a
total success after all. Similarly, you don't have to take the exact
same approach I take to get results. There are multiple ways to do
just about anything in programming—especially if you have some
experience or have been using Leaflet for a little bit, you might do
certain things differently, and that's OK!

This being a cookbook means, of course, that you don't have to read
this book in a linear way. In fact, you could read the last chapter
first and still be satisfied. Pick whatever looks most appealing to
you and get started.

So, how does this Leaflet cookbook differ from a regular cookbook?
First, almost every single recipe in this book uses the same ingredi-
ents: HTML, CSS, JavaScript, and Leaflet. Don't worry about having
to go shopping first or having to constantly acquire new skills. With
just a few basics you are good to go.

What might be unusual, at least for a programming cookbook, is the
second chapter of this book. Most programming cookbooks assume
you are familiar with the topic already and jump straight to the
recipes. This book is a little different. To begin, I'd like to address
those who are entirely new to Leaflet, i.e. those who don't know
how to create the most basic web map. If you worked with Leaflet
before, you can most likely skip the entire chapter, but you might

want to give it a quick glance, just to see if you might have missed something after all.

That's it—the second chapter is an introduction to Leaflet and the remaining chapters are classic cookbook chapters.

1.3 Code and Sample Data

Almost all recipes in this book come with one or more code files and each code file is named using the chapter and recipe number. Glancing at the number of recipes, you'll realize there must be a lot of code files. While writing the book, the only way to keep track was by naming them using their recipe number.

Each file, therefore, uses the following naming convention:

`recipe_chapterNumber_recipeNumber.html`

For instance, recipe 4.6 *Adding a Scale Bar to the Map*, is the sixth recipe in chapter four.

Therefore the file is named:

`recipe_4_6.html`

Often there are multiple code files for the same recipe, such as when optional parameters or alternative solutions are explained. These versions are then numbered as they appear chronologically in the text, such as:

`recipe_4_6_2.html, recipe_4_6_3.html`, etc.

All of the code files can be downloaded from `http://locatepress.com/leaflet_cookbook/leaflet_cookbook.zip`

Each chapter has its own directory and if sample data is used it will also contain a folder named `data`.

You'll notice that the code snippets that accompany the text are annotated with seemingly random numbers. These numbers are not random at all and simply correspond to the lines in the code file. They are a great help when looking for a short section in a much larger code file.

If the code snippet does not contain any line numbers, you'll not find it in a file. Such snippets are used for dummy code and very short examples that don't warrant a separate code file.

1.4   Separating HTML, CSS, JavaScript

If you are a web developer you know it's good practice to strictly separate the three main languages used in your web application by saving each one in its own file or files (.html, .css, .js). Not only is your application more manageable but adjusting it also becomes more flexible.

In this book, however, you will almost always find these three components in one single .html file.

The main reason for this is that most recipes are actually rather short, and it is much easier for you to look in a single place to find a recipe's code than having to open three files, especially if these files consist of only one or two lines.

When creating your own application, particularly as they become larger, you should think about strictly separating HTML, CSS, and JavaScript.

1.5   Picking a Text Editor or an IDE

All you really need to create applications with Leaflet is a simple text editor. The default text editor that comes with your operating system, however, might be just a little too simple, so you should look at an editor that includes useful functionalities or features, such as syntax highlighting. Here are a few free editors you can explore:

- Atom

- Brackets
- Notepad++
- Visual Studio Code

The only thing you should really avoid is using any complex word processors that you might otherwise use on a daily basis (e.g. Microsoft Word) as writing code is actually quite different from writing any other kind of text. The formatting applied to text in a word processor will cause issues running any application you write.

For writing code you need a plain-text editor

So what about an IDE (integrated development environment)? If you are an experienced programmer or have been in the field for a little while you most likely have a favorite IDE already, so no need to give you advice. If you're from the opposite side of the spectrum (i.e. you are a beginner), then you should, in my opinion, avoid using an IDE.

Here's my reasoning: IDEs come with extremely useful tools, but often these tools are difficult to comprehend for beginners. Often the mere setup of a project can be daunting. This not only makes everything seem much more complicated than it actually is, but it will also make you feel insecure. It can be a huge let down—after all, we just wanted to create a nice map.

Are IDEs bad? Not at all—I use one on a daily basis, and I could not imagine or enjoy programming without one anymore.

One big plus when using an IDE is that it can warn you early on when you make mistakes, and often suggest solutions. When getting started with programming or web mapping, however, making mistakes is essential and an important part of the learning process. I have introduced a great number of people to programming (JavaScript, Python) and GIS and web mapping libraries (Leaflet, OpenLayers, PyQGIS—and some proprietary libraries I dare not mention here) and I know that some of the most interesting discussions that have arisen in my classes were a direct result of a mistake that would not have been made had we used a full-fledged IDE.

Long story short, you can use whatever you want to try out what you learn in this book, but I warmly recommend that you don't let yourself be held up with anything but Leaflet logic.

1.6 Software Used In This Book

Below you will find a list of software used in this book. Does that mean you need to install all of them before you get started? Absolutely not. Most of these applications are used in a single or, at most, a handful of recipes and the vast majority of the recipes in this book can be completed using Leaflet only. In other words, installing or using any of these is completely optional. There is a high chance that the recipes you are interested in don't require any additional software. So, it is best to only install an application once you encounter a recipe that requires the software to complete it. Although, quite frankly, some of these packages are important players in GIS or web mapping and it cannot hurt to explore them.

All software used in this book is free and open source. With a few exceptions, this book will not guide you through installing software as the installation is mostly straight forward.

Apache Cordova / Adobe Phonegap

Apache Cordova is a framework that lets you create mobile applications that can be installed natively on Android, iOS, and Windows. The great thing about it is that it does not require you to learn programming languages and APIs that natively run on these operating systems. In fact, you write a normal web application (i.e, HTML, CSS, JavaScript) and Cordova packages that application so it can be installed on a smartphone. Adobe bought the company that created Cordova and then renamed the product to PhoneGap but later released an open source version named Apache Cordova. The naming can be confusing and both names are often used interchangeably. Although there are minute differences, you don't have to worry about them.

`https://cordova.apache.org/`

GeoServer

Server software to publish OGC compliant geospatial services (e.g. WMS, WFS).
`http://geoserver.org/`

jQuery

jQuery is a popular library that makes working with JavaScript much easier and therefore also lessens the time you spend writing code. In this book we use pure and plain JavaScript as much as possible, as not everyone might use the same libraries or frameworks when it comes to actual development. jQuery is only used in the few cases where we need to form AJAX requests, which are cumbersome to write in pure JavaScript.
`https://jquery.com/`

Leaflet

The one software you actually need. More information to follow over the next 300 pages.
`https://leafletjs.com/`

MBUtil

MBUtil is used to export data from the MBTiles format to a structure that web maps can directly read. Running MBUtil requires a Python installation, but you don't need to have any Python knowledge whatsoever to run it.
`https://github.com/mapbox/mbutil`
`https://www.python.org/`

PostgreSQL / PostGIS

PostgreSQL, most often referred to as Postgres, is a database management system that supports a multitude of data types and functionalities. The PostGIS extension adds spatial support to PostgreSQL, meaning that you can efficiently store spatial data and run spatial analysis.
`https://www.postgresql.org/`
`https://postgis.net/`

QGIS

QGIS is the most advanced open source geographic information system (GIS). It can read and write most vector and raster data formats and includes a wide range of tools, from classic spatial algorithms to advanced cartography. Its flexibility is increased by a plugin ecosystem that makes it easily extendable.
`https://qgis.org/`

TileMill

TileMill lets you design maps using CartoCSS, a stylesheet language that resembles CSS. Using TileMill you can create and export your own basemaps to the MBTiles format.
`https://tilemill-project.github.io/tilemill/`

Turf.js

Turf.js is a JavaScript library that brings spatial analysis and geoprocessing to the browser.
`http://turfjs.org/`

XAMPP

Getting a web server up and running with the right software and versions can be an arduous task. You might not want to go through the process just to test or learn something new. This is where XAMPP comes in. XAMPP is a package that groups some commonly combined software and programming languages to set up a server-side infrastructure. It includes an Apache web server, the MariaDB database management system, and the programming languages PHP and PERL. Within a few minutes you can get started developing web applications by never having to set up a web server. Note that XAMPP should be used for the development and testing of applications, but not as a live, production system. Since most web servers use a similar configuration, the transition from XAMPP to a production system is easy.
`https://www.apachefriends.org`

1.7   Setting Up Your Environment

The great thing about Leaflet is you don't need to install a lot of components to get started. As you will learn in the next chapter, using Leaflet comes down to downloading the source code and including it in an HTML file.

Practically any recipe in this book can be tested by simply double-clicking the file and opening it in a browser. Although opening a file this way works in most cases, it might not be the most professional way. What happens is that your browser simply opens a local file, renders its visual components and executes its scripts. This does not mean, however, that the application necessarily behaves or looks like it would if it was hosted on a web server. Ideally you test any application by running it from a web server. Since you might not have access to a web server or the skills to set one up you could download and install XAMPP, which provides you with a complete setup that resembles an actual web server:

```
https://www.apachefriends.org
```

Once installed, the xampp directory on your computer includes a directory called htdocs in which you can create further directories. Each directory reflects a web application. So, if you get started on a new project you would first create a directory. Once the development and testing processes are completed you can simply upload that folder to a server.

Let's create a folder called leafletcookbook and create a new file leafletMap.html inside that folder. If you double-click this file the browser will show its absolute path on your machine, such as:

```
file:///C:/xampp/htdocs/leafletcookbook/leafletMap.html
```

Although this file is now stored on a web server we still opened it locally, which completely defeats the purpose. To truly open this file via the built-in Apache web server you need to replace the part of the path leading up to your application's folder with localhost:

Note that by simply calling the directory you will be shown an overview of the files it contains. If your directory contains a file called index.html. It will be opened automatically. Therefore the main page of a web application is often called index.html.

```
http://localhost/leafletcookbook/leafletMap.html
```

If your browser tells you that the page cannot be reached or the connection failed, then you most likely forgot to start the actual web server. In that case start the XAMPP Control Panel, which is installed along with XAMPP, and make sure to start Apache.

Refresh your browser and see that it works. That's it! Now your file is read as if it was stored on an actual web server, which, in fact, is the correct way to run it. After all, the point of creating a web application is to host it on a web server and make it accessible via the web.

Again, almost any example in this book will function by simply double-clicking a file, no matter where that file is stored, so you don't necessarily need to worry about installing XAMPP. When working with databases, web services, and AJAX requests, however, examples often don't work, unless they are run from a server.

1.8   Browser And Developer Tools

It's probably not necessary to mention that you need a browser to run the web applications you write, but you might first want to check whether your browser is supported.

Leaflet supports the following browsers:

Desktop

- Google Chrome
- Firefox
- Safari 5+
- Opera 12+
- Internet Explorer 7–11

Mobile

- Safari for iOS 7+
- Android browser 2.2+, 3.1+, 4+

- Google Chrome for mobile
- Firefox for mobile
- Internet Explorer 10+ for Win8 devices

Notice that all current major browsers are supported. Unless you are using an outdated version your browser should already be on the list—no need to update.

Of course there are some browsers that are faster or more efficient than others, or to be frank: simply more appealing than others. One deciding factor when developing web applications is the availability of developer tools. Most modern browsers come with a set of tools that greatly assist you with the development process. Personally, I prefer Google Chrome's developer tools and I will be using that browser throughout the book. That doesn't mean you need to use it too, but be aware that screenshots of the developer tools shown in this book might look different from the ones you are using.

In this book the developer tools will be referred to as "the developer console", "the browser's console" or simply "the console". In many recipes the console plays an essential part, as it makes it possible to inspect elements, log results, or test commands. In most browsers you can press F12 to open the console, but you can also open it from a menu.

2 Getting Started

Contents

This chapter will introduce you to Leaflet. We'll start with the absolute basics, such as downloading and including Leaflet, and then we will create our very first map. Since most recipes include a map, the template we create in this chapter can be used for almost every single recipe in the book. Unlike the other chapters, this chapter reads more like a tutorial. You'll be guided step by step through creating a map. This differs from other chapters where recipes don't necessarily build upon each other, and you can selectively pick a recipe to achieve a very specific goal.

2.1 Leaflet and Why It Is Awesome

To put it simply, Leaflet is a JavaScript library that lets you create interactive web maps. Using JavaScript commands you assemble a map that can be added to an existing website or function fully on its own. While reading the book you'll learn that Leaflet has many faces and the final application you create can look different from what other people create.

Leaflet is not the only web mapping library available, but it has several advantages over others (contributing to its quick gain in popularity), having become one of the most widely-used web mapping libraries.

Let's look at some aspects that make Leaflet stand out.

Free and open source
> Leaflet is free and open source. You can use it for free and not invest a single cent. But most importantly it is open source, which means the source code is public and anyone can look at it. This has several advantages. Not only is the software more transparent, but it also means the code can be tested more thoroughly and bugs can be detected (and fixed) much faster. It also means that anyone with an interest in Leaflet can engage in its development. Take a quick look at the Leaflet GitHub repository and you'll notice there are over 500 contributors:
> `https://github.com/Leaflet/Leaflet`

License
> Leaflet's license allows you to use, change, and redistribute the source code, as long as you include a copyright notice. You can read about the details here:
> `https://github.com/Leaflet/Leaflet/blob/master/LICENSE`

Plugins
> Leaflet can be easily extended with plugins. If the Leaflet core does not include what you are looking for, there is a high chance that someone has developed a plugin that does exactly what you need. You can browse available plugins here:
> `https://leafletjs.com/plugins.html`

Documentation
> Leaflet comes with exemplary documentation. Often open source software are criticized for lacking documentation. This is not the case for Leaflet. Once you know how to read the documentation

it will become your best friend.

Mobile optimization

Leaflet runs smoothly on mobile devices. With the number of mobile devices increasing and responsive design becoming more and more important, it is crucial that your web maps are not the one part of a web page that ends up frustrating users. Leaflet is optimized for mobile devices, which includes the support of touch gestures as well as a slightly adjusted design.

Compact

Leaflet is not a huge package. If you need your web application to be a minimal burden on your users, Leaflet is a good option. Oftentimes all your page needs is a very simple map. It would be unfortunate to send a few megabytes to the client just to render that simple map. Being compact also makes Leaflet ideal for applications that are used on mobile devices: your users will be thankful for every kilobyte they don't have to download.

Easy to learn and use

It's easy to get started with Leaflet because it's easy to learn. You don't need to be a professional JavaScript developer, nor do you need to know a whole lot about web mapping. You'll see in this chapter that creating your very first web map is really not that complicated. Combined with the excellent documentation, you can quickly get to know Leaflet and start building advanced applications.

2.2   Creating an HTML Template

Before we can use Leaflet, we need to write some HTML and CSS to create a minimal web page.

First create a folder and assign it a name that you can remember, such as `myFirstLeafletApplication`. This folder will hold our application and, most importantly, the Leaflet source code.

If you are using XAMPP, create this folder in htdocs.

Next, start your preferred text editor or IDE and open an empty document.

Let's create a basic page and assign a title to it. We'll assign the title *Template* to it and you can use this template throughout the book:

Listing 2.1: HTML template

```
1  <!DOCTYPE html>
2  <head>
3    <meta charset="UTF-8">
4    <title>Template</title>
5  </head>
6  <body>
7
8  </body>
9  </html>
```

Save the file in your folder and make sure to assign an `.html` extension to it. Let's save it as `leafletMap.html` (fig. 2.1).

Figure 2.1: The HTML file

That's all we need to get started with Leaflet. In the page's **<body>** we'll insert our map, but before we do that, we need to download Leaflet.

Visit `http://leafletjs.com/` and have a look at the Download section (fig. 2.2).

Figure 2.2: Downloading Leaflet

Download Leaflet

Version	Description
Leaflet 1.4.0	Stable version, released on December 30, 2018.
Leaflet 1.3-dev	In-progress version, developed on the master branch.
Leaflet 0.7.7	Legacy version, released on November 18, 2013 and last updated on October 26, 2015.

You'll see there are several different versions available. Since we're just getting started with Leaflet, we'll stick with the stable version.

Go ahead and download Leaflet by clicking the link.

Apart from downloading Leaflet you can also use a *CDN* (Content Delivery Network) or npm.

Optional: using a CDN

Scrolling down a little, we see that a hosted version of Leaflet is also available on a CDN (fig. 2.3).

Using a Hosted Version of Leaflet

Figure 2.3: Downloading Leaflet

The latest stable Leaflet release is available on several CDN's — to start using it straight away, place this in the head of your HTML code:

```
<link rel="stylesheet" href="https://unpkg.com/leaflet@1.4.0/dist/leaflet.css" />
<script src="https://unpkg.com/leaflet@1.4.0/dist/leaflet.js"></script>
```

Optional: Installing Leaflet Using npm

We can also use the npm package manager to install Leaflet with the following command:

The npm package manager: https://www.npmjs.com/

```
npm install leaflet
```

Version

Note that the most recent version at the time of writing was 1.4.0. This version has been used throughout the book and might include features that older version don't have. If you inherited an application that uses an older version, some recipes in the book might not work for you.

To find out what version you are using, type *L.version;* in your browser's console (fig. 2.4, on the next page):

Figure 2.4: Getting the current version

2.3 Source Code and the Difference Between leaflet.js and leaflet-src.js

Copy the downloaded ZIP file into your folder and unzip it. This leaves you with a new folder: `leaflet`.

This folder holds the entire source code of Leaflet as shown in figure 2.5.

Figure 2.5: Contents of the leaflet folder

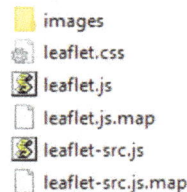

Here's what the folders and files contain:

images

Holds images used in Leaflet, such as the standard blue marker icon that is used when we add a marker to our map.

leaflet.css

The styling that Leaflet uses. This, for example, is necessary so that Leaflet can position a layer control or the attribution correctly. This file is important or things would end up looking very strange. We don't need to do anything with it, other than include it in our application—Leaflet takes care of the rest.

leaflet.js

This file contains the JavaScript that makes up Leaflet. Except for the styling rules in `leaflet.css`, Leaflet is mostly JavaScript. As soon as `leaflet.js` is included in the application we can start using Leaflet commands.

leaflet-src.js

Go ahead and open `leaflet.js` and `leaflet-src.js` in your text editor. One of them looks unusual at first, the other does not. In reality they include the same code, and it doesn't matter which one you add to your application. `leaflet.js` is minified, meaning its content has been compressed so that the file is much smaller. `leaflet-src.js` includes the code as it was written by Leaflet developers. If you want to modify the source code then you would make edits to `leaflet-src.js`. If you are only interested in using Leaflet, then you should avoid using `leaflet-src.js`, for the simple reason that it is larger, and you always want users of your application to have to download files that are as small as possible.

2.4 Including Leaflet

Let's include Leaflet in our application.

We only need to include two files, the CSS and the JavaScript:

Listing 2.2: Including Leaflet

```
3   <head>
4     <meta charset="UTF-8">
5     <title>Template</title>
6     <link rel="stylesheet" href="../leaflet/leaflet.css" />
7     <script src="../leaflet/leaflet.js"></script>
8   </head>
```

Very important: always load the CSS file before the JavaScript file. Some classes defined in the CSS file are used in the JavaScript code and these need to be available before JavaScript can use them. Loading the CSS file after the JavaScript file would be equivalent to not loading the CSS at all.

> A note about paths. If you are working with the downloaded code files you'll notice that Leaflet is stored directly in the code files folder whereas each chapter is stored in an extra folder. Therefore the above code snippet includes Leaflet by jumping up one directory (using ../). If you unzipped Leaflet next to your HTML template then the paths are `leaflet/leaflet.css` and `leaflet/leaflet.js`

Open the application in your browser and open the developer console to check if Leaflet was included correctly.

Refresh the page. If there is an error message Leaflet was not included correctly. If you followed the preceding steps carefully this is almost always linked to a typo and results in the path to Leaflet not being found. If no error message appears we can assume that Leaflet is ready to be used.

If you want to make extra sure then go ahead and type L. Figure 2.6 shows the case where Leaflet was not included correctly, while figure 2.7 shows it loaded and available.

Figure 2.6: Leaflet was not included correctly

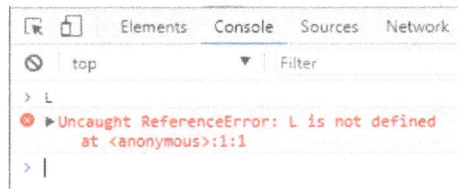

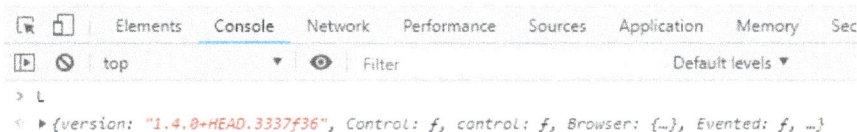

Figure 2.7: Leaflet is available

L is the global variable that represents Leaflet. L, or Leaflet for that matter, is simply an object. Any Leaflet command will therefore be called from L using dot notation, such as: `L.method(...)`;

You can see that through the letter L you can now access a number of methods (fig. 2.8, on the next page):

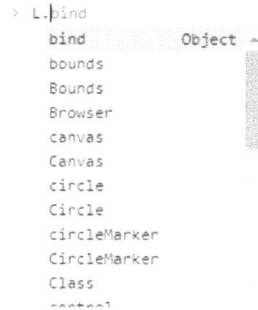

Figure 2.8: The variable L

Everything in Leaflet will be accomplished by calling different methods from L, which is representative for Leaflet.

Now that we know how to download and include Leaflet we can create our first map.

Alternative: Using a CDN

If you want to use a CDN instead of downloading and extracting Leaflet you can simply copy the **<link>** and **<script>** tags from the Leaflet website and paste them into your **<head>** section:

Listing 2.3: Including Leaflet using a CDN

```
3   <head>
4     <meta charset="UTF-8">
5     <title>Template</title>
6     <link rel="stylesheet" href="https://unpkg.com/leaflet@1.4.0/dist/
          leaflet.css" />
7     <script src="https://unpkg.com/leaflet@1.4.0/dist/leaflet.js"></
          script>
8   </head>
```

This is great if you quickly want to test something, but remember that in that case Leaflet's source code is hosted on a server that you don't control. Should the server be down or the version be updated there is a chance that your application will break. Therefore, if you develop applications and software that are going to be publicly available and you want to guarantee stability and avoid sudden bugs it's good practice to use the downloaded version instead of the CDN.

2.5   Creating a Map

HTML provides a variety of elements (table, list, paragraph, etc.), but doesn't have an element to create a map. To display our map, we need to use an existing element to which JavaScript will then add the map. That element is often referred to as the *map container* and is always a **<div>**.

Let's create a **<div>** in our page's **<body>** and assign an ID to it:

Listing 2.4: Adding the map-div

```
18      <div id="mapDIV"></div>
```

Leaflet does not automatically assign a height to our **<div>**, so we need to provide it. If we don't assign a height, our **<div>** will be zero pixels high and we'll never see the map, although it is technically there.

In the **<head>** we create a **<style>** tag and assign a width, a height and a border to our map. Only the height is needed, but we assign the other properties nevertheless. We assign a border so we can see the container before we add a map to it. The border is optional, but it helps to better understand what we are trying to achieve, or in other words, to see where our map will be displayed.

Listing 2.5: Styling the map-div

```
8       <style>
9         #mapDIV {
10          height: 700px;
11          width: 700px;
12          border: solid 1px black;
13        }
14      </style>
```

After refreshing the page we see that the empty container is now visible.

Let's now add a map to that container.

A map always needs two things:

- A center (where it is opened)
- A zoom level (how many times the map zooms in when first displayed)

The map command in Leaflet is quite simple. The only required parameter is the **<div>** the map should be rendered in. Anything else is optional.

```
L.map('mapDIV', {options});
```

We'll open the map around Glacier National Park in Montana, USA (latitude: 48.6238, longitude: -113.7661) and we will zoom in 9 times. Because we almost always want to work with the map after creating it we assign it to a variable. We'll call that variable myMap.

Now let's create our first map by assigning it to the **<div>** and giving it the coordinates and zoom level of Glacier National Park.

Listing 2.6: Creating the map
```
22    var myMap = L.map('mapDIV', {
23      center: [48.6238, -113.7661],
24      zoom: 9
25    });
```

Refresh the page and see that our map has been created (fig. 2.9):

Figure 2.9: The map

This might not be what you expected. It is important to know that creating a map in Leaflet actually means creating a map container without a basemap. Leaflet is very flexible when it comes to what is actually shown in the container and so it does not load a default basemap. In fact, a basemap is optional—we could show vector data without ever showing a basemap. This is comparable to any desktop GIS, which also does not require the loading of a basemap to show spatial data. In our case, we haven't added any data so the container is empty.

Note that you can also pass the element directly, instead of its ID:

```
22    var myMap = L.map(document.getElementById('mapDIV'), {
23      center: [48.6238, -113.7661],
24      zoom: 9
25    });
```

2.6   Adding a Basemap to the Map

After the code that creates the map, add the following to create a basemap that displays OpenStreetMap tiles:

```
27  var basemap = L.tileLayer('http://{s}.tile.osm.org/{z}/{x}/{y}.png',
        {
28  attribution: '&copy; <a href="http://osm.org/copyright">OpenStreetMap
        </a> contributors'
29  });
30
31  basemap.addTo(myMap);
```

The basemap now appears and we see that we truly are in Montana (fig. 2.10, on the next page).

2.7   Adding Basemaps from Different Providers

Basemaps are served as tiles and Leaflet can load any basemap as long as it understands the tiling scheme. Luckily this is standard-ized and most basemaps are served in the same way. The Leaflet providers repository on GitHub lists a variety of basemaps that are free to use:

```
https://github.com/leaflet-extras/leaflet-providers
```

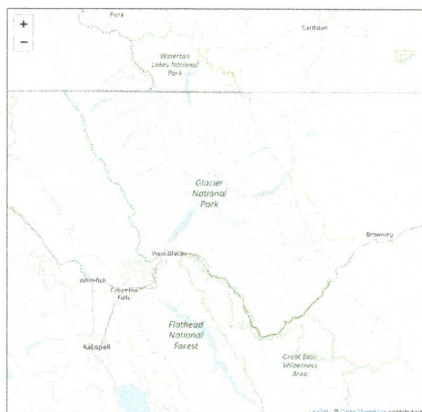

Figure 2.10: The map with a basemap

The demo page makes it easy for you to find a basemap:

`https://leaflet-extras.github.io/leaflet-providers/preview/`

All you have to do is copy the code of the selected basemap and paste it into your Leaflet application.

For instance, if you want to include Hydda.Base you select it in the right-hand panel and copy the code that appears in the box (fig. 2.11):

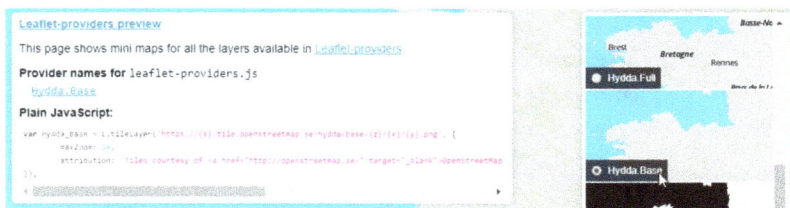

Figure 2.11: Leaflet-providers

The code that appears in the box is similar to the one in the last recipe, but since we are accessing a different provider the URL is different. The sample code even creates the variable for you, so it comes down to a matter of pasting the code into your application and adding the variable to your map:

```
Hydda_Base.addTo(myMap);
```

Note that you can add multiple basemaps to the map and switch between these basemaps using a layer control (have a look at recipe 4.8, on page 73). In the previous example we created a basemap and immediately added it to the map. When defining multiple basemaps, be careful to only add one of them to the map. It would be nonsensical to add more than one, as basemaps take up the entire map container. Although Leaflet would load all basemaps, only the one that was last added to the map would be shown, but when zooming or dragging the map, all loaded layers would request tiles. You should avoid this by adding all subsequent basemaps to the layer control, but not to the map.

2.8   Naming Variables

The way you name variables is of utmost importance. It's important to name them in a way that makes the most sense to you and also facilitates working with the application.

You noticed we called the variable holding the map myMap and the div mapDIV. Often the variable and div are simply called map, which can be confusing to beginners, as the word map exists three times, once for each of the following elements: the variable, the Leaflet command, and the div:

```
var map = L.map('map', { ...
```

Although this is not an issue to the browser as it can distinguish between the three, it can pose problems to those new to web mapping or web development. Once you have gained some experience, you'll most likely end up calling both the variable and the div map as well.

Note that in the following chapters the variable and the div will be called map.

2.9 Reading the Leaflet Documentation

Leaflet has excellent documentation. Once you've learned the basics of Leaflet, the documentation becomes essential to you and you'll consult it often. Although the book covers a lot of possibilities offered by Leaflet, it can't cover every minute detail, so the documentation is a great way to get to know Leaflet even better. Most often you'll open the documentation to look something up that you can't fully remember. Rather than browsing the book or code snippets and applications that you have previously written, the documentation often is your first choice when it comes to seeking quick help.

Leaflet documentation: `https://leafletjs.com/reference-1.3.4.html`

Let's have a look at the documentation, because once you know how to read it, it becomes extremely useful.

As an example we are going to look at the marker (`L.marker`), which you'll learn much more about in the chapters that follow.

Most elements in the documentation are described in at least some of the following categories: Usage example, Creation, Options, Events, and Methods.

The usage example in its most simple form tells you how to *instantiate* an element. Often you can simply copy this snippet and paste it into an application. Once you get to know Leaflet, take advantage of the examples—they can save you time and no need to reinvent the wheel (fig. 2.12).

Instantiate: to create an instance of an object in object-oriented programming

Usage example

Figure 2.12: A usage example

```
L.marker([50.5, 30.5]).addTo(map);
```

Everything you can create in Leaflet has a block in the documentation called Creation. Here you learn what is required to correctly instantiate an element (fig. 2.13, on the next page):

Notice for `L.marker` it says:

Creation

Factory	Description
L.marker(<LatLng> latlng, <Marker options> options?)	Instantiates a Marker object given a geographical point and optionally an options object.

```
L.marker(<LatLng> latlng, <Marker options> options?)
```

Parameters that can be or need to be passed to instantiate an element are always comma-separated. In this case a marker accepts two parameters: *latlng* and *options*. To find out what that truly means you can click on the link to the left of the parameter's name. Once you click <LatLng> you are taken to the part of the documentation that describes how to enter coordinates in Leaflet. The second parameter *options* is followed by a question mark. The question mark indicates that this parameter is optional, meaning that you don't necessarily have to enter it to instantiate the element. Leaflet has plenty of optional parameters, many that will become essential to you. Optional parameters in Leaflet are always entered as a JavaScript object, which consists of key-value pairs:

```
{
        option1: content,
        option2: content,
        option3: content
}
```

To learn what optional parameters can be entered you can look at the Options block (fig. 2.14, on the facing page):

Apart from the description, the table shows an option's name, type, and default value. The presence of a default value indicates that options are automatically added to an element when instantiating it, without explicitly stating them. This is convenient and you only need to look into these options if the defaults don't suit you.

The only thing tricky about options is they can be inherited. If you are not used to looking at documentation you might overlook

Options

Figure 2.14: optional parameters

Option	Type	Default	Description
icon	Icon	*	Icon instance to use for rendering the marker. See icon documentation for details on how to customize the marker icon. If not specified, a common instance of L.Icon.Default is used.
keyboard	Boolean	true	Whether the marker can be tabbed to with a keyboard and clicked by pressing enter.
title	String	''	Text for the browser tooltip that appear on marker hover (no tooltip by default).
alt	String	''	Text for the alt attribute of the icon

inherited options, even though they might be essential to achieve your goals.

You see that L.marker inherits options from Interactive layer and Layer and that their descriptions hide in a collapsible page element. Inherited simply means that an object can use options that are defined by its parent object(s). Instead of writing the same blocks of code multiple times, Leaflet has been developed in a modular fashion, meaning that some properties are defined once, but then "passed on" to other elements (fig. 2.15).

▶ Options inherited from Interactive layer

▶ Options inherited from Layer

Figure 2.15: inherited options

If you keep scrolling down you often bump into blocks called Events and Methods. There are a lot of recipes in the book dedicated to events and methods, so no need to dive into these topics now—just know that many of the concepts explained in the book can also be found in the official documentation.

2.10   Understanding Coordinate Systems in Leaflet

Unlike a desktop GIS that might support hundreds of coordinate systems, web mapping usually works with a very limited set of coordinate systems.

For more information about EPSG have a look at http://www.epsg.org, http://www.epsg-registry.org and http://epsg.io

By default, only two coordinate systems are used in Leaflet: WGS 84 (EPSG:4326) and Web Mercator (EPSG:3857).

As a user, all you really have to worry about is WGS 84, because every coordinate you enter in Leaflet is in WGS 84, or in other words: latitude and longitude.

Web Mercator is sometimes also called Pseudo-Mercator, Spherical Mercator, or Google Projection. Because the naming of coordinate systems can differ it is important that you always go by the EPSG code, not the name.

The map, however, is displayed in Web Mercator. Any value you enter in WGS 84 is converted on the fly to Web Mercator by Leaflet and then plotted on the map. You can ignore the specifics of Web Mercator and never have to bother about entering coordinates in Web Mercator, as Leaflet does this for you. You should only enter coordinates in WGS 84 and every dataset you add to the map should be in WGS 84. See figures 2.16 and 2.17, on the next page for a comparison of the two coordinate systems.

Figure 2.16: A world map displayed in WGS 84 (EPSG:4326)

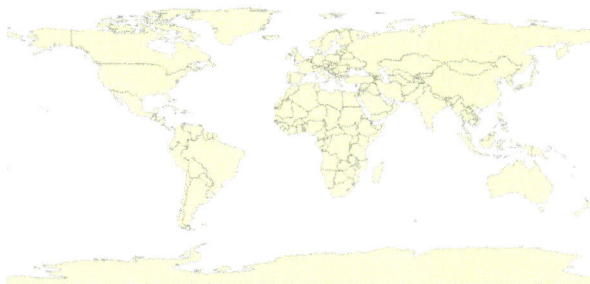

2.11   Working with Coordinates in Leaflet

As we said, all coordinates that are entered or extracted in Leaflet are displayed in WGS 84. The values always represent latitude and longitude, which are displayed as decimal degrees. If your data does not explicitly mention latitude or longitude but x and y you

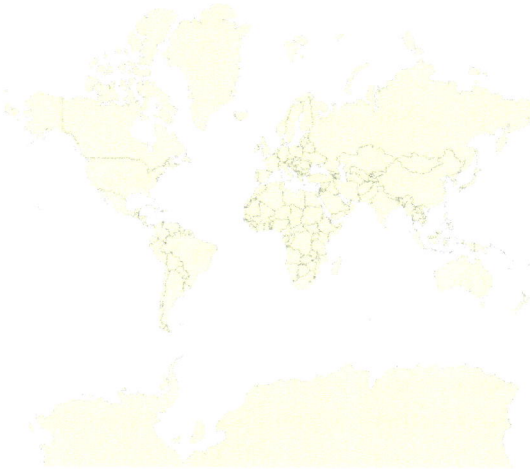

Figure 2.17: A world map displayed in Web Mercator (EPSG:3857)

should know that the x value represents longitude and the y value represents latitude.

Attention: x = longitude, y = latitude

Latitude specifies how far north or south a coordinate is and longitude specifies how far east or west a coordinate is. But north, south, east, west of what?

As a reference point the equator and the Greenwich meridian are used. Have a look at the following image (fig. 2.18):

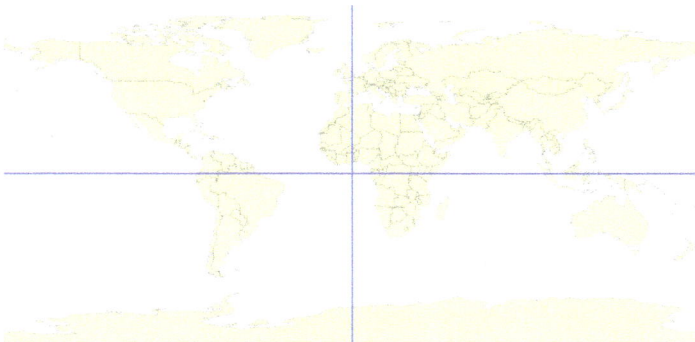

Figure 2.18: Greenwich Meridian (vertical line) and Equator (horizontal line)

Looking at this image we can derive the four cardinal directions:

- North: above the equator
- South: below the equator
- East: right of the prime meridian
- West: left of the prime meridian

A point east of the prime meridian is in the eastern hemisphere, and a point west of the prime meridian is in the western hemisphere, just like a point north of the equator is in the northern hemisphere and a point south of the equator is in the southern hemisphere.

To plot a point on a map you always need two values: the value specifying whether the point is north or south (latitude) and the value specifying whether the point is east or west (longitude). Only if you have that information can you add a point to the map.

The latitude value is always between -90 and 90 and the longitude value is always between -180 and 180—any value you enter in Leaflet has to be within these bounds.

Looking at the value you can conclude the following about its position:

- negative latitude value: southern hemisphere
- positive latitude value: northern hemisphere
- negative longitude value: western hemisphere
- positive longitude value: eastern hemisphere

You can transform spatial data using the GDAL and OGR utilities: http://gdal.org. See also https://locatepress.com/gpt for a great resource.

Should you find or be given coordinates that are higher or lower than these numbers, then you are looking at a mistake, or more likely, values in another coordinate system. These values are not necessarily wrong, but they are useless to Leaflet and you would have to transform them to WGS 84 first.

Let's look at two examples: Berlin and New York City.

Berlin is roughly 52 degrees north of the equator and 13 degrees east of the Greenwich meridian. So, Berlin's latitude is 52 and longitude is 13.

New York City is roughly 40 degrees north of the Equator and 73 degrees west of the Greenwich meridian. So, New York City's latitude is 40 and its longitude is -73.

Plotted on a map, the points would appear as shown in figure 2.19.

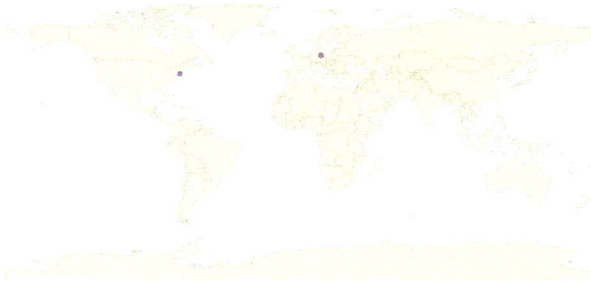

Figure 2.19: Berlin and New York City

Although this looks fine at first, if you zoomed in you would notice that both points are not entirely in Berlin or in New York City.

Depending on the scale the map is going to be used at, it's important not to use rough estimates, but exact coordinates.

Generally, the more decimal places a number has the more exact. For instance, if you use five decimal places, your accuracy is about a meter and if you use six decimal places it is about ten centimeters. In most cases five decimal places is entirely sufficient, and any more decimal places can almost always be omitted, as the user of the map would not even be able to distinguish the differences. Note that some tools, including Leaflet, often return a lot of decimal places. This has to do, not with accuracy, but with how numbers are handled internally. You can ignore this unless you plan on displaying the returned values to the user. In that case it is advised to chop the decimals to a point where they make sense to the average user.

For further detail on decimal places, have a look at this excellent answer on GIS Stack Exchange: `https://gis.stackexchange.com/a/8674/23263`

Considering accuracy, let's find something specific, a landmark, in Berlin and New York City. Berlin's Brandenburg Gate is at latitude 52.51628 and longitude 13.37773 and New York City's Chrysler Building is at latitude 40.75165 and longitude -73.97535.

In Chapter 6 you'll learn how to add points to the map. For now we're just going to look at how coordinates have to be formatted before they are passed to Leaflet.

There are three ways to format coordinates to be used in Leaflet: using L.latLng, using an object, or using an array.

`L.latLng(latitude, longitude)`
    For example: L.latLng(52.51628, 13.37773)
`{lat: latitude, lng: longitude}`
    For example: {lat: 52.51628, lng: 13.37773}
`[latitude, longitude]`
    For example: [52.51628, 13.37773]

Passing the coordinates as a simple array is clearly the easiest way and we will adopt this for the rest of the book, but feel free to do otherwise.

Latitude is specified before longitude!

Longitude is abbreviated to lng.

Methods that return coordinates in Leaflet, most often return them as an object. You'll see an example of this in the recipe Getting a click's coordinates, on page 206. There are two things you need to be careful about. First, in Leaflet latitude is always entered before longitude. This is different from other software that requires longitude before latitude. This also differs from some data formats that you'll encounter in the book, most notably GeoJSON. The second thing you should be aware of is that Leaflet abbreviates longitude to *lng*, and not *lon*.

2.12   Degrees, Minutes, Seconds (DMS) to Decimal Degrees (DD)

When it comes to coordinates, Leaflet solely accepts decimal degree (DD) notation that you have seen so far in this chapter. There are other ways to represent geographic coordinates—for instance, the coordinate pair:

    37.7527, -122.4474

could also be split up into degrees, minutes, and seconds (DMS) and be represented this way:

    37° 45' 9.71" N, 122° 26' 50.64" E

Leaflet, and most GIS software or libraries, don't understand this notation and you should always use decimal degrees instead. Unfortunately, not everyone is aware of this, and sometimes you are given data that is in DMS notation. In that case you can convert DMS to DD using this simple formula:

```
decimal degrees = degrees + minutes / 60 + seconds / 3600
```

Let's write a JavaScript function that accepts DMS and returns DD (fig. 2.20):

```
11    function dmsToDd(d, m, s) {
12
13      var dd = d + (m / 60) + (s / 3600);
14
15      return dd;
16
17    }
```

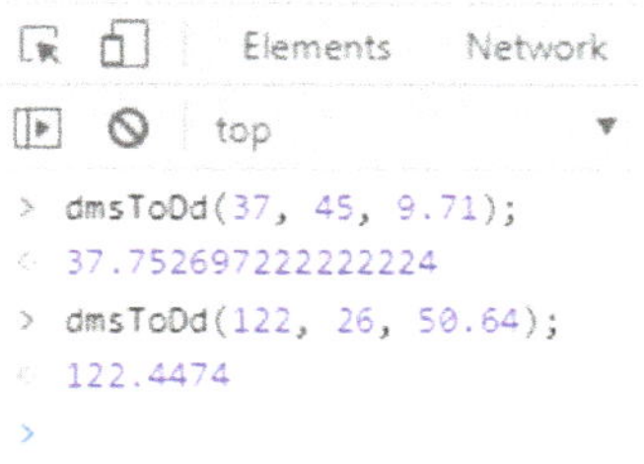

Figure 2.20: Converting DMS to DD

You can also write a function that accepts both latitude and longitude and returns them in a format that can be directly used by Leaflet (fig. 2.21, on the following page):

```
19    function dmsToDdLatLon(dLat, mLat, sLat, dLon, mLon, sLon) {
20
21      var ddLat = dLat + (mLat / 60) + (sLat / 3600);
22      var ddLon = dLon + (mLon / 60) + (sLon / 3600);
23
24      return [ddLat, ddLon];
25
26    }
```

Figure 2.21: Converting DMS to DD
for both latitude and longitude

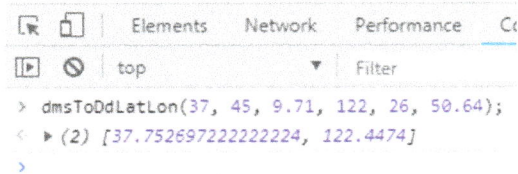

```
⌐ᵣ ☐        Elements    Network    Performance    C(

▷ ⊘   top                ▼  Filter

> dmsToDdLatLon(37, 45, 9.71, 122, 26, 50.64);
< ▶ (2) [37.752697222222224, 122.4474]

>
```

2.13   Limiting Decimal Places

Since Leaflet almost always returns a large number of decimal places,
you might want to chop them when displaying to users of the application. To do this you can use JavaScript's toFixed method. In
the following snippet, the latitude is adjusted to five decimal places:

```
var latitude = 43.46759062609431;

latitude.toFixed(5);

>>> "43.46759"
```

As mentioned in the previous recipe, Leaflet most often returns coordinates as an object. In that case you first access *lat* or *lng* and
then use toFixed:

```
var coordinates = {lat: -18.913208661776835, lng: 47.52996683120728};

coordinates.lat.toFixed(5);

>>> "-18.91320"
```

Note that toFixed returns a string. This is not an issue when displaying coordinates to users but it matters if you want to reuse the
result in calculations.

2.14   Why the Keyword "new" Is Not Used in Leaflet

By now you might have noticed that we have not yet used the keyword new, although we have created instances of classes.

For example, we assigned instances of L.map and L.tileLayer to
variables, but when doing so we did not use new like this:

```
var myMap = new L.map(...);
```

This might differ from other mapping libraries you may have used. Why do we never use new in Leaflet? The answer is actually pretty simple: Leaflet does it for us. In fact, when we instantiate a class we are not doing this directly, but we are calling a function that does it for us, a so-called class factory. Classes in Leaflet always begin with an uppercase letter and their corresponding class factories begin with a lowercase letter.

Did you notice that we only used lowercase commands so far? That's because we did not directly instantiate classes, and instead called their class factory.

Let's look at an example. In the following snippet we create a tile layer, and store it in a variable basemap:

```
var basemap = L.tileLayer(url, options);
```

But what Leaflet really does, is not instantiate the class directly, but executes a method, L.tileLayer, that sends our parameters (*url* and *options*) to the actual instantiation of the class L.TileLayer. In that function the keyword new is finally used and the returned instance of the class is stored in our variable.

```
L.tileLayer = function(url, options) {

    return new L.TileLayer(url, options);

};
```

Long story short: you never have to use the keyword new in Leaflet—and always be sure to use the lowercase notation.

3 The Map

Contents

Now that you know how to create a map and add a basemap to it, you are ready to look at the map more closely. This chapter mainly goes into options that can be specified when creating the map. From zooming animations to restricting the map's extent, there are many options that can influence the behavior and appearance of our map.

3.1 Restricting the Zoom Levels and Extent of the Map

You can use the options *maxZoom, minZoom,* and *maxBounds* to restrict the zoom levels and extent of the map.

The following map's extent is restricted to Wyoming and zooming is limited from 7 to 14.

Listing 3.1: Restricting the map's extent and zoom levels

```
22  var map = L.map('map', {
23    center: [43.5425, -107.9214],
24    zoom: 9,
25    maxBounds: [
26      [40.396, -111.445],
27      [45.996, -103.754]
```

```
28        ],
29        maxZoom: 14,
30        minZoom: 7
31      });
```

In the example, the *maxZoom* option keeps users from zooming to levels greater than 14 and the *minZoom* option keeps them from zooming to levels smaller than 7.

If the user pans the map outside the specified bounding extent (i.e. the *maxBounds*) the map bounces back automatically. The extent is defined using a rectangle which is created by providing two diagonally opposite corners (lower left and upper right).

To gain a better understanding of what this means you can add the bounding extent as a rectangle to the map by adding the following code to your application:

```
39  L.rectangle([[40.396, -111.445], [45.996, -103.754]]).addTo(map);
```

3.2   Box Zooming and Double-click Zooming

By default you can zoom to an area by holding `Shift` and drawing a box and you can zoom in one level at a specific location by double-clicking the map.

You can disable either option by setting *boxZoom* and *doubleClick-Zoom* to `false`.

Listing 3.2: Disabling box zooming and double-click zooming

```
22      var map = L.map('map', {
23        center: [35.9602, -99.2285],
24        zoom: 4,
25        boxZoom: false,
26        doubleClickZoom: false
27      });
```

3.3   Mouse Wheel Zooming

As long as your cursor is inside the map, you can zoom in and out of the map by using the mouse wheel.

To disable mouse wheel zooming, set *scrollWheelZoom* to `false`.

Listing 3.3: Disabling mouse wheel zooming

```
22    var map = L.map('map', {
23      center: [35.9602, -99.2285],
24      zoom: 4,
25      scrollWheelZoom: false
26    });
```

3.4 Zooming to the Center of the Map

When zooming with the mouse, Leaflet zooms in to the cursor's position unless you override this by setting the options *scrollWheel-Zoom* and *doubleClickZoom* to 'center'. This zooms in to the current center of the map, regardless of your cursor position.

Listing 3.4: Enabling center zooming

```
22    var map = L.map('map', {
23      center: [35.9602, -99.2285],
24      zoom: 4,
25      scrollWheelZoom: 'center',
26      doubleClickZoom: 'center'
27    });
```

3.5 Adjusting the Zoom Delta

Two options, *zoomSnap* and *zoomDelta* let you control zooming steps and granularity of zooming.

The *zoomDelta* option defines how much the zoom level changes when zooming. By increasing this number you jump more than one step, as in:

```
22    var map = L.map('map', {
23      center: [35.9602, -99.2285],
24      zoom: 4,
25      zoomDelta: 2
26    });
```

or less than a step:

```
24      zoomDelta: 0.25
```

Although we entered 0.25, the map still zooms to a full integer. That is where the *zoomSnap* option comes in. By defining a zoom snap you force the map's zoom level to always be a multiple of the defined number. By default the zoom snap is 1, meaning that you snap to the nearest integer (e.g. 2, 3, 4). To truly zoom a quarter step only, you could assign the same value to both the zoom snap and the zoom delta:

```
25        zoomSnap: 0.25,
26        zoomDelta: 0.25
```

Note that setting the zoom delta does not have an effect for mouse-wheel zooming and only applies to using the zoom control, keyboard zooming and the zoomIn and zoomOut methods.

Also, pay attention to what happens when you define a zoom that cannot be a multiple of the zoom snap:

```
24        zoom: 4,
25        zoomSnap: 3
```

Since the zoom level always needs to be a multiple of the zoom snap, the initial zoom of 4 is ignored and the map opens at 3.

To fully understand how the zoom snap and zoom delta behave you can hook the map up to the zoom event and log zoom levels to the console:

```
32        map.on('zoom', function() {
33
34            console.log(map.getZoom());
35
36        });
```

Adjusting the steps and granularity of zooming comes in handy when using no basemaps and only displaying vector layers which are not tied to specific scales, or when using your own basemaps that use scales other than the standard "full steps".

3.6   Zoom and Fade Animations

Leaflet adds zooming animations for a smoother zooming experience. Disable zoom animations by setting the option *zoomAnimation* to false and notice that zooming suddenly seems more abrupt.

Listing 3.5: Disabling zoom animations

```
22    var map = L.map('map', {
23      center: [35.9602, -99.2285],
24      zoom: 4,
25      zoomAnimation: false
26    });
```

It is also possible to enable zoom animations in general but disable them if zooming exceeds a certain threshold.

Let's look at an example to understand what this means:

Listing 3.6: Setting the zoom animation threshold

```
22    var map = L.map('map', {
23      center: [35.9602, -99.2285],
24      zoom: 4,
25      zoomAnimation: true,
26      zoomAnimationThreshold: 5
27    });
```

Hint: use the setZoom method to jump to a specific zoom level.

In the snippet we set *zoomAnimationThreshold* to 5. If we jump from zoom level 1 to 7 the animation will be skipped as we are zooming in 6 levels, which exceeds the stated threshold. If we zoom from 1 to 4, however, the zooming will be animated as the difference is 3, which is below the threshold.

The fade animation is not about zooming, but about the tiles that are loaded once the zooming is over. By default tiles are not immediately displayed once they are loaded, but they fade into view, from a low to a high opacity. Understanding this effect is best observed when disabling the *fadeAnimation* property by setting it to false:

Listing 3.7: Disabling fade animations

```
22    var map = L.map('map', {
23      center: [35.9602, -99.2285],
24      zoom: 4,
25      fadeAnimation: false
26    });
```

3.7 Adjusting Keyboard Navigation

In addition to letting you zoom and pan with the mouse, Leaflet also allows keyboard navigation. You can zoom in by pressing the

+ key and zoom out by pressing the - key of your keyboard. The map can be moved using the keyboard's arrow keys.

You can disable keyboard navigation by setting the option *keyboard* to `false`.

Listing 3.8: Disabling keyboard navigation

```
22    var map = L.map('map', {
23      center: [35.9602, -99.2285],
24      zoom: 4,
25      keyboard: false
26    });
```

Furthermore, by assigning an integer to the option *keyboardPanDelta*, you can adjust how many pixels the map pans when using the arrow keys. The default keyboard pan delta is 80 pixels.

Listing 3.9: Setting the keyboard pan delta

```
22    var map = L.map('map', {
23      center: [35.9602, -99.2285],
24      zoom: 4,
25      keyboardPanDelta: 320
26    });
```

3.8   Working with Panning Inertia

Panning inertia is another feature that makes moving the map much smoother. When panning the map and then releasing the mouse button or the finger the map pans a little further. Simply set *inertia* to `false` to see how much this effect contributes to the user's experience:

Listing 3.10: Disabling panning inertia

```
22    var map = L.map('map', {
23      center: [35.9602, -99.2285],
24      zoom: 4,
25      inertia: false
26    });
```

Let's look into a few properties that let you adjust how panning inertia behaves.

- *inertiaDeceleration*: the higher the number the quicker the movement slows down (default: 3000)
- *inertiaMaxSpeed*: the maximum number of pixels the map will move by per second after releasing the mouse button (default: Infinity)
- *easeLinearity*: the higher the number the faster the movement gets before abruptly stopping (default: 0.2)

Play with these values and observe different effects. Often you end up with a not-so-user-friendly map with funny effects. What matters is that Leaflet is flexible enough to let you adjust such properties. If the defaults are not exactly what your application requires then you can actually go ahead and change them.

3.9 Waiting Until the Map is Ready

In Leaflet the map is officially ready once it has been assigned a center and a zoom level.

Sometimes it's necessary to wait until the map is ready before you execute the rest of your code. This can be achieved by using the whenReady method:

Listing 3.11: Waiting until the map is ready

```
27    map.whenReady(function() {
28
29       console.log('The map is ready!');
30
31    });
```

You can test this by creating a map without any options and later setting the center and zoom level. As soon as you have set these, the console.log will be returned.

In the following example the map is created without options:

```
22    var map = L.map('map', {});
23
24    map.whenReady(function() {
25
26       console.log('The map is ready!');
27
```

```
28        });
```

Run this example, and in the console execute the following code:

```
map.setView([48.6238, -113.7661], 9);
```

Only after running this code is the console.log method called and the message printed.

Note that waiting until the map is ready is different from using the onload event on the **<body>** or using jQuery's ready method, which simply wait until all DOM elements have been rendered. They listen for your map container to be created but whenReady listens for the actual map inside the container to be assigned a center and a zoom level.

3.10   Destroying the Map

The remove method lets you completely remove the map and all its attached event listeners:

```
map.remove();
```

Note that this method does not remove the map container. It just removes that map you created from the container and gets rid of event listeners attached to it. In other words, it reverts the state of your application to the first part of the recipe Creating a Map, on page 36.

3.11   Completely Disable Zooming

To completely disable zooming you have to set all of the following options to false:

Listing 3.12: Completely disable zooming

```
22    var map = L.map('map', {
23      center: [35.9602, -99.2285],
24      zoom: 4,
25      zoomControl: false,
26      scrollWheelZoom: false,
27      doubleClickZoom: false,
28      boxZoom: false,
```

```
29      keyboard: false
30    });
```

You could also disable zooming by assigning the same value to the *zoom, maxZoom,* and *minZoom* properties. In other words, you load the map at a specific zoom level and don't allow the use of a higher or lower zoom level, thereby locking the map at a specific level.

Listing 3.13: Completely disable zooming by setting the maximum and minimum zoom

```
22    var map = L.map('map', {
23      center: [35.9602, -99.2285],
24      zoom: 4,
25      zoomControl: false,
26      maxZoom: 4,
27      minZoom: 4
28    });
```

3.12   Disabling Antimeridian Wrapping

When zooming out repeatedly, you'll notice that the world is repeated (fig. 3.1):

Figure 3.1: noWrap set to false

Although this is the default in many web mapping applications, you might not like this effect or think it's confusing to users. To make the world show only once, set your tileLayer's *noWrap* property to true (fig. 3.2, on the next page):

```
27  L.tileLayer('http://{s}.tile.osm.org/{z}/{x}/{y}.png', {
28    attribution: '&copy; <a href="http://osm.org/copyright">
          OpenStreetMap</a>\
29      contributors',
```

```
30    noWrap: true
31    }).addTo(map);
```

Figure 3.2: noWrap set to true

4 Map Controls

Contents

There are four controls in Leaflet, each of which, by default, occupies one corner of the map:

- Zoom (top-left)
- Layers (top-right)
- Scale (bottom-left)
- Attribution (bottom-right)

These controls help users interact with the map (Zoom and Layers) or they provide useful information about the map (Scale and Attribution). Each of these controls can be created, added to the map, and removed from the map.

The Zoom and Attribution controls are part of the map by default while the Layers and Scale controls can be added as desired. Figure 4.1, on the following page shows a map with all four controls enabled.

Figure 4.1: A map with all four controls

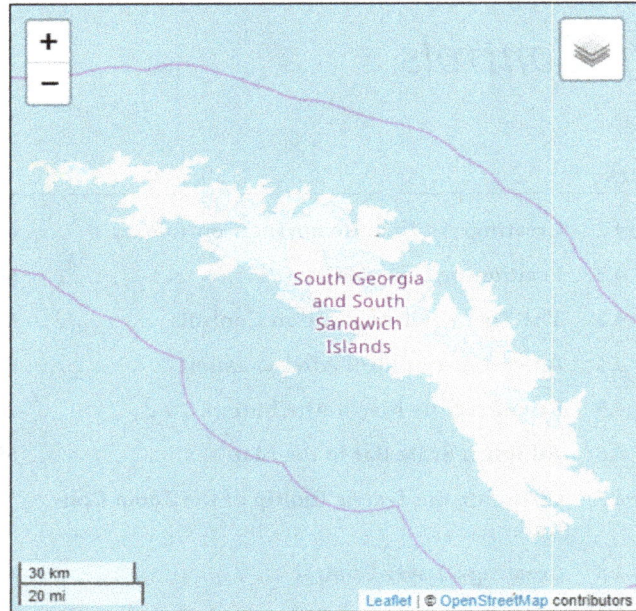

4.1   Creating, Adding, Removing Controls

Each control is created using the following syntax, nameOfTheControl being zoom, attribution, layers, or scale:

```
L.control.nameOfTheControl(options);
```

There are two ways to add and remove controls.

Imagine a variable named control, holding an instance of a control. You can add that control to the map using the control's addTo method:

```
control.addTo(map);
```

Alternatively, controls can be added using the map's addControl method:

```
map.addControl(control);
```

Removing a control can be accomplished using the control's remove method or using the map's `removeControl` method:

```
control.remove();

map.removeControl(control);
```

Note that you cannot add the same control to multiple maps. For example, if your application contains two maps, and each map should have a scale bar, then you cannot simply create one scale bar and add it to both maps. You have to create two scale bars and add each one to its respective map.

4.2 Positioning Controls

Each control can be positioned using the option *position*.

There are four possible positions, always passed as a string:

- topleft
- topright
- bottomleft
- bottomright

As in:

```
L.control.scale({position: 'topright'});
```

You can also get or set the control's position after it has been instantiated, using the methods `getPosition` and `setPosition`.

You can assign multiple controls to the same position. When doing so, the controls will be stacked towards the bottom (when using topleft, topright) or towards the top (when using bottomleft, bottomright). The controls will be stacked in the order they are added to the map, so pay attention to this, as it might result in a map that looks disordered (See figures 4.2, on the next page and 4.3, on the following page).

To position a control by not using any of the four positions have a look at recipe 9.11, on page 182.

Figure 4.2: Controls added in the order attribution, zoom, scale

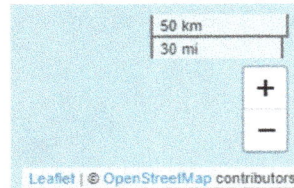

Figure 4.3: Controls added in the order attribution, scale, zoom

4.3   The Zoom and Attribution Controls

The zoom and attribution controls generally do not have to be created as they are part of the map already.

When creating the map, you can keep them from being created by
setting the options *zoomControl* and *attributionControl* to false (fig.
4.4, on the facing page):

Listing 4.1: Removing the zoom and attribution controls

```
22    var map = L.map('map', {
23      center: [36.12200, -5.34734],
24      zoom: 14,
25      zoomControl: false,
26      attributionControl: false
27    });
```

Note that removing the zoom control does not disable zooming—it
simply removes the buttons used to zoom. Mouse zooming and
double-click zooming still work. To disable zooming completely,
see recipe 3.11, on page 60.

By calling the disable method, you can also disable the buttons
without removing them (fig. 4.5, on the facing page):

```
map.zoomControl.disable();
```

Figure 4.4: A map without the default controls

Figure 4.5: A disabled zoom control

Once disabled you can always enable them again:

```
map.zoomControl.enable();
```

4.4   Accessing a Control After Creation

Sometimes you need to access a control after it's been created, either to change its options, position, or maybe even remove it entirely.

If you assigned the control to a variable you can access it through that variable. The two controls that are part of the map by default, zoom and attribution, can be accessed as follows:

```
map.zoomControl;
```

```
map.attributionControl;
```

4.5   Extending the Map's Attribution

There are two ways to extend the map's attribution.

You can add an attribution element using the attribution control's `addAttribution` method, as in:

```
map.attributionControl.addAttribution('United States Geological
    Survey');
```

Useful markup, such as anchor or span tags, can be added to the attribution as well. In the following example, the text will appear in blue (fig. 4.6):

```
map.attributionControl.addAttribution('<span style="color:blue;">
    United States Geological Survey</span>');
```

Figure 4.6: Attribution using a span element

The `addAttribution` method is mainly used to add general information that should always be visible.

Removing a specific element from the attribution control is done via the `removeAttribution` method:

```
map.attributionControl.removeAttribution('United States Geological
    Survey');
```

Note that when removing an element from the attribution, the text has to be specified exactly like it was added. So, if markup was added to the element, this markup must be included when using the `removeAttribution` method:

```
map.attributionControl.removeAttribution('<span style="color:blue;">
    United States Geological Survey</span>');
```

A second way lets you conveniently add attribution to a layer, using the *attribution* property, which is available for every layer in Leaflet. The benefit of using this method is that the attribution is directly tied to a dataset, and is only visible if that dataset is part of the map. For example, if your application contains a layer control, this adds the layer's attribution to the map when checking the layer and removes it again when unchecking it (fig. 4.7).

```
L.geoJSON(data, {attribution:'Géoportail National du Grand-Duché de Luxembourg'});
```

Figure 4.7: Extended attribution

4.6 Adding a Scale Bar to the Map

A scale bar is created using `L.control.scale();`.

Like any control in Leaflet it can be added to the map directly:

```
L.control.scale().addTo(map);
```

Or it can be assigned to a variable before adding it:

Listing 4.2: Adding a scale bar

```
33    var scale = L.control.scale();
34
35    scale.addTo(map);
```

By default the scale bar displays metric and imperal units (fig. 4.8):

Figure 4.8: Scale bar displaying metric and imperial units

Either unit can be disabled by setting it to `false` in the options object:

Listing 4.3: Disabling imperial units

```
33    var scale = L.control.scale({
34      'imperial': false
35    });
```

Listing 4.4: Disabling metric units

```
33    var scale = L.control.scale({
34      'metric': false
35    });
```

The scale bar is constantly updated when moving the map.

To update it only when the user stops moving the map, set the option *updateWhenIdle* to `true`.

Listing 4.5: Update the scale bar while moving

```
33      var scale = L.control.scale({
34        'updateWhenIdle': true
35      });
```

A good way to see this in action is by panning north or south. You will notice that by default the scale bar constantly adjusts. When setting the *updateWhenIdle* to `true` it only adjusts when panning ceases.

4.7   *Changing the Text or Tooltip of the Zoom Control*

By default the zoom control contains a plus sign to zoom in and a minus sign to zoom out. When hovering over either button, the text *Zoom in* and *Zoom out* appears, respectively.

There is no method to change the text or tooltip of the default zoom control, but you can define the text if you create your own zoom control.

A quick way to achieve this is to create the map without the default zoom control by setting the *zoomControl* option to `false` and then create your own zoom control using the options *zoomInText* and *zoomOutText* or *zoomInTitle* and *zoomOutTitle*.

Since the plus and minus symbols used in the zoom control are self-explanatory, there is often no need to change them. Using words, instead of these symbols, for instance, takes up much more room and can be distracting. In most cases, you'll go with the defaults. In addition, the plus and minus signs are often kept, but the text is still adjusted to add **<span>** tags, such as to assign colors to the signs.

Adjusting the title might be used much more frequently.   Think about creating a map that is going to be used by a non-English audience. The plus and minus symbols would still be self-explanatory but the English title might not be understood by everyone. In that case it can be useful to adjust it.

For instance, if you created a map for a German audience you might want to adjust the *zoomInTitle* to hineinzoomen and the *zoomOutTitle* to herauszoomen.

The following example shows a layer control with colored plus and minus signs, and a German text on hover (fig. 4.9):

Listing 4.6: Adjusting the layer control

```
22    var map = L.map('map', {
23      center: [50.97907, 11.32432],
24      zoom: 14,
25      zoomControl: false
26    });
27
28    L.control.zoom({
29      zoomInTitle: 'hineinzoomen',
30      zoomOutTitle: 'herauszoomen',
31      zoomInText: '<span style="color: blue;">+</span>',
32      zoomOutText: '<span style="color: blue;">-</span>',
33    }).addTo(map);
```

Figure 4.9: A styled zoom control

Instead of using a **<span>** you can also use CSS by styling the classes *leaflet-control-zoom-in* and *leaflet-control-zoom-out* (fig. 4.10, on the next page):

Listing 4.7: Changing the color of the zoom button symbols

```
15    .leaflet-control-zoom-in {
16      color: green !important;
17    }
```

```
18
19      .leaflet-control-zoom-out {
20        color: orange !important;
21      }
```

Figure 4.10: A styled zoom control,
using CSS

Apart from adding colors or changing the text you can also add
icons. This can be easily achieved using a library like Glyphicons
or Font Awesome, which include a multitude of icons that can
be assigned to **<span>** elements using CSS classes. Visit `https:
//fontawesome.com` and download Font Awesome. Once down-
loaded, all you need to add to your page's **<head>** is a CSS file:

Listing 4.8: Adding Font Awesome to the application

```
8    <link rel="stylesheet" href="font-awesome/css/font-awesome.css">
```

Font Awesome is used by adding two CSS classes to a **<span>** element. The first class is simply *fa*, stating that Font Awesome will be
used. The second class starts with *fa-* and is followed by the icon
you are going to use. Not every icon, of course, is appropriate in
a zoom control. Let's add a chevron pointing upwards (*fa-chevron-
up*) and chevron pointing downwards (*fa-chevron-down*) to our zoom
control (fig. 4.11):

Listing 4.9: Adding icons to the zoom control

```
29    L.control.zoom({
30      zoomInText: '<span class="fa fa-chevron-up"></span>',
31      zoomOutText: '<span class="fa fa-chevron-down"></span>'
32    }).addTo(map);
```

Figure 4.11: Using Font Awesome in
the zoom control

4.8   Creating a Layer Control

A layer control lets you switch between different layers that have been added to your map.

Two kinds of layers can be added to a layer control: base layers and overlays.

The difference between these two is there can only be one base layer active at a time, but there can be multiple overlays active. Which layers you define as base layers or overlays is entirely up to you, but most often your basemaps are defined as base layers and any other layer is defined as an overlay.

Have a look at figure 4.12:

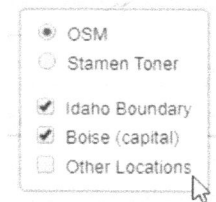

Figure 4.12: A layer control

The upper part of a layer control shows the base layers and the radio buttons indicate that only one base layer can be selected at a time. Luckily, you do not have to worry about any further logic: the layer control is not only a visual element but it also takes care of adding or removing the layers you select or unselect. If you click on Stamen Toner, the OSM map would be removed and the Stamen Toner map would be added.

The bottom part of the layer control lets you switch between overlays. You can check multiple checkboxes and each checked layer is shown on the map.

The layer control accepts two parameters: an object holding the basemaps and an object holding the overlays. The keys in these objects are used to define the text that will be shown in the layer control and the values hold variables assigned to layers. And yes, you can use spaces, special characters, and markup when naming the keys.

```
var basemaps = {
        "name 1 in layer control": basemap1,
        "name 2 in layer control": basemap2
};

var overlays = {
        "name 1 in layer control": overlay1,
        "name 2 in layer control": overlay2
};
```

When creating the layer control these objects are passed as parameters:

```
L.control.layers(basemaps, overlays);
```

Note that base layers are always passed first, and overlays second.

Let's look at a full example.

Listing 4.10: Creating basemaps and overlays to pass to a layer control

```
28    var osmBasemap = L.tileLayer('http://{s}.tile.osm.org/{z}/{x}/{y
             }.png', {
29       attribution: '&copy; <a href="http://osm.org/copyright">
             OpenStreetMap</a>\
30       contributors'
31    }).addTo(map);
32
33    var stamenBasemap = L.tileLayer(
34       'https://stamen-tiles-{s}.a.ssl.fastly.net/toner-background/{z
             }/{x}/{y}.{ext}',
35       {
36       attribution: 'Map tiles by <a href="http://stamen.com">Stamen
             Design</a>,\
37        <a href="http://creativecommons.org/licenses/by/3.0">CC BY
             3.0</a>\
38        &mdash; Map data &copy; <a href="http://www.openstreetmap.org/
             copyright">\
39        OpenStreetMap</a>',
40       subdomains: 'abcd',
41       minZoom: 0,
42       maxZoom: 20,
43       ext: 'png'
44    });
```

```
45
46      // circle marker style
47      var options = {
48        color: 'red',
49        radius: 5,
50        weight: 1
51      };
52
53      // creating a marker for Boise
54      var boise = L.marker([43.62614, -116.32050]);
55
56      // creating circle markers for all other locations
57      var idahoFalls = L.circleMarker([43.47086, -112.04681], options);
58      var ketchum = L.circleMarker([43.68029, -114.36493], options);
59      var cratersOfTheMoon = L.circleMarker([43.24120, -113.52997],
            options);
60
61      // grouping some of the points
62      var otherLocations = L.layerGroup(
63        [idahoFalls, ketchum, cratersOfTheMoon]
64      );
65
66      // adding the boundary GeoJSON to a layer
67      var idahoBoundary = L.geoJSON(idaho, {color: 'green'});
68
69      // add Boise and the Idaho boundary to the map
70      boise.addTo(map);
71      idahoBoundary.addTo(map);
72
73      var basemaps = {
74        "OSM": osmBasemap,
75        "Stamen Toner": stamenBasemap
76      };
77
78      var overlays = {
79        "Idaho Boundary": idahoBoundary,
80        "Boise (capital)": boise,
81        "Other Locations": otherLocations
82      };
```

Note that any layer can be passed to a layer control. In this example the variables osmBasemap (*line 28*) and stamenBasemap (*line 33*) hold instances of L.tileLayer, boise (*line 54*) holds an instance of L.marker, otherLocations (*line 62*) holds an instance of L.layerGroup, and idahoBoundary (*line 67*) holds an instance of L.geoJSON.

To check layers by default, simply add them to the map. Any

layer that has been added to the map using `layer.addTo(map);` or `map.addLayer(layer);` will appear as checked in the layer switcher and any layer that has not been added to the map remains unchecked. To create an empty map where the user has to select layers, create them, but don't add them to the map (fig. 4.13).

Figure 4.13: A layer control with only unchecked layers

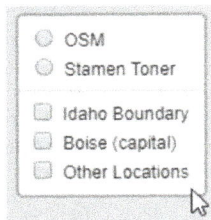

Should you create an application which contained a single or no basemaps at all, you can pass an empty object when defining the base layers, which hides the upper part of the control (fig. 4.14):

```
L.control.layers({}, overlays);
```

Figure 4.14: A layer control without base layers

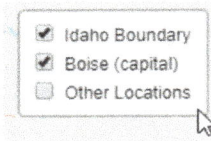

The layer control accepts a third parameter which you can use to specify options. For example, you can set the layer control so it is always expanded. By default it's collapsed and you have to hover your mouse over it to expand it (fig. 4.15):

Figure 4.15: The layer control is collapsed by default

Set the option *collapsed* to `false` to expand the layer control by default:

```
76    L.control.layers(basemaps, overlays, {
77      collapsed: false
78    }).addTo(map);
```

By setting the option *hideSingleBase* to `true`, the upper part of the layer control is hidden when the control contains only one base layer. You might wonder why this option is necessary, since you could just as well pass an empty object as the first parameter. An example where this option comes in handy is an application in which users can add their own basemaps. In that case, it makes sense to only show the base layer buttons once a user has added a layer.

```
67      L.control.layers(basemaps, overlays, {
68          hideSingleBase: true
69      }).addTo(map);
```

4.9   Sorting the Data in a Layer Control

Layers are displayed in the order in which they were added to the layer control.

To sort layers alphabetically, use the option *sortLayers* (fig. 4.16):

Listing 4.11: Alphabetical sorting

```
76      L.control.layers(basemaps, overlays, {
77          sortLayers: true
78      }).addTo(map);
```

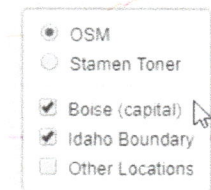

Figure 4.16: Alphabetical sorting

It is important that you take a closer look at how JavaScript sorts characters, which becomes important when you mix lowercase and uppercase. When sorting, JavaScript returns uppercase characters before lowercase. This differs from how humans sort words alphabetically and therefore a sorted layer switcher might not entirely correspond to what you might expect (fig. 4.17, on the following page).

In the above image you might have expected boundary to show up

Figure 4.17: Alphabetical sorting (case-sensitive)

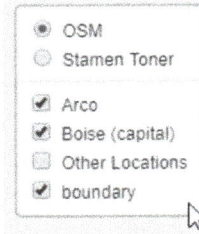

in between Boise and Other Locations.

Luckily there is another option, *sortFunction*, which lets you specify a custom sorting function. You can be creative and add complex sorting to your layer control. Most often, however, this function is used to enable case-insensitive sorting.

You can achieve this as follows (fig. 4.18):

Listing 4.12: Alphabetical sorting (case-insensitive)

```
79    function sortCaseInsensitive(layerA, layerB, nameA, nameB) {
80
81       return nameA.toLowerCase().localeCompare(nameB.toLowerCase());
82
83    }
84
85    L.control.layers(basemaps, overlays, {
86      sortLayers: true,
87      sortFunction: sortCaseInsensitive
88    }).addTo(map);
```

Figure 4.18: Alphabetical sorting (case-insensitive)

Note that when using a custom sorting function you must set *sortLayers* to `true` or the function will be ignored.

4.10   Toggling a Control Using a Checkbox

Often you create applications that contain controls that might be useful to some users, but not to others. Or you are developing a mobile application where the more controls your application contains, the less room is available on the screen.

In such cases it can be useful to add a menu which lets users check or uncheck controls using buttons or checkboxes.

Let's try to toggle the zoom control using a checkbox. First we create a checkbox:

Listing 4.13: Adding a checkbox

```
20   <label>
21    <input type="checkbox" name="zoom" value="zoom" id="cbZoom" checked>
22    Zoom Control
23   </label>
```

Then it's just a matter of hooking the checkbox up to a function that either hides or displays the control:

Listing 4.14: Toggling a control using a checkbox

```
36      function checkUncheckZoom() {
37
38        if (document.getElementById('cbZoom').checked) {
39
40
41          map.zoomControl.addTo(map);
42
43
44        } else {
45
46          map.zoomControl.remove();
47
48        }
49      }
50
51      document.getElementById("cbZoom").onclick = checkUncheckZoom;
```

Remember that the zoom and attribution controls can be accessed directly via the map and that the layer and scale controls can be accessed through the variable you created.

The controls can also be toggled using CSS. Knowing that each control has its own CSS class, you can change its display property:

Listing 4.15: Toggling a control using a checkbox

```
36   function checkUncheckZoom() {
37
38     if (document.getElementById('cbZoom').checked) {
39
40
41       document.getElementsByClassName('leaflet-control-zoom')[0].
             style.display = 'block';
42
43
44     } else {
45
46       document.getElementsByClassName('leaflet-control-zoom')[0].
             style.display = 'none';
47
48     }
49   }
50
51   document.getElementById("cbZoom").onclick = checkUncheckZoom;
```

Here's an overview of the CSS classes that are assigned to the controls:

- Zoom control: `leaflet-control-zoom`
- Layers control: `leaflet-control-layers`
- Attribution control: `leaflet-control-attribution`
- Scale control: `leaflet-control-scale`

5 *Raster Layers and Web Services*

Contents

In this chapter we'll learn how to add raster layers and web services to a Leaflet map. This chapter is rather short since using rasters in web mapping is usually confined to adding them to the map. True analysis or processing would be done in a GIS or remote sensing software. Apart from adding a raster to the map, we'll also look into working with geospatial web services. Although optional, this chapter includes a very brief introduction to GeoServer, so you can publish your own services.

Note that this chapter does not cover basemaps, as they were discussed in Chapter 2, Getting Started, on page 27. To create your own basemap, look at Chapter 9, Layout and Styling, on page 169.

5.1 *Adding a Raster to the Map*

You can add JPG and PNG images to the map. When doing so you need to specify the path to the image as well as the image's bounding box. It is important that you enter the correct bounding box or the image will end up looking skewed.

```
31    var imgPath = 'data/africa.png';
32    var bbox = [[-34.81, -17.62] , [37.34, 51.13]];
33    L.imageOverlay(imgPath, bbox).addTo(map);
```

5.2   Publishing a Service Using GeoServer

In this recipe we'll have a look at publishing a web service. This is not a Leaflet recipe per se. If you have access to web services that you would like to add to a Leaflet map, simply skip to the next recipe.

There are a number of software choices for publishing services. The reason we use GeoServer is because it is user-friendly and easy to set up. Apart from that, it has an extensive set of capabilities and is widely used. If you get into web mapping, you will run into GeoServer sooner or later.

Before you can publish a service you need to install GeoServer: http://geoserver.org/. The installation of GeoServer is flexible. You can either install it with the included web server or you can hook it up to an existing web server. If you are new to GeoServer and simply want to learn how to publish services, you should go for the easier option, meaning that GeoServer is installed as a package that includes a web server.

If you went with the defaults during the installation, you can log in as follows:
URL: http://localhost:8080/geoserver
username: admin
password: geoserver

Start GeoServer and open its interface in the browser.

Once logged in, have a look at the left-hand menu (fig. 5.1):

Figure 5.1: The left-hand menu

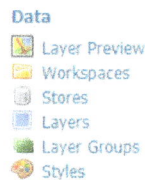

Data
Layer Preview
Workspaces
Stores
Layers
Layer Groups
Styles

For now, only three concepts are important.

Workspace:
a group of similar layers, like a directory that stores files (i.e. services)

Store:
a connection to a dataset

Layer:

a published layer (i.e. a spatial web service)

Let's first create a workspace so we can group all layers that we create in this book. Again, a workspace is simply a folder. What ends up in it is completely up to us, but one usually uses a workspace to group layers that are similar or layers that belong to a project.

In Leaflet you can access a specific layer by providing the workspace it resides in, a colon, and its name, as in workspace:layer

The URI of a workspace must be unique but it does not have to exist on the web. Usually you would associate it with a project you are working on, but this is not required

Enter a name and a URI (fig. 5.2):

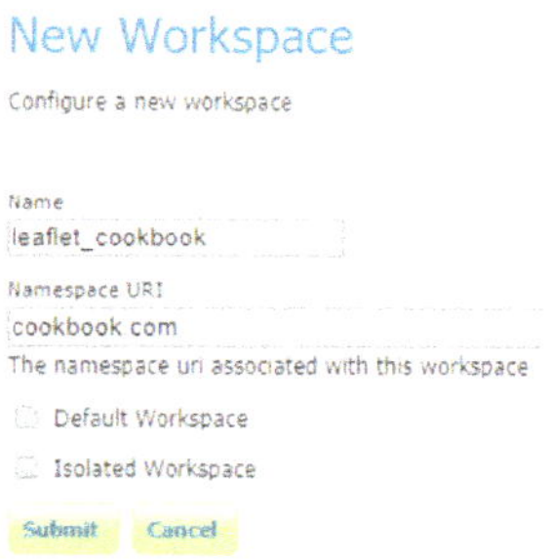

Figure 5.2: Creating a new workspace

The workspace appears—now we can create a store and add a dataset to GeoServer (fig. 5.3).

Figure 5.3: Creating a new store

We'll publish the shapefile `africa.shp`, which you can find in the `data` folder of this chapter. From the available Vector Data Sources go with the shapefile (fig. 5.4):

Figure 5.4: Available vector sources

For each store you first need to assign it to a workspace and then give it a name. This name will not be visible to others—its purpose is so you can recognize your store in the workspace later on (fig. 5.5).

Figure 5.5: Entering basic store information

Basic Store Info
Workspace *

leaflet_cookbook ▼

Data Source Name *

Africa

Description

☑ Enabled

Now navigate to `africa.shp` and upload it (fig. 5.6):

Figure 5.6: Selecting a dataset

Connection Parameters
Shapefile location *

file data/example.extension   Browse..

DBF charset

ISO-8859-1   ▼

If you installed GeoServer on your local machine you will see the computer's directory structure. If it is installed on a server you see the server's structure, and you will not be able to access your local computer. In that case you first have to upload the dataset to the server, and then create a store.

Finally, press the *Save* button and in the next interface click *Publish* (fig. 5.7):

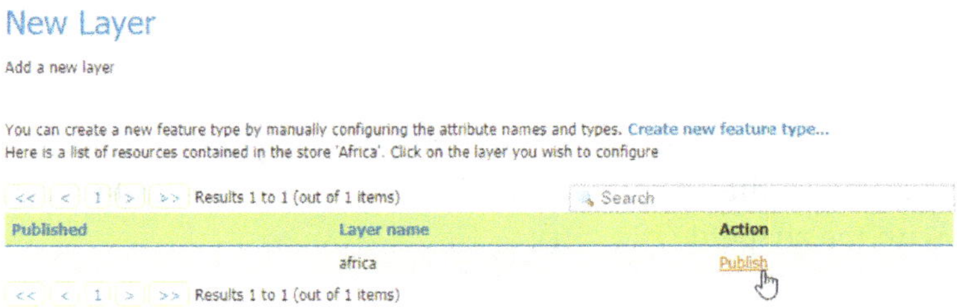

Figure 5.7: Proceeding to publish a new layer

New Layer

Add a new layer

You can create a new feature type by manually configuring the attribute names and types. Create new feature type...
Here is a list of resources contained in the store 'Africa'. Click on the layer you wish to configure

<< < 1 > >> Results 1 to 1 (out of 1 items)   Search

Published	Layer name	Action
	africa	Publish

<< < 1 > >> Results 1 to 1 (out of 1 items)

We're almost there, but a few things need to be defined still.

In the *Data* tab, define a name (you can use the default) and check both checkboxes (fig. 5.8, on the next page):

Enabled simply means that the service is available. Sometimes you might want to create a service but not immediately make it public.

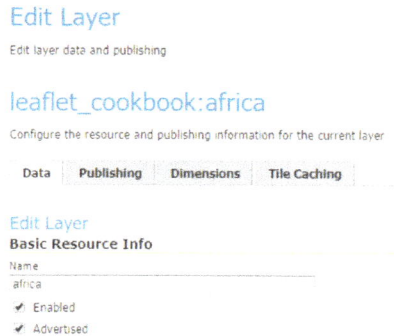

Figure 5.8: Naming, enabling and advertising a layer

Or, after a while you might want to deactivate a service, but not entirely delete it.

Advertised means that a preview of the layer is public. Anyone can see a preview of your GeoServer services, even if they are not logged in. By unchecking the box the layer will not appear in the public preview.

Scroll down to Coordinate Reference Systems and make sure the right one is displayed (EPSG:4326). GeoServer might not always detect the right coordinate system so it is essential that you double-check.

Next, compute the bounds. Every service must have a bounding box, which will be advertised in the GetCapabilities document. If we do not calculate the bounding box we cannot publish the service. We compute the bounds from the dataset (fig. 5.9):

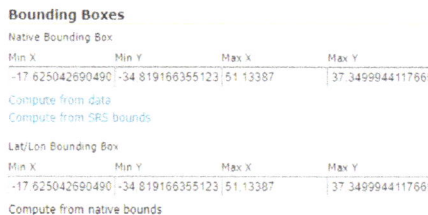

Figure 5.9: Computing the bounding box

In the Publishing tab we can pick a style. Simply choose a few from

Choosing the bounds from the SRS, in our case WGS 84, would lead to the service's bounding box covering the entire world. Since our service includes only Africa, it makes sense to use the dataset's bounds instead of those of the SRS.

the left-hand box and add them to the box on the right (fig. 5.10). Note: you can also create your own styles using SLD (Styled Layer Descriptor), an XML schema to style spatial data.

Figure 5.10: Picking a style

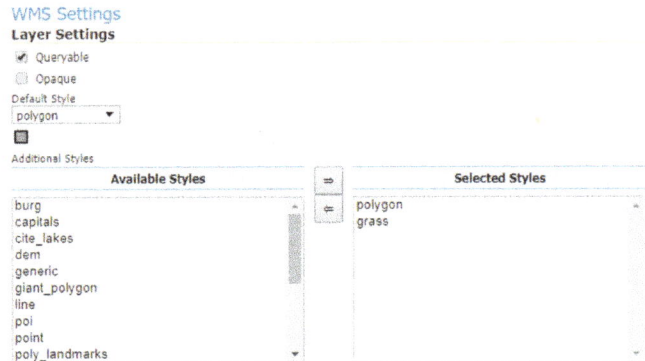

Now click the *Save* button and that's it—you just published your first service.

Open the Layer Preview menu and look for the service (fig. 5.11):

Figure 5.11: The layer now appears in the preview

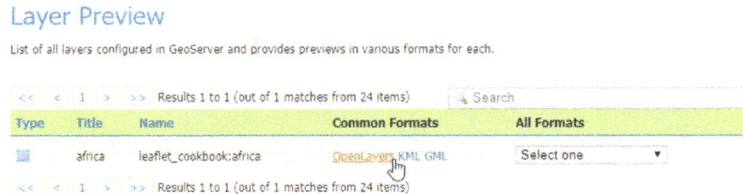

You can preview the service in an OpenLayers application and you can use the dropdown to select a WMS or WFS in a variety of formats. Choose a WMS as PNG. In the next window have a look at the browser's address bar. Anything up to *wms?* is the address of your service address—anything after is additional parameters:

```
http://localhost:8080/geoserver/leaflet_cookbook/wms?
```

This base URL is needed to add the service to a GIS or a web map—in our case a Leaflet application.

> The data you upload can be found in your GeoServer's installation folder under data_dir/data/shapefiles. You could directly copy the data in there, but you would still have to set up the store. When using a real server, instead of your local machine, this is a good option, as it enables you to copy the data to the right location, instead of first uploading it to a random location on the server and then copying it while creating the store.

Dealing with cross domain issues

In the GeoServer folder structure, navigate to:

GeoServerX.X/webapps/geoserver/WEB-INF

and open the file web.xml. Make sure to uncomment the following two blocks before restarting GeoServer:

If you are not familiar with cross-origin resource sharing (CORS) and the issues that can be linked to it, you should have a look at: https://developer.mozilla.org/en-US/docs/Web/HTTP/CORS

```
<filter>
        <filter-name>cross-origin</filter-name>
        <filter-class>org.eclipse.jetty.servlets.CrossOriginFilter</
              filter-class>
</filter>

<filter-mapping>
        <filter-name>cross-origin</filter-name>
        <url-pattern>/*</url-pattern>
</filter-mapping>
```

Note that this solution only applies to the standard installation that uses a Jetty server. If you are using GeoServer with a different web server then this adjustment will differ.

5.3   Adding a WMS to the Map

Adding a WMS to Leaflet is done using L.tileLayer.wms. The first parameter is always the URL to the service. This is identical to creating a basemap, and technically it is sufficient to request the WMS. To actually see something, however, you need to specify a layer in the options object, in the workspace:layer pattern. You can also request the images in a specific format, such as a PNG, and you can add attribution. Let's add Natural Earth to the attribution to give them credit for providing such great data.

```
31      var wms = L.tileLayer.wms("http://localhost:8080/geoserver/
            leaflet_cookbook/wms", {
32          layers: 'leaflet_cookbook:africa',
33          format: 'image/png',
34          attribution: "Natural Earth"
35      });
36
37      wms.addTo(map);
```

When you load the application you'll notice a white background. You can get rid of it by setting *transparent* to `true`:

```
34          transparent: true,
```

If your service includes multiple styles, you can control its appearance by passing the *styles* option:

```
35          styles: 'grass',
```

You can also adjust the opacity:

```
36          opacity: 0.7,
```

5.4   Filtering a WMS using Common Query Language (CQL)

Note that not all options you can pass to a service are shown in the Leaflet documentation. Some options you can send to a service are not always part of an official OGC standard either. This recipe covers a parameter that is available by services published with GeoServer.

The option *cql_filter* lets you pass a CQL query to a WMS, so only a subset is returned. As long as you know the attribute headers of the service, you can get creative.

Knowing that our WMS includes a column named ADMIN which stores country names, let's select some countries.

Using the equal sign, you can select a name exactly as it is stored in the table (that includes the case):

```
35          cql_filter: "ADMIN='Madagascar'",
```

The LIKE operator lets you enter just a part of the name and the percentage sign can be used as a wildcard for one or more characters. In the following example all countries that start with a capital *M* are selected:

```
35          cql_filter: "ADMIN LIKE'M%'",
```

The ILIKE operator works similarly to the LIKE operator but it is case-insensitive:

```
35          cql_filter: "ADMIN ILIKE'mAdaGAscAr'",
```

Note that when querying strings you need to put the search word into single quotes. When querying numbers you do not use quotes. The following snippet selects all countries with a population over 10 million:

```
35          cql_filter: "POP_EST > 10000000",
```

5.5 Changing Parameters After a WMS has Been Loaded

The method setParams lets you request a WMS again. You pass an options object just like the one you pass when creating a WMS layer. Note that you do not need to pass every parameter again—it is sufficient to only pass the ones you want to change.

Let's create an application where users can request a different style when clicking on a button. Users should also be able to type in a country's name and filter the dataset.

First create the input mask (fig. 5.12):

```
20   <input type="button" id="btnStyleGrass" value="Grass Style">
21   <input type="button" id="btnStyleDefault" value="Default Style">
22   <br><br>
23   <input type="text" id="nameInput" placeholder="Enter country name">
24   <input type="button" id="btnFilter" value="Filter">
```

Figure 5.12: Buttons to set a service's parameters

Now it is just a matter of hooking the buttons up to functions that call the setParams method:

```
46       document.getElementById('btnStyleGrass').onclick = function() {
47
48         wms.setParams({styles: 'grass'});
49
50       };
51
52       document.getElementById('btnStyleDefault').onclick = function() {
53
```

```
54        wms.setParams({styles: 'polygon'});
55
56      };
```

To filter the dataset you first read whatever name has been entered in the text input and then build a query that filters the ADMIN column:

```
58      document.getElementById('btnFilter').onclick = function() {
59
60        var name = document.getElementById('nameInput').value;
61
62        var query = "ADMIN='" + name + "'";
63
64        wms.setParams({cql_filter: query});
65
66      };
```

5.6   Getting Attributes through GetFeatureInfo

To simplify the requests we use jQuery (https://jquery.com/) in this recipe and the next.

To access attribute information from a service you can send a GetFeatureInfo request, which you can achieve by forming a simple AJAX request. It is important that you do not send latitude/longitude coordinates to the service but x and y image coordinates. For this to function correctly you need to provide the view's bounding box and the width and the height of the map container.

In the following example we send out a request on each click and then log the result.

```
43      map.on('click', function(e) {
44
45        $.get({
46          url: 'http://localhost:8080/geoserver/leaflet_cookbook/wms',
47          data: {
48            request: 'GetFeatureInfo',
49            layers: 'leaflet_cookbook:africa',
50            query_layers: 'leaflet_cookbook:africa',
51            bbox: map.getBounds().toBBoxString(),
52            height: map.getSize().y,
53            width: map.getSize().x,
54            x: e.layerPoint.x,
55            y: e.layerPoint.y,
56            version: '1.1.0'
57          },
58          success: returnFeatureInfo
```

```
59        });
60
61      });
62
63      function returnFeatureInfo(data) {
64
65        console.log(data);
66
67      }
```

Hint: getParamString

Since the parameters we send to the service are simply an object you could also define the object separately in a variable and use that variable in the AJAX request. This can be useful when testing as you can use `L.Util.getParamString` to see what the actual request string will end up looking like:

```
params = {
  request: 'GetFeatureInfo',
  layers: 'leaflet_cookbook:africa',
  ...
  ...
  version: '1.1.0'
};

var paramsString = L.Util.getParamString(params);
console.log(paramsString);
```

5.7 Adding a WFS to Leaflet

A WFS can be transmitted in a variety of formats. The easiest way to get a WFS into Leaflet is to go with the GeoJSON format, since it is natively supported by Leaflet.

Note that the server must allow cross domain requests for these examples to work.

Once you have the service address, simply form an AJAX request:

```
33      $.get({
34        url: 'http://localhost:8080/geoserver/leaflet_cookbook/ows?
              service=WFS&version=1.0.0\
35        &request=GetFeature&typeName=leaflet_cookbook:africa&&
              outputFormat=application%2Fjson',
36        contentType: 'application/json',
37        success: addGeoJsonToMap
38      });
39
40      function addGeoJsonToMap(data) {
```

```
41
42          L.geoJSON(data).addTo(map);
43
44      }
```

Since the address URL can be a bit long and therefore difficult to read or to adjust you can also request the base URL and send the rest as parameters:

```
33      $.get({
34        url: 'http://localhost:8080/geoserver/leaflet_cookbook/ows',
35        data: {
36          request: 'GetFeature',
37          service: 'WFS',
38          typeName: 'leaflet_cookbook:africa',
39          version: '1.0.0',
40          outputFormat: 'application/json',
41        },
42        success: addGeoJsonToMap
43      });
44
45      function addGeoJsonToMap(data) {
46
47        L.geoJSON(data).addTo(map);
48
49      }
```

6 *Vector Layers*

Contents

There are three geometries that can be used on a map to cartographically represent just about anything on the Earth's surface: points, lines, and polygons (fig. 6.1, on the following page). These are referred to as vector data. Vectors consist of vertices, each vertex being a coordinate pair and together these pairs make up the final geometry that will be displayed on the map. The simplest of these is the point, requiring exactly one pair. A line requires at least two pairs and a polygon requires at least three pairs. Lines and polygons can have thousands of coordinate pairs.

Figure 6.1: point, line, polygon

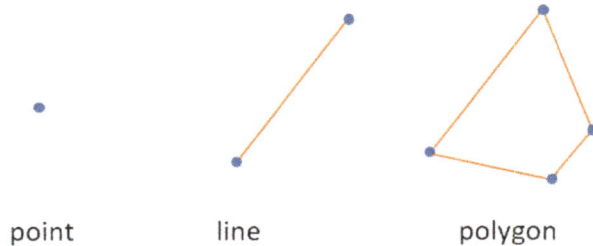

point   line   polygon

In this chapter we will learn about working with these types of vector data:

- Marker
- Polyline
- Polygon
- Rectangle
- Circle
- CircleMarker
- GeoJSON

Although Leaflet might not officially classify all of these as vector layers, we will treat them as such in this chapter, because on a conceptual level they are exactly that. Unless you are interested in the more technical aspects and inner workings of Leaflet, you can think of these layers as vectors.

We will also learn about two ways to group vector layers:

- LayerGroup
- FeatureGroup

6.1   Adding and Removing Vector Layers

After creating a vector layer you can both add it and remove it from the map.

Imagine a variable `vector`, containing a vector layer created by Leaflet.

The layer is added to the map by using:

```
vector.addTo(map);
```

and removed by using:

```
vector.removeFrom(map);
```

Note that you could also add and remove layers directly from the map using:

```
map.addLayer(vector);
```

and

```
map.removeLayer(vector);
```

Both ways of adding and removing layers result in the exact same thing, and it comes down to personal preference which one you end up using. For the remaining recipes we'll use the first method.

6.2   Markers

In this recipe we will add three points in New York City: Central Park, Times Square, and the Statue of Liberty.

Points in Leaflet are by default displayed as blue markers and each point always consists of a single pair of coordinates, holding the latitude value first, and the longitude second.

Since a marker consists of an image, it is technically not a vector layer but we'll treat it as such, and throughout this book we'll use markers as the default when adding points.

Listing 6.1: Adding markers

```
31    // creating markers
32    var centralParkMarker = L.marker([40.7805, -73.9679]);
33    var timesSquareMarker = L.marker([40.7588, -73.9852]);
34    var statueMarker = L.marker([40.6892, -74.0445]);
35
36    // adding the markers to the map
```

```
37        centralParkMarker.addTo(map);
38        timesSquareMarker.addTo(map);
39        statueMarker.addTo(map);
```

Note that we created a variable for each marker. The variable is
necessary to access the marker later on, such as programmatically
moving it or removing it when it is clicked. If we're only interested
in displaying it, we can skip creating a variable and instead add the
marker to the map directly:

```
L.marker([40.7805, -73.9679]).addTo(map);
```

This comes in especially handy when adding markers to the map in
a loop.

6.3   Adding Markers in a Loop

Assume you are given a list of markers, and imagine it contains
hundreds of points. It would be cumbersome to add each marker
individually to the map.

Listing 6.2: Array holding marker data
```
31    var markersArray = [
32      ["Central Park", 40.78059, -73.96795],
33      ["Times Square", 40.75886, -73.98521],
34      ["Statue of Liberty", 40.68921, -74.04457],
35      ["Union Square", 40.73586, -73.99058],
36      ["Bryant Park", 40.75347, -73.98311],
37      ["High Line", 40.73951, -74.00823],
38      ["Washington Square", 40.73069, -73.99795],
39      ["Brooklyn Bridge", 40.70795, -73.99912],
40      ["American Museum of Natural History", 40.78144, -73.97363]
41    ];
```

Adding the markers to the map using a loop is the preferred way to
accomplish the task:

Listing 6.3: Adding markers in a loop
```
43    for (var i = 0; i < markersArray.length; i++) {
44
45      var lat = markersArray[i][1];
46      var lon = markersArray[i][2];
47      L.marker([lat, lon]).addTo(map);
48
49    }
```

To add a popup containing the name of each marker, look at the recipe Adding Popups to Leaflet Objects, on page 107.

6.4   Marker Options

When creating markers you can pass a variety of options. Let's have a look at them.

Creating a Draggable Marker

Sometimes it's necessary to not only have static markers, but also markers that can be moved by the user. This can be achieved using the option *draggable*:

```
L.marker([0, 0], {draggable: true});
```

To get the new position after the marker has been moved or is being moved, see recipe 10.14, Getting a Moving/Moved Marker Position, on page 215.

Autopanning

Use the *autoPan* option to pan the map when you move a draggable marker towards the edge of the map.

```
var m = L.marker([51.111, 2.618], {draggable: true, autoPan: true});
m.addTo(map);
```

You can control how much the map moves by passing an integer to *autoPanSpeed* (the default is 10 pixels).

Accessing Markers Using the Keyboard

By default, many elements in your web page can be accessed using the keyboard's tab key. This includes elements of the map as well: zoom buttons, attribution, markers, etc.

Add some markers to the map and press the tab key. You'll notice that one after another, the markers will be highlighted by a rectangle, as shown in figure 6.2, on the next page.

Figure 6.2: Accessing a marker using the tab key

The benefit of accessing markers like this is that, instead of clicking them, you can also press the Enter key.

Adding a Title

Similar to HTML, where you can add a title attribute to elements, Leaflet lets you add a title to markers. The title will appear as a tooltip when hovering your mouse over them (fig. 6.3, on the facing page):

```
L.marker([0, 0], {title: 'Null Island'});
```

Note that this tooltip is equivalent to the tooltip created in HTML by assigning the title attribute. If you need more control over the tooltip or if you want a more appealing design, you should have a look at recipe 6.14, on page 112 and create a tooltip using the bindTooltip method.

Figure 6.3: Tooltip created using bind-Tooltip (left) and tooltip created using title (bottom)

Adjusting the Z-index

A marker's z-index can be adjusted by using the *zIndexOffset* property and assigning it an integer. The larger the integer, the closer to the top the marker will be when rendered. You can test this by creating overlapping markers.

Create some markers that sightly differ in latitude (fig. 6.4):

```
L.marker([51.111, 2.61]).addTo(map);
L.marker([51.112, 2.61]).addTo(map);
L.marker([51.113, 2.61]).addTo(map);
L.marker([51.114, 2.61]).addTo(map);
```

Figure 6.4: Markers with slightly different latitude and default z-indices

By default a marker with a lower latitude will be rendered higher, making the overlap effect look cleaner.

Adjust the z-index to have the third marker show on top (fig. 6.5):

```
L.marker([51.113, 2.61], {zIndexOffset: 1000}).addTo(map);
```

Figure 6.5: The third marker from the bottom has an adjusted z-index

If the markers have the exact same latitude their z-index cannot be ordered by latitude and therefore their z-index is determined by the order they have been added to the map. Generally, the first added marker has the lowest z-index and each marker that is added after has a higher z-index. Let's add four markers to observe this effect (fig. 6.6):

```
L.marker([51.1, 2.611]).addTo(map);
L.marker([51.1, 2.612]).addTo(map);
L.marker([51.1, 2.613]).addTo(map);
L.marker([51.1, 2.614]).addTo(map);
```

Figure 6.6: Markers with slightly different longitude with default z-indices

Again, you can adjust this by explicitly setting the z-index (fig. 6.7):

```
L.marker([51.1, 2.613], {zIndexOffset: 1000}).addTo(map);
```

Figure 6.7: The third marker from the right has an adjusted z-index

Rising on Hover

When hovering the mouse over a marker, its z-index can be temporarily changed to raise it above other markers. Set its *raiseOnHover* property to `true` to assign it a z-index of 250. If the default 250 is not sufficient, you can adjust it using the *riseOffset* property (fig. 6.8):

```
L.marker([51.1, 2.613], {riseOnHover: true, riseOffset: 999}).addTo(
    map);
```

Figure 6.8: The hovered marker is raised above all other markers

Adjusting the Opacity

You can adjust the transparency of a marker by using the *opacity* option. The number you assign is always between 0 (invisible) and

1 (opaque, i.e. no transparency, fig. 6.9). In the following example 0.5 means that the marker is 50% transparent (fig. 6.10):

```
L.marker([0, 0], {opacity: 0.5});
```

Figure 6.9: A marker with no transparency (default)

Figure 6.10:   A half-transparent marker

Bubbling Mouse Events

The following is true for all events, but let's look at a click event as an example.

Generally, when you register a click event on both the map and a marker, the map event is not triggered. You can bypass this by setting *bubblingMouseEvents* to `true`. In the following snippet the click on the marker also triggers a click on the map:

```
var m = L.marker([0,0], {bubblingMouseEvents: true}).addTo(map);

m.on('click', function() {

        console.log('Clicked on a marker!');

});

map.on('click', function() {

        console.log('Clicked on the map!');

});
```

6.5   Lines

At least two points are required to create a line. `L.polyLine` accepts an array of point arrays.

The following example creates a line of the Golden Gate Bridge:

Listing 6.4: Adding a line

```
31    var lineCoordinates = [
32        [37.8092, -122.4772],
33        [37.8279, -122.4795]
34    ];
35
36    var line = L.polyline(lineCoordinates);
37
38    line.addTo(map);
```

When the datasets get large, i.e. when they include many coordinate pairs, readability of your code can be increased by assigning the coordinates to a variable and then using that variable when creating the line. However, this is not required. In fact, you could have chained the three steps, not using a single variable:

Listing 6.5: Adding a line without variables

```
31    L.polyline(
32        [
33            [37.8092, -122.4772],
34            [37.8279, -122.4795]
35        ]
36    ).addTo(map);
```

6.6   Polygons

At least three points are required to create a polygon. L.polygon accepts an array of point arrays:

```
L.polygon(
  [
    [lat, lon],
    [lat, lon],
    [lat, lon]
  ]
)
```

The following example creates a polygon for Colorado:

Listing 6.6: Adding a polygon

```
31    var polygonCoordinates = [
32        [41.0016, -109.0461],
33        [40.9881, -102.0465],
34        [36.9937, -102.0301],
35        [36.9992, -109.0434]
36    ];
```

```
37
38      var polygon = L.polygon(polygonCoordinates);
39
40      polygon.addTo(map);
```

Note that in Leaflet, the first and last point don't have to coincide. Some software demands that for a shape to close properly, the first and last points must be identical.

When creating polygons with Turf.js (Geoprocessing and Analysis with Turf.js, on page 225) or when creating GeoJSON polygons, the first and last points must coincide.

6.7   Polygons with Holes

Sometimes you need to add one or more holes to a polygon. For example, the lake you want to show on your map has an island. Since the island is not part of the waterbody, you want to remove it from the polygon.

In the previous recipe you learned that you create polygons using an array holding multiple coordinate pair arrays.

If your polygon includes holes, instead of passing one array holding coordinate pairs, you will pass an array holding arrays of coordinate pairs.

The first array is the main polygon and each subsequent array is a hole within that polygon:

Listing 6.7: Adding holes to a polygon

```
L.polygon(
  [
    [polyCoordinates],
    [holeCoordinates],
    [holeCoordinates]
  ]
)
```

Figure 6.11, on the following page shows an example of a polygon depicting Central Park, excluding the Jacqueline Kennedy Onassis

Reservoir (using `recipe_6_7.html`).

Figure 6.11: A polygon with a hole

6.8   Multilines and Multipolygons

Leaflet also supports multigeometries. Multigeometries are used for features that consist of more than one geometry but should logically be treated as one. Think of the state of Florida. The Florida Keys are separate geographic entities that are not connected to the mainland and not connected to each other, yet they still belong to Florida. In a geographic dataset they would be stored as a single feature as the state of Florida. Instead of creating multiple polygon layers, we can create one and store all of the parts in it.

Creating multilines and multipolygons is fairly easy. Instead of defining coordinate arrays directly, you add an extra array for each separate geometry.

Listing 6.8: Creating a multiline

```
32    var lineCoordinates = [
33      [
34        [23.79540, -46.05469],
35        [32.16631, -38.67188]
36      ],
37      [
38        [20.21066, -28.47656],
39        [10.73618, -36.91406]
40      ],
41      [
42        [2.71261, -9.84375],
```

```
43            [8.30934, -17.57813]
44          ]
45        ];
46
47        var line = L.polyline(lineCoordinates);
48
49        line.addTo(map);
```

Listing 6.9: Creating a multipolygon

```
51        var polygonCoordinates = [
52          [
53            [41.60312, -37.26563],
54            [36.55819, -43.06641],
55            [31.61129, -37.96875]
56          ],
57          [
58            [48.42556, -9.84375],
59            [47.24568, -2.10938],
60            [44.42986, -8.08594]
61          ]
62        ]
63
64        var polygon = L.polygon(polygonCoordinates);
65
66        polygon.addTo(map);
```

Note that the setup of a multipolygon dataset and a polygon dataset with holes is identical. Leaflet is smart enough to distinguish whether to add a new part or cut out a part.

6.9   Rectangles and Squares

To create rectangles or squares you can use L.rectangle, instead of L.polygon. To create a rectangle using L.polygon requires you to specify each corner individually. L.rectangle, however, accepts two corners and the rest will be taken care of for you. As long as the corners you provide are diagonally opposite, it does not matter which corners you provide or in what order. For example, you could provide the lower left corner and the upper right corner, but you could just as well provide the upper left corner and the lower right corner.

The following example creates a rectangle around South Georgia:

Listing 6.10: Creating a rectangle

```
31    var rectangle = L.rectangle([[-53.9, -38.3], [-55.1, -35.6]]);
32
33    rectangle.addTo(map);
```

6.10   Circles

L.circle lets you create a perfect circle by specifying the center and radius, always provided in meters.

Listing 6.11: Creating a circle

```
31    var circle = L.circle([33.984, -118.465], {
32      radius: 200
33    });
34
35    circle.addTo(map);
```

6.11   Creating Regular Shapes: Circle Markers

Another way to create a perfect circle is to use a circle marker. The creation of a circle marker is identical to a normal circle:

Listing 6.12: Creating a circle marker

```
31    var circleMarker = L.circleMarker([33.984, -118.465], {
32      radius: 200
33    });
34
35    circleMarker.addTo(map);
```

The difference is that the units provided to create a circle marker are not meters but pixels.

Since the width of the circle marker is an absolute value in pixels, the circle marker will have the same size at every zoom level. This means that when you zoom out, the marker will encompass a larger area on the ground and, although it might appear that the circle marker is growing in size, it has the exact same width on every zoom level. The normal circle seen in the previous recipe will cover the exact same area on the ground, no matter what the zoom level. This means that it appears smaller the more you zoom out.

You can observe this when adding both a circle and a circle marker

to the map using the following code and comparing figures 6.12 and
6.13, on the following page:

Listing 6.13: Creating a circle

```
31    var circle = L.circle([33.984, -118.465], {
32      radius: 200,
33      color: 'red'
34    });
35
36    var circleMarker = L.circleMarker([33.984, -118.465], {
37      radius: 200
38    });
39
40    circle.addTo(map);
41    circleMarker.addTo(map);
```

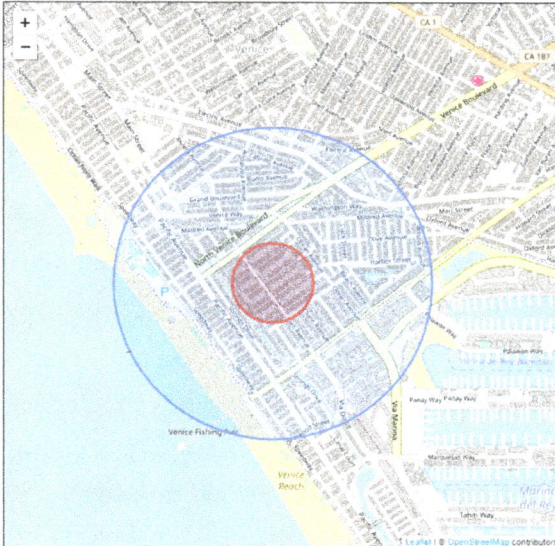

Figure 6.12: Circle (red) and circle marker (blue) on zoom level 15

6.12 Adding Popups to Leaflet Objects

You can add popups to the map, markers, polylines, and polygons.

Popups can be placed directly on the map:

Listing 6.14: Adding a popup to the map

```
31    var eastRiverPopup = L.popup();
32    eastRiverPopup.setLatLng([40.707, -73.995]);
```

Figure 6.13: Circle (red) and circle
marker (blue) on zoom level 13

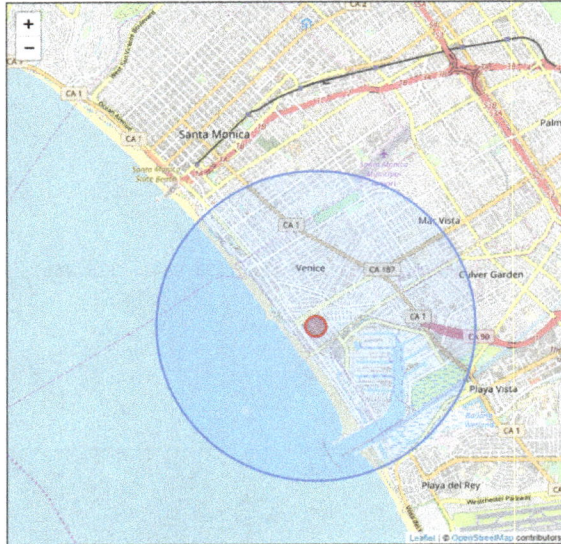

```
33        eastRiverPopup.setContent('Swimming in the East River!');
34        eastRiverPopup.openOn(map);
```

As always, you could chain the commands instead of using a variable, although this might be harder to read:

```
L.popup().setLatLng([40.7078, -73.9951])
.setContent('Swimming in the East River!')
.openOn(map);
```

In newer versions of Leaflet you don't even have to instantiate L.popup; you can use the map's openPopup method directly:

```
map.openPopup('Swimming in the East River!', [40.7078, -73.9951]);
```

Most often popups are not added to the map, but are bound to a vector layer using the bindPopup method:

Listing 6.15: Adding a popup to a marker

```
31        var statueMarker = L.marker([40.6892, -74.0445]);
32        statueMarker.bindPopup("Statue of Liberty");
33        statueMarker.addTo(map);
```

Note that it doesn't matter whether you first bind the popup to the dataset and then add the dataset to the map or add the dataset first and then bind the popup.

6.13   Popup Options

Numerous options can be entered to adjust the popup appearance or behavior. The options object is entered as a second argument, right after the popup text.

Adjusting the Size of a Popup

By default, a popup has a minimum width of 50 pixels and a maximum width of 300 pixels. This means that even if the content is very short, such as one character, the popup is still 50 pixels wide. When the content grows, the text will break at 300 pixels and continue in a new line. A popup does not have a maximum height by default, meaning that it grows and adjusts to the content.

You can override the defaults as follows:

```
marker.bindPopup('Hello!', {
  minWidth: 75,
  maxWidth: 90,
  maxHeight: 150
});
```

Should your content not fit anymore after you adjusted the maximum width and height, a scrollbar will be added to the popup. If you add an image that is larger than the maximum size, it might still overlap, instead of becoming scrollable. In that case you could use CSS to specify the *max-width* and *max-height* properties of the image:

```
marker.bindPopup("<img src='image.jpg' style='max-width:90px;max-
    height:150px;'>", {
  minWidth: 90, maxWidth: 90, maxHeight: 150
});
```

Panning the Map on Opening a Popup and Keeping it in View

If you open a popup that does not entirely fit into the view, the map will pan to make the popup fit, leaving a margin of 5 pixels between the popup and the map's border. You can deactivate the panning by setting *autoPan* to `false`:

```
marker.bindPopup('Hello!', {autoPan: false});
```

You can also adjust the margin between the edge of the popup and the map's border by specifying *autoPanPaddingTopLeft* and *autoPanPaddingBottomRight*:

```
marker.bindPopup('Hello!', {
  autoPanPaddingTopLeft: [45, 0],
  autoPanPaddingBottomRight: [75, 15]
});
```

In the above snippet, if the popup opens close to a corner or an edge of the map the following padding is added:

- top left corner: 45 px from the left, 0 px from the top
- bottom right corner: 75 px from the right, 15 px from the bottom
- top right corner: 75 px from the right, 0 px from the top
- bottom left corner: 45 px from the left, 15 px from the bottom

If you plan on using the same padding for both the top left and bottom right corners then you can use the shortcut property `autoPanPadding`:

```
marker.bindPopup('Hello!', {autoPanPadding: [25, 25]});
```

By setting *keepInView* to `true` you can also force an opened popup to stay in view, even after panning the map. If the map is moved so the popup disappears outside of the border, the map bounces back to keep the popup in view. The farther you pan the map the stronger the bounce effect gets, potentially confusing users, so think twice about using this option.

```
marker.bindPopup('Hello!', {keepInView: true});
```

Managing How Popups are Closed

You can remove the popup's close button by setting *closeButton* to `false`:

```
marker.bindPopup('Hello!', {closeButton: false});
```

You might have noticed that opening a popup first closes another opened popup. By default only one popup can be opened. To change this, set *autoClose* to `false`.

```
marker.bindPopup('Hello!', {autoClose: false});
```

The *closeOnClick* option lets you define whether a popup closes or not when clicking the map:

```
marker.bindPopup('Hello!', {closeOnClick: false});
```

To globally define that no popups close when clicking the map, set the map's *closePopupOnClick* option, which is more convenient than remembering to set the *closeOnClick* option for each marker you add:

```
var map = L.map('map', {
  center: [33, -117],
  zoom: 11,
  closePopupOnClick: false
});
```

Settings of individual popups override the map's setting. If your *closePopupOnClick* is set to `false`, but an individual marker's *closeOnClick* option is set to `true`, the popup closes when clicking on the map.

Popups can also be closed by pressing the `ESC` key. To deactivate this, set *closeOnEscapeKey* to `false`:

```
marker.bindPopup('Hello!', {closeOnEscapeKey: false});
```

Note that pressing the `ESC` key only works if the popup has the focus. When opening a popup by clicking a marker, the focus resides with the marker and you first have to click inside the popup for it to get the focus.

Assigning a CSS Class to a Popup

A popup consists of multiple CSS classes, each of which can be accessed and styled. Often you don't want to change the default classes used by Leaflet. You can use the option *className* to assign your own CSS class to a popup.

In the following snippet we assign a class named myPopup.

```
marker.bindPopup('Hello!', {className: 'myPopup'});
```

If you inspect the popup in your browser you'll notice it now contains the class (fig. 6.14):

```
<div class="leaflet-pane leaflet-popup-pane">
 <div class="leaflet-popup myPopup leaflet-zoom-animated" style=...
  ...
```

Figure 6.14: Markup of a popup

```
▼<div class="leaflet-popup myPopup leaflet-zoom-animated" style="opacity: 1; tr
 ▼<div class="leaflet-popup-content-wrapper">
    <div class="leaflet-popup-content" style="width: 51px;">Hello!</div>
  </div>
 ▶<div class="leaflet-popup-tip-container">…</div>
   <a class="leaflet-popup-close-button" href="#close">×</a>
 </div>
</div>
```

With the class set, you are free to do whatever you want, as every other element in the popup is a child of the element that has been assigned your class. To change the text color to purple you could, for example, simply select every descendant **div** and change its *color* property:

```
.myPopup div {
  color: purple;
}
```

6.14   Adding Tooltips to Markers, Polylines, and Polygons

Tooltips are similar to popups except they don't open on click, but on hover. They also look different. A tooltip can be attached to a vector layer using the bindTooltip method:

```
statueMarker.bindTooltip('Statue of Liberty');
```

Tooltips can also be bound to the map. In that case they are opened by default:

```
map.openTooltip('Null Island', [0, 0]);
```

6.15   Tooltip Options

Similar to popups, tooltips have a number of options to control their appearance and behavior.

Adjusting the Opacity

By default a tooltip has an opacity of 0.9, meaning that you can see through it just a bit. You can assign a number between 0 and 1 to adjust the opacity, the lower the number the higher the transparency (see figures 6.15 and 6.16):

```
marker.bindTooltip('Statue of Liberty', {opacity: 0.3});
```

Figure 6.15: A tooltip with default opacity

Figure 6.16: A tooltip with adjusted opacity

Adjusting the Offset

You can add an offset to a tooltip by specifying a Leaflet point:

```
L.point(x, y)
```

In the following snippet the tooltip moves 15 pixels to the right and 25 pixels to the bottom (fig. 6.17):

```
marker.bindTooltip('Statue of Liberty', {offset: L.point(15, 25)});
```

Figure 6.17: A tooltip with an offset

Adjusting the Direction

Leaflet places a tooltip either to the left or to the right of the element it is attached to. You can force the position to always be the same by assigning one of the following positions to *direction* (fig. 6.18):

- right
- left
- top
- bottom
- center
- auto (default)

```
marker.bindTooltip('Statue of Liberty', {direction: 'center'});
```

Figure 6.18: A tooltip placed at the center of a marker

Permanent Tooltips

A tooltip can be made permanent by setting *permanent* to `true`.

```
marker.bindTooltip('Statue of Liberty', {permanent: true});
```

Sticky Tooltips

A sticky tooltip follows the mouse cursor once you are hovering over the feature it is attached to:

```
marker.bindTooltip('Statue of Liberty', {sticky: true});
```

Interactive Tooltips

An event is triggered when interacting with a layer or a feature. The tooltip has a neat option that makes it react to the same events the layer it is bound to is listening to. Set *interactive* to `true` and make the marker listen to clicks to notice that the click is triggered even when clicking on the tooltip:

```
marker.bindTooltip('Statue of Liberty', {
  permanent: true,
  interactive: true
});

marker.on('click', function() {
```

```
    console.log('The marker was clicked!');

  });
```

6.16 Working with Layer Groups

Sometimes you would like to group vector layers, so you can work with them as one (for example, removing multiple layers from the map at once, adding the same popup to multiple layers). To do this you can use a layer group.

You can think of the layer group as an array to which layers are added. Unlike when working with single layers, you don't add each layer to the map individually, but you add the layer to the group, which in turn is added to the map. Have a look at recipe 6.2, on page 95 in which we added markers to the map. Instead of adding them to the map, you could also add them to a group:

Listing 6.16: Creating a layer group

```
31    // creating markers
32    var centralParkMarker = L.marker([40.7805, -73.9679]);
33    var timesSquareMarker = L.marker([40.7588, -73.9852]);
34    var statueMarker = L.marker([40.6892, -74.0445]);
35
36    // creating a LayerGroup
37    var layerGroup = L.layerGroup();
38
39    // adding the markers to the LayerGroup
40    centralParkMarker.addTo(layerGroup);
41    timesSquareMarker.addTo(layerGroup);
42    statueMarker.addTo(layerGroup);
43
44    // adding the group to the map
45    layerGroup.addTo(map);
```

At first you don't see any difference. In fact, there is no visual difference. It is only when working with this group that the benefits of using groups become clear.

Open your browser's console and type:

```
    layerGroup.removeFrom(map);
```

You'll notice that all markers are now removed from the map. Now imagine that your map contains hundreds of markers, and you would like to remove all of them. In recipe 6.1, Adding and Removing Vector Layers, on page 94 we removed individual markers using the method removeFrom, but if we were dealing with hundreds of markers, it would be much more convenient to store them in a group from the beginning.

Note that in the above example we added the markers to the group before we added the group to the map. You don't have to take this approach and could just as well add the empty group to the map and add markers to it afterwards. If the group is already in the map, markers are displayed as soon as they are added to the group.

Listing 6.17: Creating a layer group

```
31    // creating a LayerGroup
32    var layerGroup = L.layerGroup();
33
34    // adding the group to the map
35    layerGroup.addTo(map);
36
37    // creating markers and adding them to the group
38    L.marker([40.7805, -73.9679]).addTo(layerGroup);
39    L.marker([40.7588, -73.9852]).addTo(layerGroup);
40    L.marker([40.6892, -74.0445]).addTo(layerGroup);
```

Note that in this example we also saved some lines of code by not defining any variables and adding the markers to the group right away.

6.17 Working with Feature Groups

A feature group works much in the same way as a layer group, but there are a few additional things you can do with it.

The creation of a feature group differs only in that you use L.featureGroup instead of L.layerGroup:

Listing 6.18: Creating a feature group

```
31    // creating markers
32    var centralParkMarker = L.marker([40.7805, -73.9679]);
33    var timesSquareMarker = L.marker([40.7588, -73.9852]);
34    var statueMarker = L.marker([40.6892, -74.0445]);
```

```
35
36    // creating a LayerGroup
37    var featureGroup = L.featureGroup();
38
39    // adding the markers to the LayerGroup
40    centralParkMarker.addTo(featureGroup);
41    timesSquareMarker.addTo(featureGroup);
42    statueMarker.addTo(featureGroup);
43
44    // adding the group to the map
45    featureGroup.addTo(map);
```

One of the additional things you can do with a feature group is using the methods bindPopup and bindTooltip. Instead of adding a popup or a tooltip to each element in a group individually, you can assign the popup or the tooltip to the entire group and every element will automatically receive it (fig. 6.19):

Listing 6.19: Binding popups and tooltips to a feature group

```
47    // bind a popup to the feature group
48    featureGroup.bindPopup('You clicked on a marker in the feature
         group!');
49
50    // bind a tooltip to the feature group
51    featureGroup.bindTooltip('You hovered over a marker in the
         feature group!')
```

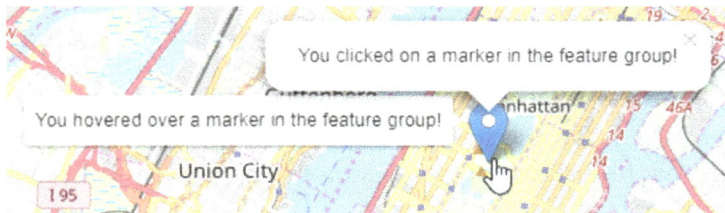

Figure 6.19: A feature group with pop-ups and tooltips

The other great benefit of using a feature group over a layer group is that you can bind events to a feature group, which are then propagated to all layers in the group. This includes all event handlers described in Chapter 10, Events and Event Objects, on page 199 as well as *layeradd* and *layerremove* events, which are fired when a layer is added to the group or removed from the group:

Listing 6.20: Binding event handlers to a feature group

```
47    // adding a click handler to the group
```

```
48    featureGroup.on('click', function() {
49
50      console.log('You clicked on a layer in the group.');
51
52    });
53
54    // adding a layeradd handler to the group
55    featureGroup.on('layeradd', function() {
56
57      console.log('A new layer was added to the group');
58
59    });
60
61    // adding a layerremove handler to the group
62    featureGroup.on('layerremove ', function() {
63
64      console.log('A layer was removed from the group');
65
66    });
```

Execute the following in the console to test the *layeradd* event:

```
var marker = L.marker([40.7423, -73.9879]);
marker.addTo(featureGroup);
```

6.18   Layer Group and Feature Group Methods

Some methods can be applied to both layer groups and feature groups.

Adding and Removing Layers

In the previous two recipes we added layers to the group using the layer's addTo method, but you can also directly use the group to add a layer to it:

```
var marker = L.marker([40.7423, -73.9879]);
featureGroup.addLayer(marker);
```

And you can remove a layer from it:

```
featureGroup.removeLayer(marker);
```

Emptying a group

You can remove all layers from a group by calling clearLayers:

```
featureGroup.clearLayers();
```

The benefit of this is the ability to keep using the same group, clearing it from time to time, instead of having to destroy and create an instance each time.

Converting the Group to GeoJSON

You can export the entire group to GeoJSON using the `toGeoJSON` method:

Listing 6.21: Returning the group as a GeoJSON

```
47    var groupGeoJSON = featureGroup.toGeoJSON();
48    console.log(JSON.stringify(groupGeoJSON));
```

For more about this method have a look at recipe 7.10, on page 148.

Checking if the Group Contains a Layer

To check whether a layer is within a group, use the `hasLayer` method. The following snippet first logs `false`, then `true`:

```
var marker = L.marker([40.7423, -73.9879]);
featureGroup = L.featureGroup();
console.log('Marker in group?', featureGroup.hasLayer(marker));
featureGroup.addLayer(marker);
console.log('Marker in group?', featureGroup.hasLayer(marker));
```

Executing a Function for Each Layer in the Group

You can execute a function for each layer in a group. If you are stuck with a layer group instead of a feature group, you could use this as a workaround to assign a popup to each layer.

The first parameter in the function you define always holds the layer of the current iteration.

Listing 6.22: Binding a popup to each layer in the group

```
47    layerGroup.eachLayer(function(layer) {
48
49       layer.bindPopup('This popup was assigned using a function!');
50
51    });
```

Knowing that the first parameter holds the layer, we can call any method that can be used on layers. In this case, all of the layers are markers, and we know that markers expose the method `getLatLng`. So, we could use `eachLayer` to extract the coordinate from each marker and add it to the popup (fig. 6.20):

Listing 6.23: Adding coordinates to a popup

```
47    layerGroup.eachLayer(function(layer) {
48
49      var coor = layer.getLatLng();
50
51      layer.bindPopup('Lat: ' + coor.lat + '<br>Lon: ' + coor.lng);
52
53    });
```

Figure 6.20: A popup showing the marker's coordinates

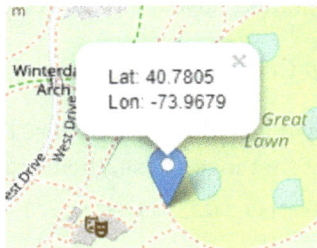

Getting Layers from the Group

Let's work with the group we created in recipe 6.17, on page 116 and test some commands in the console.

To get an array that includes all layers of a group you call `getLayers`:

```
featureGroup.getLayers();
```

But often you'd rather grab a single layer. For instance, you'd like to add a popup to a single marker in a group. To access a layer in a group you need to know its ID, which you can get as follows:

```
var id = featureGroup.getLayerId(statueMarker);
```

Once you know the ID you can request the layer and execute whatever method the layer allows:

```
var marker = featureGroup.getLayer(id);
marker.bindPopup('famous landmark');
```

Note that by knowing the ID you can also remove a layer from a group:

```
featureGroup.removeLayer(id);
```

Bringing a Group to the Front

Create a group with overlapping polygons:

```
31    var poly1 = L.polygon([
32      [40.75754, -73.99311], [40.75644, -73.99404],
33      [40.75418, -73.98831], [40.75538, -73.98743]
34    ], {color: 'black', fillOpacity: 1});
35
36    var poly2 = L.polygon([
37      [40.75473, -73.99163], [40.75657, -73.99022],
38      [40.75532, -73.98726], [40.75358, -73.98874]
39    ], {color: 'yellow', fillOpacity: 1});
40
41    var group1 = L.featureGroup([poly1]).addTo(map);
42    var group2 = L.featureGroup([poly2]).addTo(map);
```

You can bring groups to the front or send them to the back using `bringToFront` and `bringToBack`. To observe the effect, run the example and in the console execute:

```
group1.bringToFront();
```

and then:

```
group1.bringToBack();
```

Setting the Style of Each Layer in a Group

Using the data from the previous example, let's assign the same style to each layer in the group by calling `setStyle` and passing a *Path*:

Have a look at the recipe Understanding Path, on page 173 for more detail about styling vector layers.

```
group1.setStyle({
  color: 'green',
  fillOpacity: 0.4,
  weight: 6
});
```

This method will work on each layer that has a `setStyle` method. Note that our example includes only one layer.

Invoking a Method for Each Layer

If you need to call the same method for each layer in a group you
can call invoke and pass the method name as a string. For example,
to call the remove method for each layer in the group you would run
the following:

```
group.invoke('remove');
```

If the layer does not implement the method it will be ignored, so no
need to worry about calling invoke with different types of layers.

Getting the Bounds of a Group

Using getBounds you can get the bounding extent of a group.

This is especially useful when wanting to fit all layers into the map
view at once:

```
var bounds = group1.getBounds();
map.fitBounds(bounds);
```

6.19   Getting Marker Coordinates

A marker's coordinates can be retrieved using the method getLatLng,
which returns coordinates as an object:

```
someMarker.getLatLng();
```

To get latitude or longitude directly, use (fig. 6.21, on the facing
page):

```
someMarker.getLatLng().lat;

someMarker.getLatLng().lng;
```

Listing 6.24: Getting a marker's coordinates

```
31    '
32        var someMarker = L.marker([43.76802, 11.25315]).addTo(map);
33
34        var markerCoordinates = someMarker.getLatLng();
35        var markerLat = someMarker.getLatLng().lat;
36        var markerLon = someMarker.getLatLng().lng;
37
38        console.log(markerCoordinates);
```

```
39      console.log(markerLat);
40      console.log(markerLon);
```

```
▶M {lat: 43.76802, lng: 11.25315}
 43.76802
 11.25315
> |
```

Figure 6.21: Logging a marker's coordinates

Admittedly, getting the coordinates of a marker that you just created is not a common scenario. We simply picked this example to get the concept across. So, when does this method come in handy? Think of an application, a digitizing application, for example, where users can move markers. Before saving the data you would have to get the new position of each marker.

6.20   Changing a Marker's Position

The position of a marker can be changed programmatically using the method `setLatLng`.

Test this by creating a marker and adding it to the map:

```
var marker = L.marker([30.51, 119.96]).addTo(map);
```

Then, in your browser console, change the position:

```
marker.setLatLng([31.22, 121.47]);
```

6.21   Calculating the Distance Between Two Coordinates

The map offers a method to calculate the shortest distance in meters between two coordinates:

```
map.distance([lat, lon], [lat, lon]);
```

To calculate the distance between two markers on the map you can use the method `getLatLng` to first extract the markers' coordinates and then pass them to `distance` (fig. 6.22, on the next page):

```
map.distance(marker1.getLatLng(), marker2.getLatLng());
```

Remember that in Leaflet coordinates can almost always be represented using arrays or objects. Therefore we can directly pass the result of `getLatLng` and we don't have to explicitly mention latitude and longitude, which would end up being much longer:

```
map.distance(
        [
                marker1.getLatLng().lat,
                marker1.getLatLng().lng
        ],
        [
                marker2.getLatLng().lat,
                marker2.getLatLng().lng
        ]
);
```

Listing 6.25: Calculating the distance between two markers

```
31      var marker1 = L.marker([52.51627, 13.37771]).addTo(map);
32      var marker2 = L.marker([52.52082, 13.40941]).addTo(map);
33
34      var distance = map.distance(marker1.getLatLng(), marker2.
            getLatLng());
35
36      console.log('The distance between the two markers is', distance,
            'meters.');
```

```
The distance between the two markers is 2203.767350395619 meters.
>
```

Figure 6.22: The distance between the two markers

Note that Leaflet returns a large number of decimal places and you almost always want to limit the decimal places using JavaScript's `toFixed` method (see Limiting Decimal Places, on page 50).

6.22 Using DivIcons

Instead of using images for markers you can also use pure HTML and CSS. A `DivIcon` simply creates a div, and you can populate that div with whatever comes to your mind. The option *html* lets you define a string that contains HTML or pure text, and the option *className* lets you specify a CSS class.

In the following snippet we create a DivIcon to which we assign a CSS class and a simple text. Then in the CSS block of our page we style the text:

```
47      var textIcon = L.divIcon({className: 'text', html: 'Sudan'});
48      L.marker([19, 28], {icon: textIcon}).addTo(map);
```

Listing 6.26: Styling text

```
15    .text {
16      color: purple;
17      font-size: 80%;
18      text-decoration: underline;
19    }
```

Note that assigning a border-radius of 25 pixels to a div makes its corners completely round, meaning that you can achieve a circle effect by creating an empty div and assigning each corner a radius of 25 pixels:

```
50    var circleIcon = L.divIcon({className: 'circle'});
51    L.marker([19, 35], {icon: circleIcon}).addTo(map);
```

Listing 6.27: Assigning a border radius to create a circle

```
21    .circle {
22      background-color: blue;
23      border-radius: 25px;
24    }
```

To create a square simply leave the div empty and assign it a background color:

```
53    var squareIcon = L.divIcon({className: 'square'});
54    L.marker([13, 32], {icon: squareIcon}).addTo(map);
```

Listing 6.28: Assigning a background-color

```
26    .square {
27      background-color: green;
28    }
```

See figure 6.23 for the styled symbols.

Figure 6.23: DivIcons

There are many more things you can do with a DivIcon. Think about the jaw-dropping things you can achieve with pure CSS and get started!

Working with GeoJSON

Contents

Now that you know how to create markers, lines, and polygons, you might wonder what happens when you already have geographic data that you would like to add to your map. It would be a pity to manually retrace these datasets, especially if they're polygons that consist of hundreds of coordinate pairs. Key to adding that vector data to Leaflet is first converting it to a format that Leaflet understands—that's where the GeoJSON format comes in.

GeoJSON is the most widely used data format in web mapping and definitely deserves its own chapter. The format's popularity is partly due to the fact that GeoJSON consists of pure JavaScript. This has one unique benefit: in addition to being supported by almost all web mapping libraries, GeoJSON can also be read, queried, and changed with pure JavaScript. In other words: you do not even need a map to work with GeoJSON.

Apart from directly including GeoJSON in an application's code, it can also be stored as a separate text file. Most software will save it under the .geojson or .json file extension, but as you will learn in this chapter, often GeoJSON is simply stored in a JavaScript file.

Another great thing is you can convert about any existing vector dataset to GeoJSON. There are numerous ways to do this, such as using QGIS or ogr2ogr. Before learning how to convert existing datasets to GeoJSON, let's have a look at what GeoJSON is and what its inner structure looks like.

7.1   The Anatomy of GeoJSON

At the most basic level, let's look at three concepts that are crucial to understanding the GeoJSON format: position, geometry, and feature.

A *position* is simply a pair of coordinates, stored in array form, such as the following position, representing Berlin:

```
[13.377, 52.516]
```

This pair looks like a point at first, and to us it might be one, but in GeoJSON it takes a little bit more to classify this as a point.

This is where the *geometry* comes in. A geometry is a construct of one or more positions. GeoJSON supports seven geometry types that have to be spelled exactly as shown in the following list:

- Point
- LineString
- Polygon
- MultiPoint
- MultiLineString
- MultiPolygon
- GeometryCollection

Let's skip multigeometries for now, and we'll skip the rarely used GeometryCollection entirely.

Here's what GeoJSON geometries look like for a spot in Berlin (point), the Golden Gate Bridge (line) and the Bermuda Triangle (polygon):

Listing 7.1: GeoJSON Point geometry

```
{
  "type": "Point",
  "coordinates": [13.377,52.516]
}
```

Listing 7.2: GeoJSON LineString geometry

```
{
  "type": "LineString",
  "coordinates": [
    [-122.477, 37.809],[-122.479, 37.827]
  ]
}
```

Listing 7.3: GeoJSON Polygon geometry

```
{
  "type": "Polygon",
  "coordinates": [
    [
      [-64.775, 32.276],
      [-65.017, 18.348],
      [-80.299, 25.271],
      [-64.775, 32.276]
    ]
  ]
}
```

Notice that a geometry is simply a JavaScript object that consists of a *type* and *coordinates*. The way the coordinates, i.e. the positions, are stored is linked to their type. The simplest geometry consists of a single position, where lines and polygons use arrays or nested arrays of positions.

When creating either of the above it is extremely important that you enter longitude before latitude as a GeoJSON position requires the longitude to be entered first. This is fundamentally different from Leaflet where latitude is always entered before longitude, so pay special attention to this when manually creating GeoJSONs or working with Turf (Chapter 11, on page 225).

Do you create erroneous data when confusing latitude and longitude? Not necessarily. Remember that any number from -90 to 90 can exist as both latitude and longitude. The meaning is an entirely different one but it's geographic data either way, just not likely to be in the place you intended.

Another thing to keep in mind is that polygons must be *closed*. Did you notice that our Bermuda Triangle consists of four positions, instead of three? Yes, a GeoJSON triangle consists of four coordinate pairs. The first and last positions of a GeoJSON polygon must be identical, and identical means that the coordinates share the exact same decimal values.

Now that we have our basic geometries down it's time to look at what makes a geographic dataset truly interesting: attributes. In GeoJSON, an attribute is called a *property*. Any geometry can be linked to an indefinite number of attributes and they are stored as key-value pairs in an object called *properties*. Once a geometry has been grouped with its properties, we call it a feature. Each *feature* is simply a JavaScript object that includes three keys:

- *type*: always the string "Feature"
- *properties*: a JavaScript object
- *geometry*: a GeoJSON geometry

Should your dataset include unique identifiers for each feature you can optionally add a fourth key called *id*, whose value is either a number or a string.

Let's add some attributes to our data and create features:

Listing 7.4: GeoJSON Point feature

```
{
  "type": "Feature",
  "properties": {
    "name": "Berlin",
    "country": "Germany"
  },
  "geometry": {
    "type": "Point",
```

```
    "coordinates": [13.377, 52.516]
  }
}
```

Listing 7.5: GeoJSON LineString feature

```
{
  "type": "Feature",
  "properties": {
    "name": "Golden Gate Bridge",
    "height": " 227m"
  },
  "geometry": {
    "type": "LineString",
    "coordinates": [
      [-122.477, 37.809],
      [-122.479, 37.827]
    ]
  }
}
```

Listing 7.6: GeoJSON Polygon feature

```
{
  "type": "Feature",
  "properties": {
    "name": "Bermuda Triangle",
    "situation": "totally lost!"
  },
  "geometry": {
    "type": "Polygon",
    "coordinates": [
      [
        [-64.775, 32.276],
        [-65.017, 18.348],
        [-80.299, 25.271],
        [-64.775, 32.276]
      ]
    ]
  }
}
```

For a feature to be recognized as a feature it needs to include a properties object. If your feature does not include any attributes you can simply include the object but leave it empty:

Listing 7.7: GeoJSON feature without attributes

```
{
  "type": "Feature",
  "properties": {},
```

```
  "geometry": {
    "type": "Point",
    "coordinates": [13.377, 52.516]
  }
}
```

That's it—now you know how to create a GeoJSON feature.

Before we continue and add GeoJSON features to the map, we should look into one more essential concept: the *featureCollection*. A feature collection does exactly what its name implies—it collects features. A good amount of geographic datasets consist of more than one feature. For example, a city has multiple neighborhoods, a country has multiple cities, a continent has multiple rivers. It would not make too much sense to save all of these as individual files.

A feature collection is simply an object containing two keys:

- *type*: always the string "FeatureCollection"
- *features*: always an array including one or more features

Listing 7.8: Structure of a GeoJSON FeatureCollection

```
{
  "type": "FeatureCollection",
  "features": [
    ...
  ]
}
```

Let's create a feature collection holding three features, each one describing a city:

Listing 7.9: A GeoJSON FeatureCollection

```
{
  "type": "FeatureCollection",
  "features": [
    {
      "type": "Feature",
      "properties": {
        "name": "Addis Ababa"
      },
      "geometry": {
        "type": "Point",
        "coordinates": [38.767, 8.995]
```

```
      }
    },
    {
      "type": "Feature",
      "properties": {
        "name": "Tokyo"
      },
      "geometry": {
        "type": "Point",
        "coordinates": [139.711, 35.711]
      }
    },
    {
      "type": "Feature",
      "properties": {
        "name": "Antananarivo"
      },
      "geometry": {
        "type": "Point",
        "coordinates": [47.531, -18.897]
      }
    }
  ]
}
```

What you might not expect, but what is entirely valid, is that feature collections can contain features that have different geometry types. A feature collection really is just a collection of features, no matter what geometries and properties these features contain. Go ahead and create a feature collection holding Berlin, the Golden Gate Bridge, and the Bermuda Triangle. You'll learn how to add it to the map soon.

Depending on your needs, you may want to think twice about adding features with different geometry types to a feature collection. If you only want to add the data to a map, you don't have to worry about it, but once you start filtering or running analysis on a feature collection with different geometries it can quickly turn into a frustrating to nearly impossible task.

Coordinate Systems in GeoJSON

All data in GeoJSON must use the WGS 84 coordinate reference system, meaning that all values entered represent longitude and

World Geodetic System 1984, EPSG:4326

latitude in decimal degrees.

In older versions, the GeoJSON format was not tied to a specific coordinate system and some current software still lets you use Geo-JSON with coordinate systems other than WGS 84. The current standard explicitly states that only WGS 84 must be used, and you should absolutely avoid using anything else.

If you have older datasets that are not in WGS 84, transform them, as neither Leaflet nor Turf will be able to interpret them correctly.

That being said, there is still a way to explicitly state that WGS 84 is being used in GeoJSON, by creating a *crs* property:

Listing 7.10: The crs object

```
"crs": {
  "type": "name",
  "properties": {
    "name": "urn:ogc:def:crs:OGC::CRS84"
  }
}
```

You often see this property at the top level of a feature collection:

Listing 7.11: A FeatureCollection with a crs object

```
{
  "type": "FeatureCollection",
  "crs": { "type": "name", "properties": { "name": "urn:ogc:def:crs:
       OGC::CRS84" } },
  "features": [
    { "type": "Feature", "properties": { ...
```

Note that you do not need to specify this for Leaflet or Turf to recognize your data.

Multigeometries

With every geometry type there is also a corresponding multigeometry. Apart from specifying a different geometry type, you wrap the coordinates in an additional array.

Listing 7.12: GeoJSON MultiPoint feature

```
{
```

```
  "type": "MultiPoint",
  "coordinates": [
    [-23.21, 44.41],
    [-20.59, 46.74]
  ]
}
```

Listing 7.13: GeoJSON MultiLineString feature

```
{
  "type": "MultiLineString",
  "coordinates": [
    [[-26.87, 40.83], [-24.74, 41.16], [-24.36, 42.22]],
    [[-24.09, 43.07], [-23.16, 41.98]]
  ]
}
```

Listing 7.14: GeoJSON MultiPolygon feature

```
{
  "type": "MultiPolygon",
  "coordinates": [
    [[[-26.87, 42.18], [-25.561, 41.61], [-26.435, 40.91], [-26.87,
        42.18]]],
    [[[-24.41, 42.46], [-23.048, 42.58], [-23.103, 41.57], [-24.41,
        42.46]]]
  ]
}
```

Holes

Polygons and multipolygons can include one or more holes. When adding multiple polygons to the coordinate array, the first polygon defines the main polygon and any subsequent polygon defines a hole within the main polygon. In other words, any subsequent polygon is cut out from the main one:

Listing 7.15: GeoJSON Polygon with a hole

```
{
    "type": "Polygon",
    "coordinates": [
        [[-16.34, 44.72], [-17.39, 44.08],[-16.29, 43.73],
            [-16.34, 44.72]],
        [[-16.83, 44.25], [-16.81, 44.04], [-16.49, 44.19],
            [-16.83, 44.25]]
    ]
}
```

The GeoJSON Specification

We did not cover every detail of the GeoJSON format in this recipe, just what we needed to start using the format in a web map.

If you want to find out about further features you should consult the official specification at: http://geojson.org/

7.2   Converting Vector Data to GeoJSON with QGIS

Start QGIS and load the berlin_districts shapefile from this chapter's data folder.

Converting to GeoJSON in QGIS could not be easier. Simply right-click the dataset in the layer list, click *Save As*, then choose the format, location, and CRS (fig. 7.1):

Figure 7.1: Saving the layer as GeoJSON

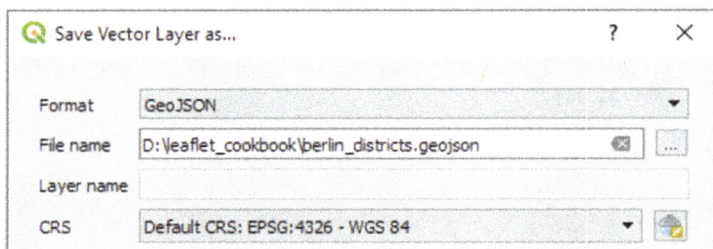

When saving it you have to be careful not to blindly accept defaults, as often the defaults differ from what you are trying to achieve. Make sure to select GeoJSON under Format and EPSG:4326 (WGS 84) under CRS. If the dataset you want to convert has any coordinate system other than WGS 84 it is important that you transform it.

In our example, Berlin's districts use EPSG:3068, which is a local coordinate system used in Berlin, and has no meaning to Leaflet whatsoever. By selecting WGS 84 from the CRS dropdown we make sure that the dataset is transformed when it is exported.

To learn more about coordinate precision, look at the recipes Working with coordinates in Leaflet, Limiting decimal places, and Adjusting coordinate precision.

Another thing to watch out for when converting to GeoJSON is coordinate precision, which defaults to 15 decimal places. Fifteen dec-

imal places is a lot, and much more than Leaflet can even render.
Let's change the precision to five (fig. 7.2):

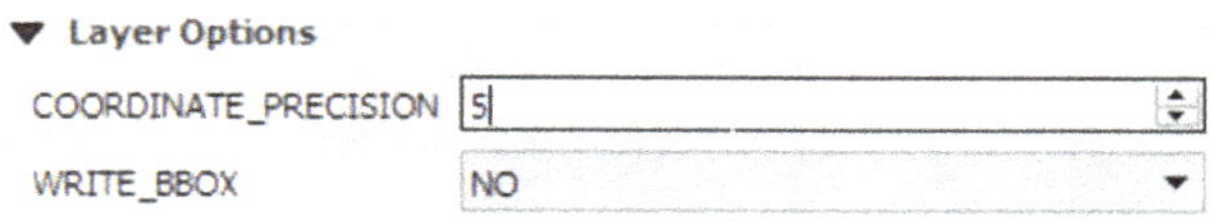

Figure 7.2: Saving the layer as GeoJSON

Once exported you can open the file in a text editor (fig. 7.3):

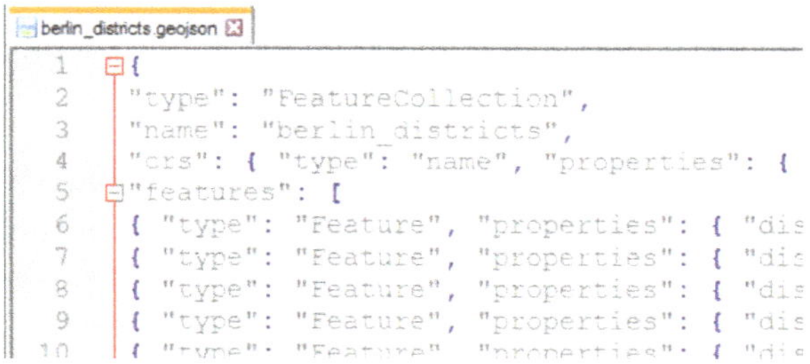

Figure 7.3: Opening the file in a text editor

Notice that QGIS always exports a feature collection, even when
you export a single feature.

7.3 Converting Vector Data to GeoJSON with ogr2ogr

There are multiple ways to convert between data formats. If you
need to automate your conversions it can be convenient to use a
command line tool. The most famous tool for converting geospatial
data is ogr2ogr. You can install it manually or, if you have installed
QGIS using the OSGeo Network Installer, you can access it through
the OSGeo Shell.

Running ogr2ogr is straightforward. The tool requires three arguments: the format into which you want to convert, the output
dataset, including its extension, and the input dataset, with extension:

```
ogr2ogr -f format output input
```

In the above snippet -f stands for the output file format.

Let's convert a shapefile (ohio.shp) to GeoJSON (ohio.geojson):

```
ogr2ogr -f GeoJSON ohio.geojson ohio.shp
```

If you need to transform from one coordinate system into another, use the *t_srs* (transform spatial reference system) option. The output coordinate system is always passed using its EPSG code. Remember that in Leaflet all datasets must be in WGS 84, so always use it:

```
ogr2ogr -f GeoJSON -t_srs EPSG:4326 ohio.geojson ohio.shp
```

The ogr2ogr utility has numerous options. Have a look at https://www.gdal.org/ogr2ogr.html to find out more.

Note that it is important to specify the output format. To find out what formats are available and what they are called in ogr2ogr, use:

```
ogr2ogr --formats
```

Run the command with the *sort* option to get a sorted list:

```
ogr2ogr --formats | sort
```

The case of the output format is not important but other than that, the output format needs to be spelled exactly as stated in the list. If the name of the output format consists of more than one word you need to use double quotes, as in:

```
ogr2ogr -f "ESRI Shapefile" rivers_4326.shp rivers.kml
```

Run the following snippet from the command lime to convert all shapefiles in a directory to .geojson files:

```
for %i in (*.shp) do ogr2ogr -f geojson "%~ni.geojson" "%i"
```
(Windows)

```
for i in *.shp; do ogr2ogr -f geojson ${i%%.*}.geojson $i; done
```
(Linux/macOS)

7.4 Adding GeoJSON to an Application and Exploring it with JavaScript

Now that we know how to get a GeoJSON file by manually creating or converting it, we can explore it with JavaScript.

Let's use the exported districts from the QGIS example. If you did not follow along, you can copy the file from the chapter's data folder.

You can either copy the GeoJSON directly into your JavaScript or you can load it from a separate file.

Storing the GeoJSON in a script tag

Copy your GeoJSON and paste it into an application's **<script>** tag. Once you have assigned it to a variable (e.g. districts) you can explore it with JavaScript.

Listing 7.16: Copying a GeoJSON into a script tag

```
9   <script>
10
11    var districts = {
12      "type": "FeatureCollection",
13      "name": "berlin_districts",
14      "crs": { "type": "name", "properties": { "name": "urn:ogc:def:crs
              :OGC:1.3:CRS84" } },
15      "features": [ ...
```

Open your browser's console and type the variable name (fig. 7.4):

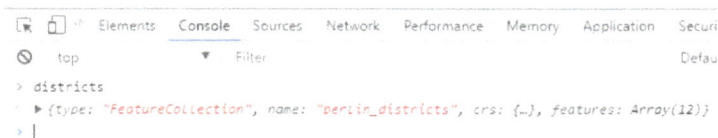

Figure 7.4: The GeoJSON in the console

You see that the entire feature collection is returned and that you can click your way through specific keys.

Or, you can programmatically explore it. We learned that a GeoJSON object consists of pure JavaScript and as long as you know how to access objects and arrays, you will be able to dig into any GeoJSON.

When you access the feature collection's *features*, you see that each feature from the original dataset is now included as a separate Geo-JSON feature (fig. 7.5):

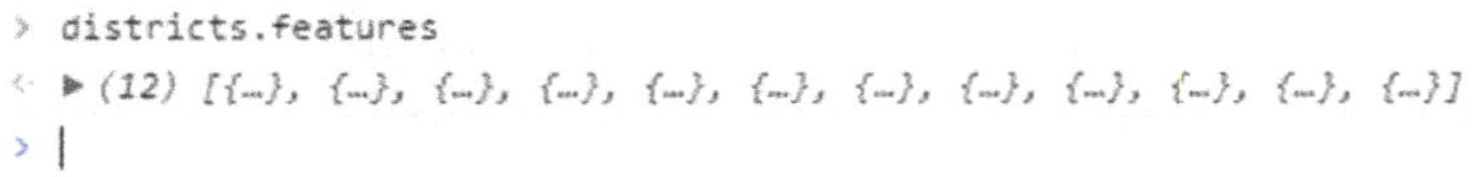

Figure 7.5: The GeoJSON's features

```
> districts.features
< ▶ (12) [{…}, {…}, {…}, {…}, {…}, {…}, {…}, {…}, {…}, {…}, {…}, {…}]
> |
```

As these features are stored in an array you can access an individual feature using its index (fig. 7.6):

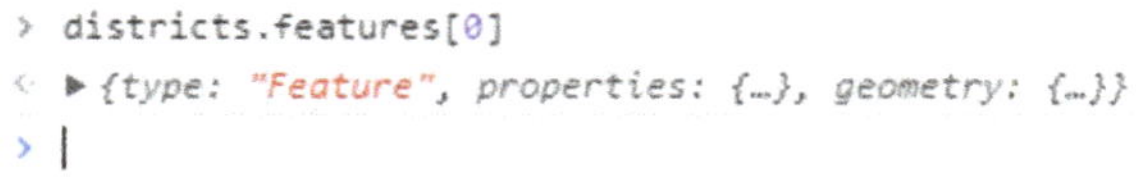

Figure 7.6: Accessing the first feature in the GeoJSON

```
> districts.features[0]
< ▶ {type: "Feature", properties: {…}, geometry: {…}}
> |
```

Once you access a single feature you can observe what we learned at the beginning of this chapter—that each GeoJSON feature has two properties: *geometry* and *properties* (fig. 7.7).

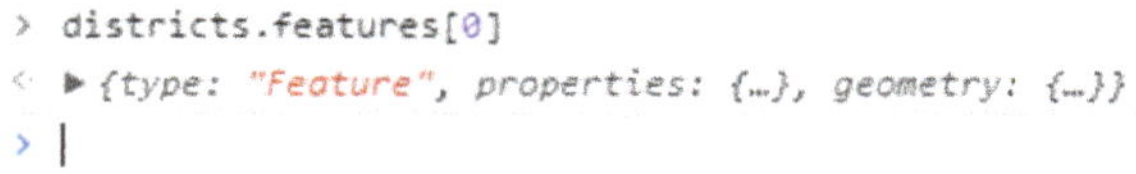

Figure 7.7: Accessing a single feature

```
> districts.features[0]
< ▶ {type: "Feature", properties: {…}, geometry: {…}}
> |
```

It's important to remember how to access these as you might need them later on, such as when working with popups (fig. 7.8).

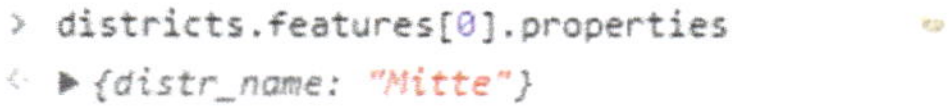

Figure 7.8: A feature's properties

```
> districts.features[0].properties
< ▶ {distr_name: "Mitte"}
```

You can also access the geometry and each single coordinate pair in the dataset. Although this can occasionally be of use, you can most often ignore it as Leaflet handles adding the dataset for you (fig. 7.9).

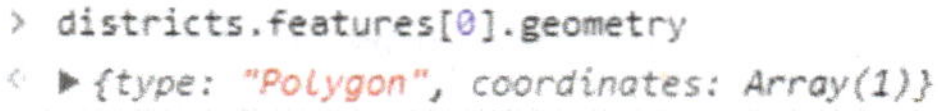

Figure 7.9: A feature's geometry

```
> districts.features[0].geometry
< ▶ {type: "Polygon", coordinates: Array(1)}
```

Storing the GeoJSON in a JavaScript file

Depending on how large your GeoJSON is, you might have noticed that your editor slowed down after copying it into the **<script>** tag. To boost performance or enhance readability, it's generally not recommended to copy datasets into your code, but rather store them separately. Since GeoJSON is JavaScript, the quickest way to get it into an application is by saving it as a JavaScript file (.js) and then including it in your application's **<head>**.

For instance, a file named berlin_districts.js and stored in a directory named data would be loaded as follows:

```
<script src="data/berlin_districts.js"></script>
```

To access it programmatically you must assign the GeoJSON to a variable (fig. 7.10):

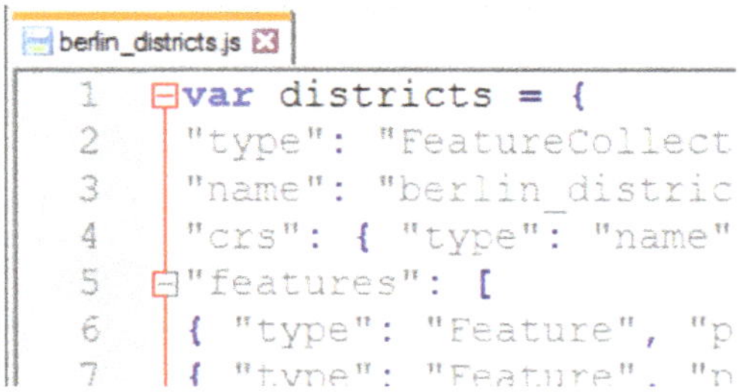

Figure 7.10: A feature's geometry

Now you can work with the GeoJSON just like before, but since it is stored in a separate file your editor's performance does not take a toll.

Another option is to load the .geojson file directly using an AJAX request, which you can read about in the recipe Loading a .geojson file, on page 316.

7.5   Creating a Table from GeoJSON

Just to deepen your understanding that GeoJSON is a spatial data format that does not require a GIS or spatial software to be read, let's iterate through a GeoJSON object and add its contents to a table in a web page (see fig 7.11, on the facing page).

Add `cities.js` to the application's head (don't forget to assign it to a variable) and create and style a table:

Listing 7.17: Creating the table

```
19    <table id="countriesTable"></table>
```

Listing 7.18: Styling the table

```
10    table, tr, td {
11      border-collapse: collapse;
12      border: 1px solid black;
13      padding: 2px;
14    }
```

Then we add a header to the table and iterate through the GeoJSON to create a new row on each iteration:

Listing 7.19: Adding GeoJSON properties to the table

```
23      var table = document.getElementById("countriesTable");
24
25      var header = table.createTHead();
26      var firstRow = header.insertRow(0);
27      firstRow.insertCell(0).innerHTML = '<b>Name</b>';
28      firstRow.insertCell(1).innerHTML = '<b>Country</b>';
29      firstRow.insertCell(2).innerHTML = '<b>Continent</b>';
30
31      for (var i = 0; i < cities.features.length; i++) {
32
33        var properties = cities.features[i].properties;
34        var row = table.insertRow(-1);
35        row.insertCell(0).innerHTML = properties.name;
36        row.insertCell(1).innerHTML = properties.country;
37        row.insertCell(2).innerHTML = properties.continent;
38
39      }
```

7.6   Adding a GeoJSON Object to the Map

Once you have added your GeoJSON object to an application you can add it to the map, but not directly. What you need to add to the map is not the raw GeoJSON but a Leaflet GeoJSON layer, which is instantiated using `L.geoJSON` and requires only one parameter: a raw GeoJSON object or a variable holding one.

Name	Country	Continent
Madrid	Spain	Europe
Paris	France	Europe
Brussels	Belgium	Europe
Portland	USA	North America
Seattle	USA	North America
Bogotá	Colombia	South America
Nairobi	Kenya	Africa
Dhaka	Bangladesh	Asia

Figure 7.11: A table created from a GeoJSON object

Let's add any GeoJSON object, such as the one we exported from QGIS, to the map. In order for this to work we either need to pass the entire GeoJSON object to `L.geoJSON` or we assign the object to a variable:

Listing 7.20: Creating and adding a GeoJSON layer

```
32    var districtsGeoJSON = L.geoJSON(districts);
33
34    districtsGeoJSON.addTo(map);
```

Note that you can create a GeoJSON layer by passing any of the following entities:

- geometry
- feature
- feature collection

Older versions

In most versions of Leaflet, GeoJSON layers were created using `L.geoJson`, which only recently has been renamed to `L.geoJSON`. Keep this in mind when working with an older version.

7.7   *Executing a Function for each Feature in a GeoJSON Layer*

One of `L.geoJSON`'s most useful options is called *onEachFeature*. It accepts a function that is executed once for each feature in the layer:

Listing 7.21: onEachFeature

```
32    var districtsGeoJSON = L.geoJSON(districts, {
```

```
33
34          onEachFeature: function() {
35
36              console.log('hello');
37
38          }
39
40      });
```

How often this function is executed always corresponds to the number of features in the layer. In our case the word *hello* is logged to the console 12 times, which corresponds to the number of districts in Berlin (fig. 7.12).

Figure 7.12: Executing a function for each feature in a GeoJSON layer

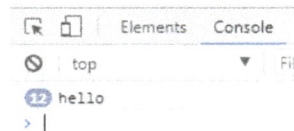

You get the idea, but before you start wondering what the point of *onEachFeature* is, let's expand the example.

The function includes two parameters, generally named *feature* and *layer*, although the naming is irrelevant. What is important is that you know that on each iteration the first parameter is automatically assigned the original GeoJSON object and the second one is assigned the layer that is created by Leaflet and added to the map.

To provide a concrete example, attaching a popup holding the district name to each feature in the dataset, you extract the name from the original feature and add the popup to the newly created layer:

Listing 7.22: Adding a popup using an anonymous function

```
32      var districtsGeoJSON = L.geoJSON(districts, {
33
34          onEachFeature: function(feature, layer) {
35
36              var districtName = feature.properties.distr_name;
37
38              layer.bindPopup(districtName);
39
40          }
```

```
41
42      });
```

In this case we defined an anonymous function but you could also define your function separately and then simply assign it. This is especially useful when using the same function for multiple layers. When doing so, be careful not to accidentally add parentheses to the function's name when assigning it to *onEachFeature*.

Listing 7.23: Adding a popup using a named function

```
32      function assignPopup(feature, layer) {
33
34          var districtName = feature.properties.distr_name;
35
36          layer.bindPopup(districtName);
37
38      }
39
40      var districtsGeoJSON = L.geoJSON(districts, {
41
42          onEachFeature: assignPopup
43
44      });
```

Also, as mentioned above, the parameters can be named differently:

```
onEachFeature: function(f, l) { ...
```

Executing a Function for each Feature after the Layer has been Created

onEachFeature only works when creating a new GeoJSON layer. If you need to iterate through the features after the layer has been created, use the eachLayer method. In the following example we add the above GeoJSON to the map, then after it is created we add the popups:

```
32      var districtsGeoJSON = L.geoJSON(districts).addTo(map);
33
34      districtsGeoJSON.eachLayer(function(layer) {
35
36        var districtName = layer.feature.properties.distr_name;
37
38        layer.bindPopup(districtName);
39
40      });
```

Note that eachLayer works on the map as well as layer and feature groups.

7.8   Filtering a GeoJSON According to Attributes

Assume you have a GeoJSON point feature collection that includes a property *type*. The value of *type* can be restaurant, hotel, or shop:

```
{
  "type": "FeatureCollection",
  "name": "restaurantHotelShop",
  "features": [
    { "type": "Feature", "properties": { "type": "restaurant" }, ...
    { "type": "Feature", "properties": { "type": "hotel" }, ...
    { "type": "Feature", "properties": { "type": "shop" }, ...
```

But what if you would like to add restaurants only? Instead of manually deleting features or filtering the feature collection in a GIS, you can do this programmatically using L.geoJSON's *filter* property.

The *filter* property accepts a function that is executed once for each feature in the dataset and the function's only parameter assumes the iteration's current feature. By default the function returns true for each feature:

```
function(feature) {

  return true;

}
```

You can interrupt this behavior by introducing a simple if statement. In the following snippet we return a feature only if its *type* property equals "restaurant":

Listing 7.24: Using the filter property

```
32    var restaurants = L.geoJSON(restaurantHotelShop, {
33
34      filter: function(feature) {
35
36        if (feature.properties.type === 'restaurant') {
37
38          return true;
39
40        }
```

```
41
42        }
43
44      });
45
46      restaurants.addTo(map);
```

This also means that by using a single GeoJSON dataset on disc you can create multiple vector layers.

In the following snippet, a vector is created for each type and then added to a layer control (see fig. 7.13, on the following page):

Listing 7.25: Creating three vector layers using one GeoJSON

```
32      var restaurants = L.geoJSON(restaurantHotelShop, {
33        filter: function(feature) {
34          if (feature.properties.type === 'restaurant') {
35            return true;
36          }
37        }
38      });
39
40      var hotels = L.geoJSON(restaurantHotelShop, {
41        filter: function(feature) {
42          if (feature.properties.type === 'hotel') {
43            return true;
44          }
45        }
46      });
47
48      var shops = L.geoJSON(restaurantHotelShop, {
49        filter: function(feature) {
50          if (feature.properties.type === 'shop') {
51            return true;
52          }
53        }
54      });
55
56      var overlays = {
57        "Restaurants": restaurants,
58        "Hotels": hotels,
59        "Shops": shops
60      };
61
62      L.control.layers({}, overlays).addTo(map);
```

Figure 7.13: Displaying hotels only

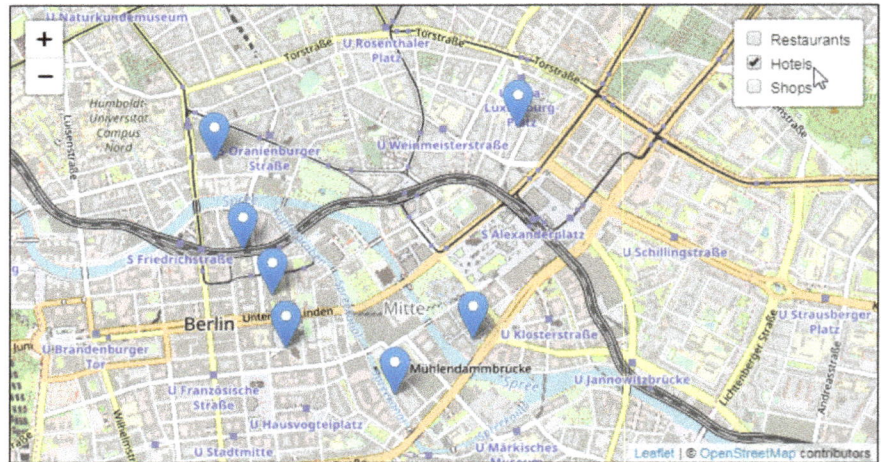

7.9   Adding features to a GeoJSON Layer

You can add features to a GeoJSON layer using the `addData` method and passing a geometry, a feature, or a feature collection:

```
var geometry = {
       "type": "Point",
       "coordinates": [38.7671, 8.9951]
}

geojsonLayer.addData(geometry);
```

A convenient feature is that the *onEachFeature* and *filter* functions will be executed if they have already been defined for the layer.

7.10   The toGeoJSON Method

The `toGeoJSON` method lets you turn the following into a GeoJSON object:

- marker
- polyline
- polygon
- circle marker
- layer group

Add a single line of code to some of the previous recipes to try this.

For example, to output the Colorado polygon from recipe 6.6, on page 102 use (see fig. 7.14):

```
31      var polygonCoordinates = [
32          [41.00167, -109.04617],
33          [40.98819, -102.04651],
34          [36.99378, -102.03003],
35          [36.99926, -109.04343]
36      ];
37
38      var polygon = L.polygon(polygonCoordinates);
39
40      var polyGeoJson = polygon.toGeoJSON();
41
42      console.log(polyGeoJson);
```

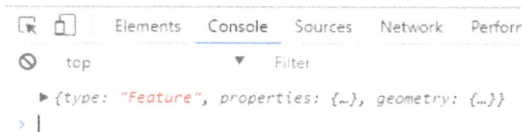

Figure 7.14: The polygon logged as a GeoJSON object

7.11   Converting a GeoJSON Object to a String

It can be extremely useful to convert a GeoJSON object to a string. For instance, when you log a GeoJSON object to the console, you can explore it by clicking and expanding it. Although this is often a good way to explore your data, it can also pose problems, especially when trying to copy it. You will end up copying formatting and information that is not directly part of the object, such as additional information that the browser displays.

Another issue is showing a GeoJSON object in a page element, such as a **<textarea>** or a **<div>**, where objects are shown as [object Object]:

```
46      document.getElementById('output').innerHTML = polyGeoJson;
```

That's why we need to convert the GeoJSON to a string first. Once it is a string it can be copied and displayed in page elements easily.

This is done using JavaScript's JSON object, which contains a method called stringify. This method converts any JavaScript object to a string (fig. 7.15):

Listing 7.26: Converting a GeoJSON to a string

```
44    var geojsonString = JSON.stringify(polyGeoJson);
45
46    console.log('Log of the GeoJSON');
47    console.log(polyGeoJson);
48    console.log('Log of the GeoJSON as a string');
49    console.log(geojsonString);
```

Figure 7.15: Logging GeoJSON as both an object and a string

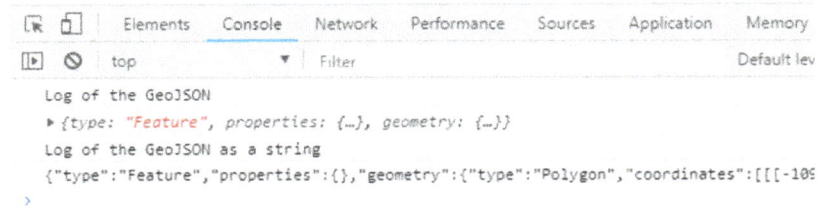

Copy the logged GeoJSON string and paste it into `http://geojson.io/`. Alternatively, you can also paste it into your text editor and save it as a `.geojson` file and then open it in QGIS.

geojson.io is a website that lets you import, export, display, and digitize GeoJSON objects.

This is incredibly convenient as it allows you to quickly transfer your vector data from Leaflet to other software. It can also save a lot of time when working with geoprocessing, as we will see in Chapter 11: Geoprocessing and Analysis with Turf.js, on page 225.

7.12   Converting a string to GeoJSON

If your GeoJSON is stored as a string you can call `JSON.parse` to convert it to a JavaScript object. When reading GeoJSON from an HTML element, such as a text area or when getting it from a request it, will be transferred as a string. In that case it's important to first parse the string so the result can be added to the map:

Listing 7.27: Parsing a GeoJSON geometry stored as a string

```
31    var geojsonString = '{"type": "Point","coordinates":
         [13.377,52.516]}';
32    var geojsonParsed = JSON.parse(geojsonString);
33    L.geoJSON(geojsonParsed).addTo(map);
```

7.13   Styling GeoJSON Point Features

When adding a point GeoJSON, the points will be shown as markers. If the points are close to each other this can be disruptive as the individual markers may overlap, as seen in figure 7.16.

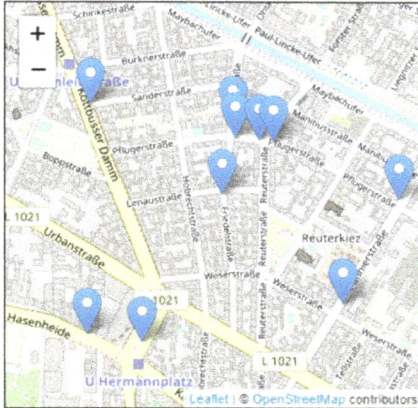

Figure 7.16: Overlapping markers

Luckily you do not have to go with the marker, but you can just as well add point features as circles or circle markers. You can pass a *pointToLayer* function, which is executed once for each point feature in the dataset.

The first parameter receives the point feature of the current iteration and the second parameter receives the point's latitude and longitude. By default, this function is executed to create markers, but you can override this behavior by either creating circles or circle markers. The *pointToLayer* option lets you pass a function that is executed once for each point feature in the dataset (fig. 7.17, on the following page).

Listing 7.28: Using pointToLayer

```
32    var style = {
33        radius: 5,
34        fillColor: "red",
35        color: "green",
36        weight: 1,
37        opacity: 1,
```

```
38        fillOpacity: 0.8
39     };
40
41     L.geoJSON(randomPoints, {
42
43       pointToLayer: function(feature, latlng) {
44
45         return L.circleMarker(latlng, style);
46
47       }
48
49     }).addTo(map);
```

Figure 7.17: Styling the features using circle markers

This uses the same style for every single point, but what if we want to use different styles? Since the first parameter in the *pointToLayer* function gives you access to the original GeoJSON feature, you can access its properties. Imagine that each feature in your GeoJSON includes an attribute, *color*, that contains a color value. In the following snippet, that property is used to override the *fillColor* defined in the style object (fig. 7.18, on the next page).

Listing 7.29: Styling by attributes

```
41     L.geoJSON(randomPoints, {
42
43       pointToLayer: function(feature, latlng) {
44
45         style.fillColor = feature.properties.color;
46
47         return L.circleMarker(latlng, style);
```

```
48
49        }
50
51     }).addTo(map);
```

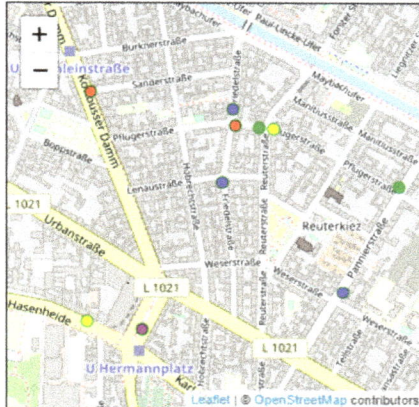

Figure 7.18: Styling the features using an attribute

You can be creative when styling layers, and you do not necessarily need to have an attribute with predefined color values. In the following snippet the property *rating*, an integer between 0 and 10, is read, and based on a conditional statement, the circle marker's color and size is assigned (fig. 7.19, on the following page).

Listing 7.30: Styling by attributes using if statements

```
41     L.geoJSON(randomPoints, {
42
43       pointToLayer: function(feature, latlng) {
44
45         var rating = feature.properties.rating;
46
47         if (rating < 5) {
48
49           style.fillColor = 'red';
50           style.radius = 4;
51
52         } else {
53
54           style.fillColor = '#00ff11';
55
56         }
57
58         return L.circleMarker(latlng, style);
```

```
59
60          }
61
62      }).addTo(map);
```

Figure 7.19: Styling determined by conditions

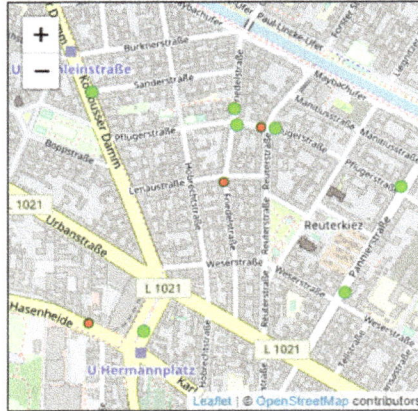

And what if you'd like to create default markers after all, but only if a condition applies? In that case, simply return a Leaflet marker in an if statement:

Listing 7.31: Styling by attributes using if statements

```
32      L.geoJSON(randomPoints, {
33
34        pointToLayer: function(feature, latlng) {
35
36          var rating = feature.properties.rating;
37
38          if (rating < 5) {
39
40            return L.marker(latlng);
41
42          }
43
44        }
45
46      }).addTo(map);
```

8 *Getters and Setters*

Contents

Many libraries include *getters* and *setters*. The names are self-explanatory: getters return the current state of an element and setters set the state of an element.

Let's look at some examples:

Getters:

- get the center of the map
- get the zoom level of the map
- get the size of the map container
- get a marker's coordinates

Setters:

- set the center of the map (zoom to a location)
- set the zoom level of the map (zoom in, zoom out)
- set the size of the map container (increase or decrease the width)
- set a marker's coordinates (change its location)

In short, a getter simply returns the state of something, whereas a setter actually changes something.

Often, a getter method starts with the word *get* and a setter method starts with the word *set*, but this is not always the case. When browsing the documentation don't simply search for get and set, but look at other methods as well.

Setter methods often come in handy to change map properties that were defined at the beginning and need to be adjusted. For example, you might restrict your map to a specific extent using the *maxBounds* property, but later on a dataset is loaded that is outside these bounds. In that case you could adjust the maximum bounds to accommodate the dataset.

This chapter introduces you to some of the most important getters and setters used in Leaflet. The getters and setters listed in this chapter mostly apply to the map, so be aware that additional getters and setters are found in other chapters.

8.1 Getting Information About the Map Container

You can get the map container height and width by calling `getSize` and then extracting *x* and *y*:

```
var width = map.getSize().x;
var height = map.getSize().y;
```

To select the entire map container, use:

```
map.getContainer();
```

This is equivalent to selecting the container via JavaScript's `getElementById`:

```
document.getElementById('map');
```

8.2 Getting the Current Zoom Level and Center

You can get the current zoom level using:

```
map.getZoom();
```

And you can get the current center using:

```
map.getCenter();
```

Remember that coordinates can exist in three different ways in Leaflet. See Working with Coordinates in Leaflet, on page 44 The `getCenter` method returns the coordinates as an object, such as:

```
{lat: -18.913208661776835, lng: 47.52996683120728}
```

You can then extract the latitude and longitude individually:

```
var center = map.getCenter();
var lat = center.lat;
var lon = center.lng; // the longitude is shortened to lng, not lon!
```

Of course, you could also achieve this without declaring an intermediate variable to hold the center:

```
var lat = map.getCenter().lat;
var lon = map.getCenter().lng;
```

Although optional, you might want to limit the decimal places:

```
var lat = map.getCenter().lat.toFixed(5);
```

A Common Scenario

The above methods are used often when creating a new map. Instead of getting the center coordinates of the view from a website or a GIS, you should define the map with a random center and zoom level, load the map, move to the location where you want your map to initialize, open your browser's console, extract the current zoom level and center, and then update your code accordingly.

8.3 Getting the Current Zoom Level and Center on Button Click

Let's write a short application that gets the zoom and center of the map after clicking on a button.

First, add a button and two paragraphs to the page:

Listing 8.1: Adding elements to the page

```
19    <input type="button" id="zoomCenterButton" value="Get Zoom and
          Center">
20    <p id="currentLatLon"></p>
21    <p id="currentZoom"></p>
```

After clicking the button the paragraphs will hold the current center and zoom level.

Now it's just a matter of writing a function that reads the map center and zoom, and then displays those in the paragraphs:

Listing 8.2: Displaying center and zoom in the page

```
34   function getZoomAndCenter() {
35
36      // get the map's center and extract its lat and lon
37      var center = map.getCenter();
38      var lat = center.lat.toFixed(4);
39      var lon = center.lng.toFixed(4);
40
41      // get the map's zoom level
42      var zoom = map.getZoom();
43
44      // display lat, lon, zoom in the page
45      document.getElementById('currentLatLon').innerHTML = '<b>Lat</b
          >: ' + lat + ' <b>Lon</b>: ' + lon;
46      document.getElementById('currentZoom').innerHTML = '<b>Zoom</b
          >: ' + zoom;
47
48   }
49
50   // on button click, fire getZoomAndCenter function
51   document.getElementById('zoomCenterBtn').onclick =
          getZoomAndCenter;
```

Figure 8.1: Getting the current center and zoom on button click

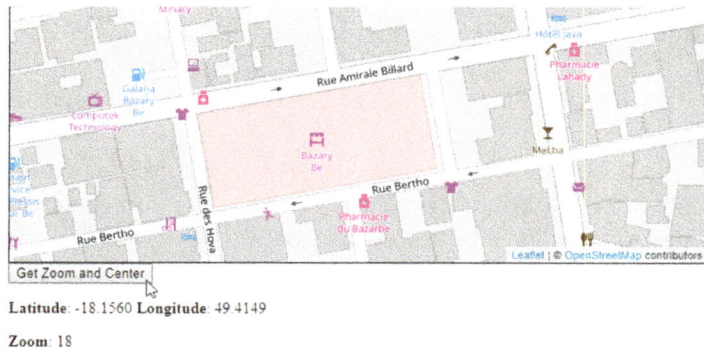

Get Zoom and Center

Latitude: -18.1560 **Longitude**: 49.4149

Zoom: 18

Note that in the example (fig. 8.1) we limited the coordinate decimal places to four, which corresponds to an accuracy of about 11 meters. Although limiting the decimal places is optional, it's good practice.

Showing all of the decimals returned by Leaflet is, in most cases, not only nonsensical, but it can also be confusing to users and reduce the readability.

To automatically get the center during or after moving the map, refer to recipe 10.13, on page 214.

8.4 Panning to a Location

You can pan to a location using the `panTo` method:

```
map.panTo([49.61, 6.12]);
```

Instead of panning to an exact location, you can also pan the map a specified number of pixels, starting from the current position. You always provide an x value (right-left) and a y value (top-bottom).

If the x value is positive the map pans to the right. If the x value is negative the map pans to the left.

If the y value is positive the map pans to the bottom. If the y value is negative the map pans to the top.

```
map.panBy([x, y]);
```

Let's have a look at a few examples.

The map pans 500 pixels to the right:

```
map.panBy([500, 0]);
```

The map pans 500 pixels to the left:

```
map.panBy([-500, 0]);
```

The map pans 500 pixels to the bottom:

```
map.panBy([0, 500]);
```

The map pans 500 pixels to the top:

```
map.panBy([0, -500]);
```

The map diagonally pans 500 pixels to the right and 500 pixels to the bottom:

```
map.panBy([500, 500]);
```

The map diagonally pans 500 pixels to the left and 500 pixels to the top:

```
map.panBy([-500, -500]);
```

8.5 Setting the Map View

The setView has the exact same effect as the panTo method but optionally takes a zoom level as a second parameter. Whereas panTo always keeps the current zoom level, setView lets you change it.

```
map.setView([49.61, 6.12]);
```
```
map.setView([49.61, 6.12], 15);
```

The setView method is one of the most often used methods in Leaflet, as it quickly allows you to jump to a specific coordinate. You commonly see people create a map without assigning *center* and *zoom* and then call setView right afterwards:

```
L.map('map').setView([49.61, 6.12], 15);
```

8.6 Programmatic Zooming

Leaflet has methods to easily zoom the map from within your code.

Zooming In and Out

You can programmatically zoom in one level using the zoomIn method

```
map.zoomIn();
```

and you can zoom out one level using the zoomOut method:

```
map.zoomOut();
```

These methods are equivalent to using the zoom buttons and they always zoom at the current view's center.

Optionally you can pass a parameter to define how many steps Leaflet should zoom in or out. In the following snippet the map does not zoom in one level, but three:

```
map.zoomIn(3);
```

Setting the Zoom Level

Instead of zooming in and out step by step you can also jump to a specific zoom level by using the setZoom method :

```
map.setZoom(7);
```

When zooming using the mouse wheel or by double-clicking, the map zooms in to the cursor position. To duplicate this effect pro-grammatically, you can use setZoomAround, which zooms in while a specified point stays at the same location.

The best way to test this is by setting a marker and then setting the zoom around that marker. You will notice that the marker stays in the exact same spot:

```
L.marker([43,12]).addTo(map);
map.setZoomAround([43,12], 6);
```

Note that this does not actually zoom to the specified point—if the point is outside of the view it remains outside of the view.

Setting the Minimum and Maximum Zoom

The map's *minZoom* and *maxZoom* options can be changed after cre-ating the map by calling setMinZoom and setMaxZoom and passing the desired zoom level.

8.7   Working with Bounding Boxes

Bounding boxes in Leaflet are defined by specifying two diagonally opposite corners.

Getting the Bounding Box of an Element

You can get the bounding box of the following elements using the getBounds method:

• Map

- ImageOverlay
- Polyline
- Polygon
- Circle
- FeatureGroup

Note that you can get the bounds of a feature group but not of a
layer group.

The bounds are always returned as an object, exposing the southwest corner and the northeast corner, but remember that when creating bounds yourself, it does not matter which corners are added,
as long as the corners are diagonally opposite.

In the following snippet we create a line and then log its bounding
box (fig. 8.2):

Listing 8.3: Getting the bounding box of a line

```
31    var line = L.polyline([
32        [37.80921, -122.47726],
33        [37.82792, -122.47953]
34    ]).addTo(map);
35
36    var bbox = line.getBounds();
37
38    console.log(bbox);
```

Figure 8.2: The bounds of the line

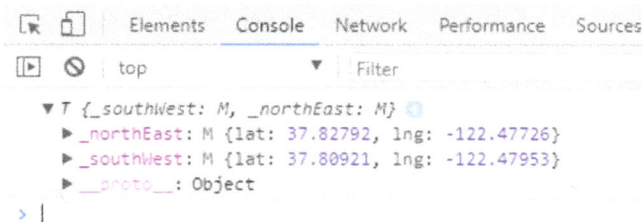

To display the bounds you can create a rectangle instead of a polygon, as L.rectangle requires only two coordinate pairs. The following snippets would both work, as it does not matter which pair
is passed first:

```
L.rectangle([bbox._southWest, bbox._northEast]).addTo(map);
```

```
L.rectangle([bbox._northEast, bbox._southWest]).addTo(map);
```

Note that, unlike the bounds of a vector or an image, the bounds of the map are variable. Every time you move the map or zoom in, the bounds change.

The map has an additional method, which can be useful: `getBoundsZoom`. This method takes a bounding box as a parameter and returns either the maximum zoom level which is necessary for the bounding box to fit entirely into the map view (*line 35*) or it returns the minimum zoom level the map view can fit entirely into the bounds (*line 36*):

Listing 8.4: Using getBoundsZoom

```
31    var neCorner = [43.622, 12.897];
32    var swCorner = [37.796, 5.207];
33    var bbox = L.latLngBounds(neCorner, swCorner);
34
35    var max = map.getBoundsZoom(bbox);
36    var min = map.getBoundsZoom(bbox, true);
37
38    console.log('Max:', max);
39    console.log('Min:', min);
```

Turning a Bounding Box into a String

All bounding boxes can be converted to a string using `toBBoxString`. Test this by running the following in the console:

```
var bbox = map.getBounds();
bbox.toBBoxString();
```

Fitting a Bounding Box

To set the map view according to a bounding box instead of a center point and zoom level, you can use the `fitBounds` method. This method zooms in as far as possible to make the entire bounding box fit.

```
map.fitBounds([
  [38.47, -18.98],
  [-38.35, 54.49]
]);
```

Have a look at recipe 10.16, on page 216 to see this in action.

Fitting the World

Leaflet contains a convenient method to make the entire world fit: `fitWorld`. This method does not simply set the zoom level to 0, but it zooms in to the maximum zoom level that can encompass the entire world.

```
map.fitWorld();
```

The effect of this method, i.e. what it takes to make the world fit, is dependent on the size of the map container.

Setting the Maximum Bounds

You can change the map's *maxBounds* property by calling `setMaxBounds` and passing a bounds array.

8.8   Flying Animations

Flying to a location

The `flyTo` method takes you to a location, just like the `setView` and `panTo` methods, but it uses a flying animation when doing so:

```
map.flyTo([49.61, 6.12]);
```

The animation does the following. While panning to the new location, the map zooms out from the current location and descends again once it is getting close to the new location, similar to a plane taking off and landing. How elaborate this animation is depends on the distance between the two locations.

Flying to a Bounding Box

If you'd like to add a flying animation when zooming to a bounding box you can use `flyToBounds`, which works exactly like `fitBounds` but adds a flying animation to the process:

```
map.flyToBounds([
  [38.47, -18.98],
```

```
    [-38.35, 54.49]
  ]);
```

Adding Padding to Bounds Methods

You can pass the options *paddingTopLeft, paddingBottomRight,* or the
shortcut *padding* when using `fitBounds` and `flyToBounds`. The options function exactly as for popups.

Deactivating Zooming Animations

Methods that let you change the zoom levels, such as `zoomIn`, `zoomOut`,
`setView`, and `setZoom` come with an animation. To deactivate the
animation, simply pass the option *animate* and set it to `false`, as in:

```
map.setView([65, -18], 6, {animate: false})
```

8.9   Zooming to a Location on Button Click

Sometimes you need to add one or more buttons in your application
that, when clicked, zoom to a specific location.

Let's create an application with a button that lets you zoom to
Tokyo.

First you need to create a button:

Listing 8.5: Creating a zoom button

```
20    <input type="button" id="zoomToLocation" value="Zoom to Tokyo">
```

Then write a function that zooms to a location, assigning it to the
button's click event:

Listing 8.6: Zooming to a location on button click

```
33    function zoomToLocation() {
34
35      map.setView([35.521, 139.952], 9);
36
37    }
38
39    document.getElementById('zoomToLocation').onclick =
            zoomToLocation;
```

The map now zooms to Tokyo anytime you click the button.

Instead of adding a button that zooms to a single location you could also create an application that lets the user enter a coordinate and zoom level before clicking the button.

First create a button with a more generic name, such as *Zoom to Location*. You also need to add input fields so users can enter coordinates and the zoom level. It would be advisable to add separate fields for latitude and longitude. Letting users add both the latitude and longitude to one field can be error prone if they don't pay close attention to how the coordinates must be formatted.

Listing 8.7: Creating input elements and a button

```
34    Latitude: <input type="text" id="latInput">
35    Longitude: <input type="text" id="lonInput">
36    Zoom: <input type="text" id="zoomInput">
37    <br>
38    <input type="button" id="zoomToLocation" value="Zoom to Location">
```

Instead of zooming to a fixed location and zoom level, the function first reads the contents of the input fields, and then passes them to the setView method (fig. 8.3):

Listing 8.8: Reading from the input elements on button click

```
51    function zoomToLocation() {
52
53      var lat = document.getElementById('latInput').value;
54      var lon = document.getElementById('lonInput').value;
55      var zoom = document.getElementById('zoomInput').value;
56
57      map.setView([lat, lon], zoom);
58
59    }
60
61    document.getElementById('zoomToLocation').onclick =
            zoomToLocation;
```

Figure 8.3: Zooming to an entered location

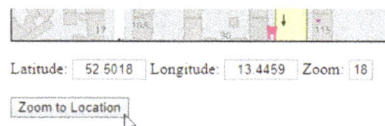

8.10   Creating Your Own Zoom Buttons

Sometimes you don't want to use the standard zoom buttons. A good example of this is when creating an application that includes a toolbar. The toolbar might include digitizing tools, a download button, and perhaps the zoom buttons to give the application a more consistent look.

When doing this you should first add the new buttons to the HTML. In the following snippet the buttons are added straight to the **<body>**, but in most cases you would add the buttons to other elements, such as the toolbar mentioned above (fig. 8.4).

Listing 8.9: Creating zoom buttons

```
19    <input type="button" value="Zoom In" id="btnZoomIn">
20    <input type="button" value="Zoom Out" id="btnZoomOut">
```

Zoom In   Zoom Out

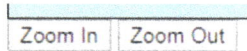

Figure 8.4: HTML buttons used to zoom in and out

It's also important to remove the zoom control, since it's redundant when using your own zoom buttons.

Listing 8.10: Disabling the zoom control

```
24    var map = L.map('map', {
25      center: [34.1618, -97.7343],
26      zoom: 4,
27      zoomControl: false
28    });
```

Finally, write functions that execute the zoomIn and zoomOut methods, and then hook them up to the buttons:

Listing 8.11: Writing zoom functions

```
34    function zoomIn() {
35
36      map.zoomIn();
37
38    }
39
40    function zoomOut() {
41
42      map.zoomOut();
```

```
43
44        }
45
46        document.getElementById('btnZoomIn').onclick = zoomIn;
47        document.getElementById('btnZoomOut').onclick = zoomOut;
```

9 *Layout and Styling*

Contents

In this chapter we'll take a look at styling vector datasets as well as the map container. The end of the chapter shows you how to create your own basemap and add it to Leaflet.

9.1 Creating a Full Screen Map

Creating a map that takes up the entire browser window is accomplished using CSS and assigning a width and a height of 100% to the map **<div>**. For this to work, we have to assign a width and height of 100% to the **<body>** and **<html>** tags as well.

Initially you'll notice that the map does not actually take up the entire height and width and a scrollbar appears on the right-hand side. This is because our browser comes with certain default settings for the **<body>**, such as a default margin or padding.

By setting the body's margin and padding to 0 using CSS, we can make the map take up the entire web page:

Listing 9.1: Creating a fullscreen map

```
10     body {
11       padding: 0;
12       margin: 0;
13     }
14
15     html, body, #map {
16       height: 100%;
17       width: 100%;
18     }
```

Feel free to resize your browser and see that the map always adjusts to the screen.

Although automatic resizing is convenient, there are cases where you want to disable it. Do this by setting the map's *trackResize* option to `false`:

```
28     var map = L.map('map', {
29       center: [44.1347, 9.6834],
30       zoom: 18,
31       trackResize: false
32     });
```

9.2   *Labeling*

You can label features by simply adding tooltips. This, however, comes with a default styling.

You can get rid of the default styling, i.e. showing text only, by using the following CSS:

```
19
20     .leaflet-tooltip {
21       background-color: initial;
22       border-style: none;
23       box-shadow: none;
24     }
25
26     .leaflet-tooltip-left:before {
27       border-left-color: transparent;
```

```
28        }
```

Of course, based on that you can come up with your own styling as well.

Possibly a quicker way is to use a DivIcon, which you can read about in the recipe Using DivIcons, on page 124.

9.3   Extending Popups with Custom HTML and CSS

Instead of adding simple text to a popup, you can also add HTML and CSS. Almost any HTML element can be added to a popup and CSS can be used for positioning, sizing, and coloring the contents.

When creating popups this way it helps to write the contents on multiple lines, as it increases readability.

In the following example, we add an image and multiple HTML elements (fig. 9.1):

Listing 9.2: Adding markup to a popup

```
31      var brewery = L.marker([33.11598, -117.12005]);
32
33      var popupContent = '<b>Type</b>: brewery';
34      popupContent += ' <img src="icons/hopBlack.png" width="15">';
35      popupContent += '<br>';
36      popupContent += '<b>Comment</b>: ';
37      popupContent += '<i>if you like hops this place is for you!</i>';
38
39      brewery.bindPopup(popupContent);
40
41      brewery.addTo(map);
```

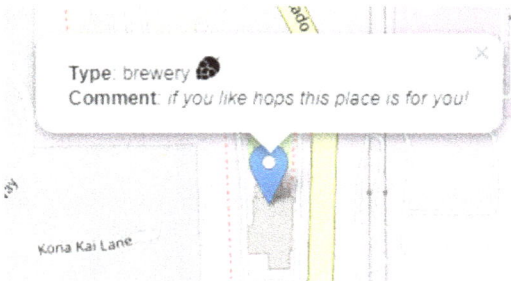

Figure 9.1: A popup using markup

Adding CSS can be done using the style attribute, which can be assigned to any HTML element (fig. 9.2):

Listing 9.3: Using the style attribute

```
33    var popupContent = '<h4>Comment</h4>';
34    popupContent += '<p style="color: blue; font-style: italic;">
          Truly awesome place.</p>';
```

Figure 9.2: Styling added using the style attribute

Since CSS often consists of multiple rules, using the style attribute can get messy. The code gets harder to read the longer it gets, and also becomes harder to adjust. Therefore, it is advisable to transfer your styling to a separate file or the **<style>** tag and select the element by assigning a CSS class:

Listing 9.4: Assigning a class

```
39    popupContent += '<p class="popupStyle">Truly awesome place.</p>';
```

Listing 9.5: Selecting the class and assigning styling

```
15    .popupStyle {
16      color: blue;
17      font-style: italic;
18    }
```

Just like in normal web design, the **<span>** element can come in handy. In the following snippet we use a **<span>** element to style a single word (fig. 9.3, on the next page):

Listing 9.6: Using a span element to access a word

```
39    popupContent += '<p>Truly <span style="font-size: 150%">awesome</
          span> place.</p>';
```

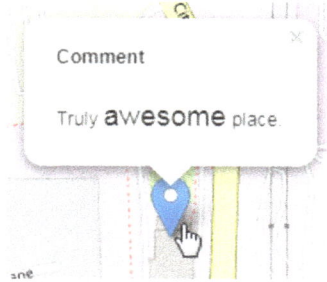

Figure 9.3: Styling using a span element

9.4   Understanding Path

When looking for available styling options in Leaflet you have to search the documentation for `Path`.

`Path` is never created directly. Vector layers inherit `Path`, and it becomes automatically available in the options object. Any option you find in the documentation under `Path` can therefore simply be added to the vector layer options object.

Also note that `Path` cannot be used for markers. Since markers are loaded as images in Leaflet and not rendered as geometries, they cannot be changed with code. In recipe 9.7, on page 177 we'll learn how to replace a marker's default image. Alternatively you could create a circle or a circle marker, which can be styled using `Path`.

Styles are always passed as an object, and the name of the keys are straightforward. The following options are available when styling vector layers:

- stroke
- color
- weight
- opacity
- lineCap
- lineJoin
- dashArray
- dashOffset

- fill
- fillColor
- fillOpacity
- fillRule
- bubblingMouseEvents
- renderer
- className

In the next recipe, we'll have a look at some of the `Path` options.

9.5   Styling Vector Layers

Let's use the line we created in recipe 6.5, on page 101 and paint the Golden Gate Bridge red.

When we search the Leaflet documentation for `polyLine` options we see that besides the options that are specific to `polyLine`, there are also options that have been inherited, which includes `Path` (fig. 9.4).

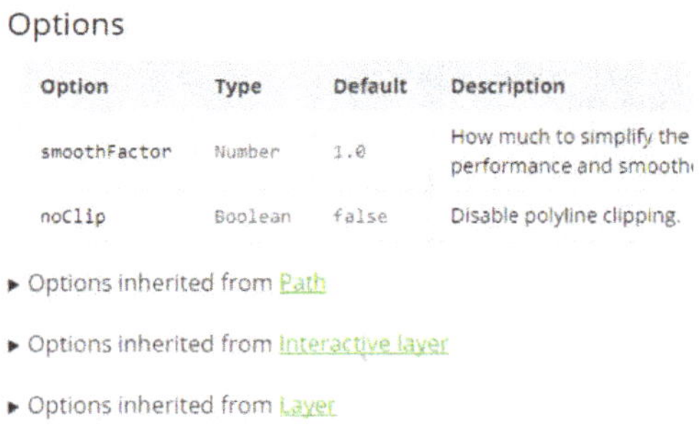

Figure 9.4: Options for L.polyLine

Options

Option	Type	Default	Description
smoothFactor	Number	1.0	How much to simplify the performance and smooth
noClip	Boolean	false	Disable polyline clipping.

▸ Options inherited from Path

▸ Options inherited from Interactive layer

▸ Options inherited from Layer

Instead of having to create an instance of `Path`, we can simply look at the available properties in `Path` and add those to the line's options object. Unlike most classes in Leaflet, `Path` is never instantiated and it is always used by assigning its properties to a vector layer's options.

```
var line = L.polyline(lineCoordinates, {color: 'red'});
```

Just like in CSS you are not limited to color names—you can also use hex values or RGB/RGBA notation.

Let's assign the actual color (International Orange), make the line a little wider, and 20% transparent:

Listing 9.7: Styling a line

```
36    var line = L.polyline(lineCoordinates, {
37      color: '#F04A00',
38      weight: 10,
39      opacity: 0.8
40    });
```

Note that opacity always takes a value between 0 and 1, 0 being 100% transparent and 1 being 0% transparent. A value of 0.8 means it is 20% transparent.

Also note that instead of using opacity we could have used an rgba sequence when assigning the color: rgba(240, 74, 00, 0.8).

The effect of *color* differs depending on the geometry type you assign it to. In the case of lines, color refers to the line. In the case of polygons, color refers to both the outer line and the inner area. To style the inner part differently, you have to use the *fillColor* option.

In the following example, we assign *color* and *opacity* to both Colorado's outer boundary and inner area:

Listing 9.8: Styling a polygon

```
38    var polygon = L.polygon(polygonCoordinates, {
39      color: '#BF0A30',
40      opacity: 0.8,
41      fillColor: '#002868',
42      fillOpacity: 0.8
43    });
```

To remove a polygon fill color, you should not assign it an opacity of 0, but should rather set its *fill* option to false.

9.6   Creating a Dashed Line

A dashed line is created using Path's *dashArray* property. The first thing you need to know is that this is actually not provided as a JavaScript array, but as a string. The string includes comma-separated integers, such as '5, 5' (you can also separate the values by an empty space).

The first value is the solid dash and the second value is the space in between dashes.

For instance: '20, 15' means that there is dash that is 20 pixels long, followed by an empty space of 15 pixels. This pattern is then repeated as often as necessary to complete the line.

You can also use more advanced patterns, such as '20, 15, 10, 15', which returns a line that has the following pattern: 20 pixel dash, 15 pixel space, 10 pixel dash, 15 pixel space.

It's straightforward as long as you use an even number of values in your pattern. When using an odd number of values it gets slightly more complicated, although it is a way to generate complex line styles. What happens is that internally your pattern is doubled, so it turns into a pattern with an even number of values. For instance, the pattern '20, 15, 10' will turn into '20, 15, 10, 20, 15, 10'. The result is the following pattern: 20 pixel dash, 15 pixel space, 10 pixel dash, 20 pixel space, 15 pixel dash, 10 pixel space. Note that in that case the values alternate between being a dash and a space between dashes.

Let's create a simple line and add it to the map. Once you get this to work, feel free to adjust the pattern and refresh your page. The best way to get a good understanding of how dash patterns work is to play with the values and see what happens.

Listing 9.9: Creating a dashed line

```
31    var options = {
32      dashArray: '20, 15, 10',
33      weight: 1,
34      color: 'black'
35    };
36
37    var line = L.polyline([[0, -179.9], [0, 179.9]], options);
38
39    line.addTo(map);
```

A few examples of dash patterns follow (figures 9.5 through 9.9).

Figure 9.5: Dash pattern '20, 20'

Figure 9.6: Dash pattern '20, 10'

Figure 9.7: Dash pattern '10, 20'

Figure 9.8: Dash pattern '20, 15, 10'

Figure 9.9: Dash pattern '20, 15, 10, 15'

9.7 Adding Your Own Image to a Marker

Replacing Leaflet's default marker can be done in two ways. Either you replace the actual file in Leaflet's source code (marker-icon.png) or you assign a different image when creating markers.

How many parameters you have to enter depends on what your new icon looks like. If you keep using the original marker and simply adjust its colors in an image editor, then adding the image is rather simple. You create the new icon using L.icon and then you assign it to the marker's *icon* option:

```
31      var greenMarker = L.icon({
32          iconUrl: 'images/green-marker-icon.png',
33      });
34
35      L.marker([24, -69], {icon: greenMarker}).addTo(map);
```

If the new marker has a different shape and size then you might have to pass some or all of the following options:

- *iconSize*
- *iconAnchor*
- *popupAnchor*
- *shadowSize*
- *shadowAnchor*

All of these options are assigned an array holding an x and y value, and getting the marker, its shadow, and popups to appear in the correct spot is just a matter of adjusting these numbers and perhaps some trial and error.

You can also define your own shadow image by passing *shadowUrl*.

If you are using markers that are hosted on a different server or if you have other reasons to expect that your marker icon is not always accessible, then you should assign some text to the marker's *alt* option (fig. 9.10):

```
35        L.marker([24, -69],  {icon: greenMarker, alt: 'green icon'}).
              addTo(map);
```

Figure 9.10: Text that is displayed when the marker image is not found or cannot be accessed

9.8 Changing the Style of a Vector Layer

Sometimes you would like to change a vector layer's style after it has been created—we can do this using the `setStyle` method that takes a simple object containing `Path` properties and values.

Test this by creating a polygon:

```
31        var polygon = L.polygon([
32          [25.3611, -80.2551],
33          [32.2393, -64.8632],
34          [18.3895, -65.6543]
35        ], {
36           color: 'black',
37           fillColor: 'yellow'
38          });
39
40        polygon.addTo(map);
```

Now in the console execute:

```
polygon.setStyle({color: 'green', fillColor: 'pink'});
```

followed by:

```
polygon.setStyle({weight: 15});
```

You'll notice that first the polygon stroke and fill colors are updated, and then the width is updated, but all other properties remain the same. Just like in CSS, using `setStyle` adds to an element's style, and existing properties will not be changed unless you pass them again (i.e. override them).

To revert back to a layer's original style you have to pass the original styling again, plus any additional properties you adjusted that were not part of the original style:

```
polygon.setStyle({color: 'black', fillColor: 'yellow'});
```

The only exception is the GeoJSON layer, which exposes a `resetStyle` method.

9.9   Resetting the Style of a GeoJSON Layer

The GeoJSON layer is the only vector layer that has a method to reset its original style. Let's create a simple GeoJSON object and add it to the map:

```
32    var polygon = {
33      "type": "Polygon",
34      "coordinates": [
35        [
36          [-80.2551, 25.3611],
37          [-64.8632, 32.2393],
38          [-65.6543, 18.3895]]
39        ]
40    };
41
42    var polygon_geojson = L.geoJSON(polygon, {
43      color: 'black',
44      fillColor: 'yellow'
45    });
46
47    polygon_geojson.addTo(map);
```

In the console change its style using `setStyle`:

```
polygon_geojson.setStyle({
  color: 'green',
  fillColor: 'pink',
  weight: 6
});
```

Now we'd like to revert back to the GeoJSON layer's original style, which can be achieved with the resetStyle method. The tricky detail is that resetStyle only works for single features and not an entire layer, so we cannot call the method directly on the layer.

The quickest way to access individual layers in GeoJSON is by looping through the layer using the eachLayer method:

```
polygon_geojson.eachLayer(function(e) {

  polygon_geojson.resetStyle(e)

});
```

This may seem a little cumbersome at first, but it is mostly used with events, such as clicking or hovering. Skip to recipe 10.17, on page 217 to see resetStyle in action.

9.10 Creating Draggable DOM Elements

Any HTML element in your page can be made draggable using Leaflet:

```
var element = document.getElementById('elementId');
var draggableElement = new L.Draggable(element);
draggableElement.enable();
```

The element does not need to be part of the page from the beginning—you can create an element using JavaScript and then make it draggable using Leaflet.

When creating an element be careful where you add it.

An element that is added to the body becomes draggable in the entire web page:

```
document.body.appendChild(element);
```

An element appended to the map is only available within the map:

```
document.getElementById('map').appendChild(element);
```

Make sure you test draggable elements carefully as they might disappear behind other elements. By default an element that is positioned statically will disappear behind the map, as the map has a high z-index. Therefore, if you want to drag an element over the map it is essential that you increase its z-index. Remember that adjusting the z-index of an element only has effect if the element is not positioned statically. An element must use relative, absolute, or fixed positioning in order for its z-index to work.

In the following example we create a **<div>** that we add to the map and then make it draggable. We change it's position to relative in order to be able to set its z-index and we set the z-index to 999, which is high enough to make it appear on top of the basemap but below the zoom control. We use the top and left properties to position it next to the zoom control.

Listing 9.10: Creating a draggable div

```
31    var div = document.createElement('div');
32    div.style.width = '100px';
33    div.style.height = '50px';
34    div.style.background = 'blue';
35    div.style.color = 'white';
36    div.innerHTML = 'I am a draggable!';
37    div.style.position = 'relative';
38    div.style.left = '55px';
39    div.style.top = '10px';
40    div.style.zIndex = '999';
41
42    document.getElementById('map').appendChild(div);
43
44    var draggableDiv = new L.Draggable(div);
45    draggableDiv.enable();
```

You can even make map controls draggable. Since they do not have an ID you can grab them by their class. The following snippet makes the zoom and attribution controls draggable.

Listing 9.11: Making the zoom and attributions controls draggable

```
31    var attribution = document.getElementsByClassName('leaflet-
          control-attribution')[0];
32    var draggableAttribution = new L.Draggable(attribution);
33    draggableAttribution.enable();
34
35    var zoom = document.getElementsByClassName('leaflet-control-zoom'
          )[0];
36    var draggableZoom = new L.Draggable(zoom);
37    draggableZoom.enable();
```

9.11   Adjusting Controls Using CSS

The controls you create in Leaflet are automatically assigned classes. These classes, defined in the Leaflet source code in the file `leaflet.css`, are used internally to style and position controls. To change the appearance of a control in ways that Leaflet does not let you do via options (e.g. using a position other than the four default positions) then these classes are a convenient way to access a control using CSS or JavaScript in order to adjust it in detail.

Each control has one main class that lets you access it:

- leaflet-control-zoom
- leaflet-control-layers
- leaflet-control-attribution
- leaflet-control-scale

Besides the main class there are additional classes, some of which are shared by multiple controls. Sometimes you have to directly use these classes to achieve your goals. A convenient way to find out which classes are available for a control is by using your browser's developer tools to inspect the DOM (fig. 9.11).

Figure 9.11: Inspecting the DOM

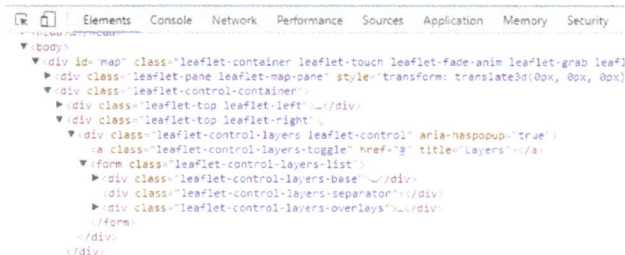

Let's look at an example. In the following snippet we change the appearance of the attribution control. We adjust the text colors, assign a border to the top, add some padding, and change the background color opacity:

```
.leaflet-control-attribution {
  color: blue;
  padding: 5px;
```

```
    border-top: 1px red solid;
    border-left: 1px red solid;
    background-color: rgba(255, 255, 255, 1) !important;
}

.leaflet-control-attribution a {
    color: green;
}
```

Let's look at another example.

In recipe 4.2, on page 65 you learned that a control can be placed
in any corner of the map. If you add more than one control to the
same corner of the map, the controls are stacked (fig. 9.12). Let's
say your upper left corner of the map includes the default zoom
buttons but you would also like to add a layer control to it. In that
case the layer control will appear directly below the zoom control.
But what if you want it to be placed to the right of the zoom control
(fig. 9.13)? You could assign a relative position to it using CSS:

```
.leaflet-control-layers {
    position: relative;
    left: 50px;
    bottom: 75px;
}
```

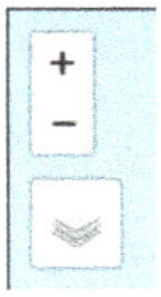

Figure 9.12: Stacked controls

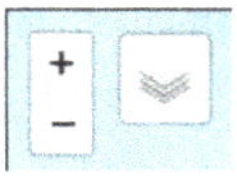

Figure 9.13: Controls next to each
other

Sometimes you need to adjust the zoom control so it matches your
application's design. Here again, if you are not sure how to do it,
you can inspect the zoom control using the developer tools in your
browser.

Doing so, you'd find that the class leaflet-bar can be used to style
a zoom control. Let's select that class and assign it a different color

for its normal and hover states (figures 9.14 and 9.15):

Listing 9.12: Adjusting the zoom control's color

```
16    .leaflet-bar a,
17    .leaflet-bar a:hover {
18      background-color: #2d35bf;
19      color: whitesmoke;
20    }
21
22    .leaflet-bar a:hover {
23      background-color: #4f57ff;
24    }
```

Figure 9.14: Zoom buttons with adjusted color

Figure 9.15: Zoom buttons with adjusted hover effect

9.12   Reloading the Basemap After Resizing the Map Container

When resizing the map container you'll notice that the map itself does not update and it will appear as if tiles from the basemap were not loading. In general, your application will appear buggy and this should absolutely be fixed.

Let's create a map with a container width of 450 pixels and height of 350 pixels (fig. 9.16, on the next page).

Now open your browser console and update the map's width:

```
document.getElementById('map').style.width = '700px';
```

You'll notice that the map container is updated, but the map stays the same (fig. 9.17, on the facing page).

Although it looks like the map was updated because it now includes the area east of Puerto Rico, this is actually not the case, as that area

Figure 9.16: The original map

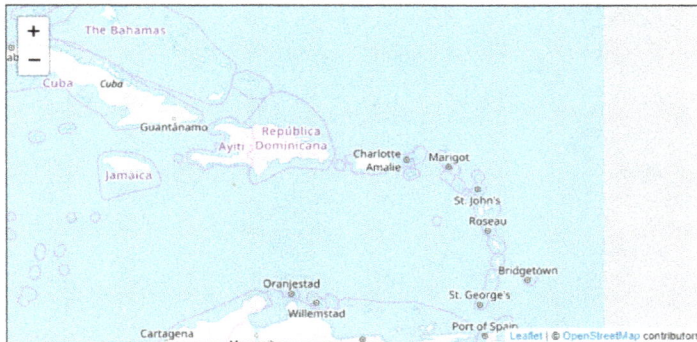

Figure 9.17: The map after changing its width

is covered by one tile. That tile was requested when the application first loaded and so that area has been there from the beginning.

Fixing this is not a simple matter of zooming and panning to request new tiles. When zooming out you notice that although some new tiles are loaded, the area to the right remains gray (fig. 9.18, on the next page).

Luckily there is a method that lets us reload the entire map so it adjusts to the map container: invalidateSize:

```
map.invalidateSize();
```

After executing the command the map updates and correctly adjusts to the map container (fig. 9.19, on the following page).

Figure 9.18: The map after zooming out

Figure 9.19: The map after using invalidateSize

By default, `invalidateSize` comes with a panning animation, but you can disable it by passing `false`:

```
map.invalidateSize(false);
```

Note that the map's resize event is triggered when the actual map is resized (e.g. `invalidateSize` is called), not when the container is resized.

For instance, register a resize event on the map that simply logs to the console:

```
map.on('resize', function() {

  console.log('resized!');

});
```

Now resize the **<div>** and you notice that the event is not fired—then use `invalidateSize` and you see that the event is fired.

Therefore, if you plan on automatically firing `invalidateSize` each time the map container is resized, you'll not achieve your goal by listening to the resize event. Make sure to explicitly fire `invalidateSize` after resizing the container.

9.13   Assigning an Image to the Map Container

By default, the map container has a gray background. Since the map container is a **div**, you can assign it a different color to fit the general design of your website:

```
 9      #map {
10        height: 750px;
11        width: 750px;
12        border: solid 1px black;
13        background-color: pink;
14      }
```

And since the **div** allows background images, you can do that as well:

```
 9      #map {
10        height: 750px;
11        width: 750px;
12        border: solid 1px black;
13        background-image: url('images/grayLines.png');
14      }
```

9.14   Dealing with Side Panels

If your application contains a collapsible side panel that overlaps the map you occasionally run into issues when working with certain event handlers, such as when zooming to a clicked feature. In many cases the feature disappears partially behind the panel.

Let's create a rudimentary panel:

```
41     <div id="panel">I am a side panel!</div>
```

Assign a styling to the panel:

```
24      #panel {
25        background-color: #cbe22f;
26        width: 600px;
27        height: 100%;
28        position: fixed;
29        top: 0px;
30        right: 0px;
31        z-index: 999;
32      }
```

Now hook up a click event to each feature. On click the feature's bounding box is read so we can pass it to the fitBounds method. You'll notice that you never see the entire feature on click, as the panel overlaps.

Luckily this is easily fixed, as fitBounds accepts *paddingTopLeft*, *paddingBottomRight*, and *padding* options, which work exactly like the popup options of the same name:

```
56      L.geoJSON(africa_subset, {
57
58        onEachFeature: function(feature, layer) {
59
60          layer.on('click', function(e) {
61
62            map.fitBounds(e.target.getBounds(), {
63              paddingBottomRight: [600,0]
64            });
65
66          });
67
68        }
69
70      }).addTo(map);
```

9.15   *Creating a Tileset*

To run the code example associated with this recipe you need to first extract the tiles from the file berlin.mbtiles, stored in the tiles folder. Further down in this recipe you'll learn how to extract tiles.

Although vector tiles are currently one of the most talked about topics in web mapping, often there is a need to create good old raster tiles.

Mapbox developed TileMill, software that lets you create raster tiles. Although not maintained by Mapbox anymore the software still does the job.

First install TileMill: `https://tilemill-project.github.io/tilemill/`

Once TileMill is installed you can load data and style it using the styling language CartoCSS, often simply called Carto (not related to the CARTO software, although that one makes use of CartoCSS as well). As the name indicates, CartoCSS is similar to CSS. It uses an almost identical syntax—elements are selected using IDs and classes, and the concept of cascading is essential. This recipe covers a few basics of CartoCSS, but if you want to dig into it more, have a look at: `https://tilemill-project.github.io/tilemill/docs/manual/carto/`

This recipe only shows you how to style data and export it to a tileset that can be used in Leaflet, so don't expect the most beautiful map. Creating a visually appealing map takes some practice and, most importantly, a fair bit of time.

Start TileMill and click the *New project* button. Assign a filename and click *Add*. When you open the project you'll notice that by default, TileMill adds a countries dataset.

The lower left includes a button that resembles a layer switcher (fig. 9.20):

Figure 9.20: Adding a layer to TileMill

Click this button and remove the countries. Then press *Add layer*, which opens the interface shown in Figure 9.21, on the following page.

Navigate to the chapter's `data` directory and one by one, load the following datasets:

- `berlin.shp`
- `buildingsSmall.shp`
- `roadsPrimarySecondarySmall.shp`
- `residentialSmall.shp`

The data used in this chapter was extracted from OpenStreetMap. As the generation of tiles can take very long, a subset of these datasets was provided in this chapter's data folder. Note that some screenshots in this chapter still show Berlin in its entirety.

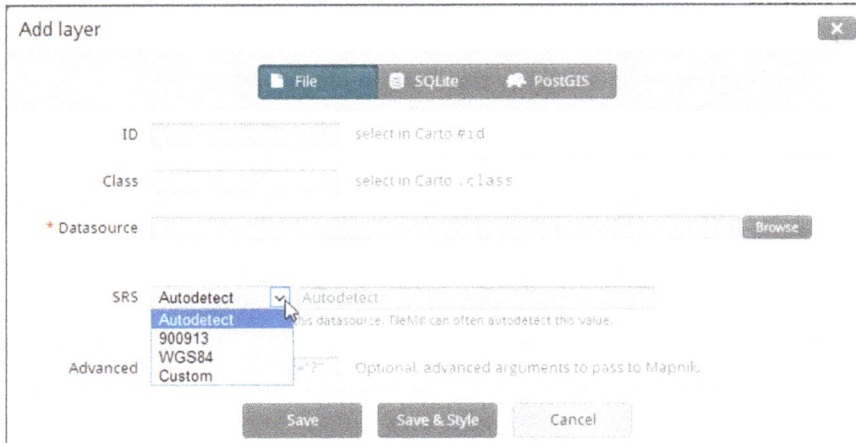

Figure 9.21: The Add layer interface

- `hydroSmall.shp`

For each dataset it is important that an ID is assigned. Just like in CSS, an ID can be used to select and style a dataset. By default the ID is identical to the dataset name, so if the name is a bit long it makes sense to shorten the ID.

Assign the IDs as shown in figure 9.22:

Figure 9.22: The layers menu

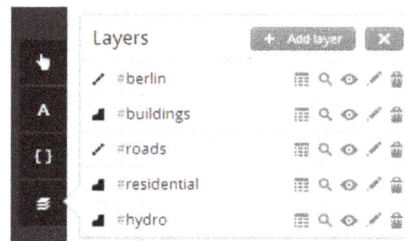

What is 900913? If you read this number in the leet alphabet, you notice that it stands for Google. Google came up with the WebMercator coordinate system, and before it was officially registered as EPSG:3857 it was referred to as 900913.

It is also essential that you define the SRS (spatial reference system). As the autodetect option often does not work, it is best to explicitly state the SRS. In our case all our datasets are provided in WGS 84. Note that this does not transform a dataset. If need be, first use a GIS or the GDAL/OGR utilities to transform the dataset to the right coordinate system and then load it in TileMill.

Once added we can start styling the datasets. Although loaded, a dataset is not visible until we assign a style to it.

Feel free to remove the `style.mss` file, as it contains styling for the countries layer which we removed.

Create a new stylesheet and simply call it `berlin`.

As a proof of concept, it is sufficient to create a simple style. CartoCSS has quite a few things to offer but we will only look at a subset:

- line-color: the color of a line
- line-opacity: the opacity of a line or polygon outer boundary
- line-width: the width of a line or polygon outer boundary
- polygon-fill: the inner color of a polygon
- polygon-opacity: the opacity of a polygon

You can define styles for specific zoom levels only, by specifying the level(s) in brackets, right after the ID selector:

```
#datasetId[zoom<15] {...}
#datasetId[zoom<=15] {...}
#datasetId[zoom>15] {...}
#datasetId[zoom=8], [zoom=10] {...}
#datasetId[zoom>5][zoom<=8] {...}
```

And you can select features with specific attributes by adding a query to the brackets:

```
#datasetId[NAME="Belgium"] {...}
#datasetId[population>20000000] {...}
```

So, let us style the loaded datasets by using some of the above properties and concepts:

```
1   #berlin {
2     line-color: black;
3     line-width: 2;
4   }
5
6   #roads {
7     line-color: #5e5e5e;
8     line-width: 0.6;
9   }
```

```
10
11   #residential[zoom<15] {
12     line-color: black;
13     polygon-fill: #e29a12;
14     line-width: 0.3;
15   }
16
17   #residential[zoom>=15] {
18     line-color: black;
19     polygon-fill: #e29a12;
20     polygon-opacity: 0.3;
21   }
22
23   #hydro {
24     line-color: blue;
25     line-opacity: 0.5;
26     line-width: 0.5;
27     polygon-fill: #28c7cf;
28     polygon-opacity: 0.3;
29   }
30
31   #buildings[zoom>13] {
32     polygon-fill: #234;
33     line-width: 0.3;
34     line-color: white;
35   }
```

That's it—the data has been styled.

Now we'd like to export our design to tiles that can be added to a web mapping application (fig. 9.23). The format the tiles are stored in is called MBTiles and its file extension is `.mbtiles`.

Figure 9.23: The Export menu

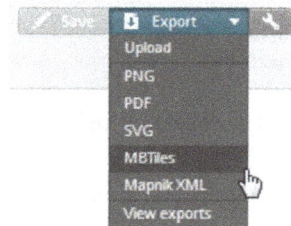

In the next interface it is extremely important that we adjust the tileset extent. We are only interested in a tiny part of the world—a few blocks in Berlin. By default, TileMill exports the entire world, which would result in an enormous dataset.

First manually zoom in to Berlin and then define the extent by hold-ing Shift, holding the left mouse button and dragging the mouse. Once you release the mouse a rectangle will be drawn. This rectan-gle is your bounding box. Luckily you can adjust it after drawing by holding the edges and moving the mouse. This is almost always necessary since the rectangle is not shown while drawing (fig. 9.24).

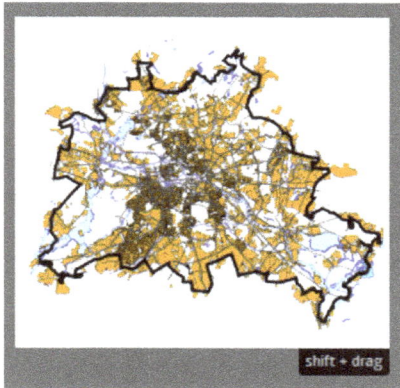

Figure 9.24: Defining the tileset's extent

Now make sure to adjust the zoom levels. The more zoom levels, the bigger the dataset. The higher zoom levels will make your tilesets dramatically increase in size. Adjust the slider and see how much of a difference it makes when excluding some of the higher zoom levels (fig. 9.25).

Note that the standard Open-StreetMap basemap we include in almost every map in this book has a maximum of 18 zoom levels.

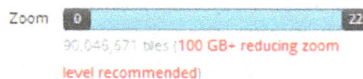

Figure 9.25: A tileset too large to han-dle!

Let's include zoom levels 1-17; plenty of detail and a size that is still manageable (fig. 9.26).

Figure 9.26: Decreasing the zoom levels

Also, you need to click inside the rectangle once to set the tileset's center. It does not matter where you click but it needs to be within the rectangle (fig. 9.27, on the following page):

Figure 9.27: Setting the center of the
tileset

Center   13.4129,52.5187,9
Click to move starting center point.

Now click on *Export*. If nothing happens, expand the Export drop-down again (figure 9.23, on page 192) and choose *View exports*. Now you can keep an eye on the exporting process. If you followed this recipe's instructions carefully, this should take just a few minutes. For a global dataset including all zoom levels the export might take days or weeks.

TileMill exports your tileset to an .mbtiles file, which is stored in the MapBox folder that is created when TileMill is installed:

- Mac OS X: /Users/<user>/Documents/MapBox
- Linux: /home/<user>/Documents/MapBox
- Windows: C:/Users/<user>/Documents/MapBox

Once exported to MBTiles, you'd like to add these to Leaflet. Natively, however, Leaflet does not support MBTiles, so you need to use a tool that lets you export the tiles to a folder structure that Leaflet understands.

9.16   *Extracting Tiles from an MBTiles File*

The MBTiles format is based on a SQLite database. In fact, an .mbtiles file is a SQLite database, but with the specific purpose of storing tilesets that can be used for web maps. Tiles are stored efficiently and the good thing is, since we are dealing with a single file we can easily transfer it. The downside is that we cannot simply add the file to an application and read it. Therefore we first need to extract the individual tiles and store them as individual images.

SQLite: https://sqlite.org

In this recipe we are going to use the berlin.mbtiles file we created in the last recipe and extract its information to create a directory structure that contains a folder for each zoom level that can be easily linked to a Leaflet application. The tool we are going to use is MBUtil, developed by Mapbox and available on GitHub. MBUtil

https://github.com/mapbox/
mbutil

can be executed from the command line. First download MBUtil and extract the zip file—it does not matter where you extract it (fig. 9.28).

Figure 9.28: Downloading mbutil

To execute MBUtil, we first need to make it executable by assigning a Python extension to the file named `mb-util`. Simply rename the file and add a `.py` extension to it (figures 9.29 and 9.30):

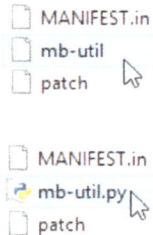

To run mb-util.py, you'll need to have Python installed.

Figure 9.29: The mb-util file with no file extension

Figure 9.30: mb-util.py

We can now execute `mb-util.py` Python script using our operating system's command line.

Before running `mb-util`, you need to place the MBTiles into the folder that contains `mb-util.py`, then open your command line and change to that directory. The command is rather simple as it only takes two parameters: the `.mbtiles` file and a folder that will be created to hold the extracted files:

```
mb-util.py ourFile.mbtiles newFolder
```

As in:

```
mb-util.py berlin.mbtiles berlin
```

The script now creates a new folder named `berlin` and extracts the tiles from `berlin.mbtiles`, exporting each tile to a single PNG.

Have a closer look at the exported folder and notice that a directory has been created for each zoom level.

9.17   Adding a Tileset to Leaflet

Now we can add the exported tiles to our Leaflet application (fig. 9.31):

```
var tiles = L.tileLayer("XXX/{z}/{x}/{y}.png", {});
tiles.addTo(map);
```

Note that we created a folder `tiles` first, and then stored `berlin` in that folder.

Simply copy the exported directory into an existing application and create a new `tileLayer`:

```
33   var berlinTiles = L.tileLayer("tiles/berlin/{z}/{x}/{y}.png", {});
34   berlinTiles.addTo(map);
```

Figure 9.31: Our tileset

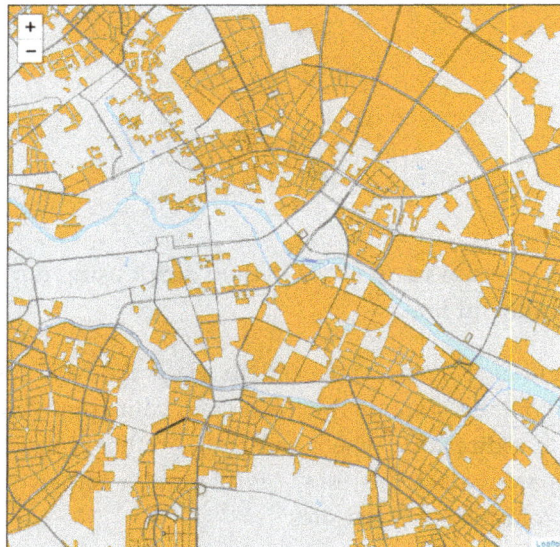

Zoom in and notice that the design changes, just like we defined in the CartoCSS (fig. 9.32, on the facing page).

Since we didn't add a polygon as a background, we could techni-

Figure 9.32: Our tileset (zoomed in)

cally add two basemaps, our own tiles being on top of the Open-StreetMap tiles (fig. 9.33).

Figure 9.33: Our tileset on top of the OpenStreetMap basemap

10 Events and Event Objects

Contents

Events and event objects are some of the most useful features of any web mapping application and they can greatly enrich the user experience and usefulness of an application.

An *event* is something that happens. For example: the basemap is changed, the map is moved, a popup is opened, someone clicked on the map. Often you would like to detect when these things happen so you can react to them. For instance, when a user clicks on the map you would like to display the click's coordinates or maybe even display a marker where the user clicked. Reacting to such an event and executing code, always as a function, is called *listening* to an event or handling an event, and the function itself is generally referred to as an *event handler*.

Often it is not sufficient to simply know that an event happened, but you would also like to know about its specifics.

For example, it might not be enough to know that a user clicked on the map, but you might actually want to know where it happened (i.e. get the coordinates).

This information is contained in an *event object*. In Leaflet, each time an event happens you are provided with an event object, a simple JavaScript object that contains additional information about the event.

There are 14 event objects in Leaflet:

- KeyboardEvent
- MouseEvent
- LocationEvent
- ErrorEvent
- LayerEvent
- LayersControlEvent
- TileEvent
- TileErrorEvent
- ResizeEvent
- GeoJSONEvent
- PopupEvent
- TooltipEvent
- DragEndEvent
- ZoomAnimEvent

Let us have a closer look at how this all fits together.

10.1 *Looking at Available Events and Event Objects*

If an element allows events, the documentation includes a block called Events. In that block you can read about what events are available, what the individual events are called, and also what events have been inherited from other classes. The following image from the official Leaflet documentation shows the events for the class `FeatureGroup`. It has two events, `layeradd` and `layerremove`, and it inherits further events from the class `Layer` (fig. 10.1).

Events

Event	Data	Description
layeradd	LayerEvent	Fired when a layer is added to this FeatureGroup
layerremove	LayerEvent	Fired when a layer is removed from this FeatureGroup

▸ Events inherited from Layer

▸ Popup events inherited from Layer

▸ Tooltip events inherited from Layer

Figure 10.1: The Events block for the class FeatureGroup

It is crucial that you know the name of the event (the content of the Event column), as it is always the first parameter of the on or once methods, described in the next recipe.

The Data column reveals what event object is used. In the above example the event object LayerEvent is used. Every event object is described in detail in the documentation (fig. 10.2):

LayerEvent

Property	Type	Description
layer	Layer	The layer that was added or removed.

Figure 10.2: The event object LayerEvent

Remember that event objects are simply JavaScript objects, which consist of properties and values. In this example, the event object LayerEvent has a property called layer, whose value is an instance of the class `Layer`.

Reading the documentation to find out about event objects can be time consuming and challenging for beginners. Often it is easier to simply explore the event object in the browser's console (see Understanding event objects, on page 204).

10.2   Adding Event Listeners: on and once

When registering an event listener, you should first think about how often the code should be executed. You have to ask yourself whether it should be executed the very first time an event happens or each time the event happens.

To register the event, you use the methods on and once on any element that allows events.

The first parameter of the on or once methods is always the name of the event. The second parameter is the function that is executed when the event happens, a so-called event handler.

The code then looks as follows:

```
element.on('eventName', function() { ... });
```

Instead of using an anonymous function you can also use a named function that you define:

```
function doSomething() {
  ...
};

element.on('eventName', doSomething);
```

Listing 10.1: Example: registering a click event (anonymous function)

```
31      map.on('click', function() {
32
33        console.log('A click on the map was registered.');
34
35      });
```

Listing 10.2: Example: registering a click event (named function)

```
31      function doSomethingOnClick() {
32
```

```
33        console.log('A click on the map was registered.');
34
35      }
36
37      map.on('click', doSomethingOnClick);
```

10.3   Removing Event Listeners: off

An event listener can be removed using the off method on the element it was registered on.

You can either remove an event listener by stating its name:

```
element.off('eventName');
```

Or you can remove all listeners of the element by calling off without any parameters:

```
element.off();
```

10.4   Adding and Removing Multiple Event Listeners at Once

Instead of calling on, once and off multiple times you can also define an object that holds your event listeners. The properties in the object correspond to the names of the events and the values refer to the functions that will be executed.

```
var eventListeners = {
  eventName1: function1,
  eventName2: function2
};

element.on(eventListeners);
```

Listing 10.3: Example: registering multiple event listeners at once

```
31      function doSomethingOnClick() {
32
33        console.log('A click on the map was registered.');
34
35      }
36
37      function doSomethingOnMouseOut() {
38
39        console.log('The mouse left the map.');
40
41      }
```

```
42
43      var eventListeners = {
44        click: doSomethingOnClick,
45        mouseout: doSomethingOnMouseOut
46      };
47
48      map.on(eventListeners);
```

10.5 Registering Event Listeners for a Layer Versus a Feature

When handling events that work with vector layers it is important to know that listening to events can be done at two different levels: either the listener can be registered for the entire layer, or it can be registered for a single feature within that layer.

Towards the end of this chapter you will learn how to highlight features, read attributes on hover, and also how to zoom to a clicked feature. It is essential that the listeners are registered for each single feature instead of the entire layer.

Let's say you have a polygon dataset that holds multiple countries and you would like to register an event that zooms to a clicked country. If you register this event on the layer you will end up zooming to entire layer's extent, no matter which country you click. If you register it to each single feature within that layer, however, you will zoom to a single feature.

10.6 Understanding Event Objects

As stated in the introduction, an event object is an object that contains information about the event that just happened.

Accessing this event object is fairly easy—all you have to do is define a parameter in your event listener function. The event object is automatically passed to the first parameter when the event happens.

In the following example we define a parameter called eventObject:

```
function doSomething(eventObject) {
  ...
```

```
};
```

The event object is passed to eventObject each time the event happens. It really doesn't matter what you name this first parameter. Regardless of what it's called, it will hold the event object. Often the parameter is abbreviated to e:

```
function doSomething(e) {
  ...
};
```

In the remaining recipes this parameter will always be called e, but feel free to assign it a different name.

Knowing that this parameter holds an object, we can access its values using e.someProperty.

The available properties of each event object are described in the Leaflet documentation under Event objects. In addition to an event object's specific properties, each event object contains default properties inherited from a base event object called Event. The base object includes essentials, such as which event was fired and which element fired it.

Instead of using the documentation you could also pass the event object to a global variable, and then explore that variable in your browser's console after the event happened (fig. 10.3, on the next page). In the following example the variable eGlobal is assigned the event object:

Listing 10.4: Example: defining a global variable to hold the event object

```
31      function doSomethingOnClick(e) {
32
33        eGlobal = e;
34
35      }
```

After exploring this global variable and finding the information you were looking for you should delete it to prevent cluttering your application with global variables.

Figure 10.3: Using the global variable

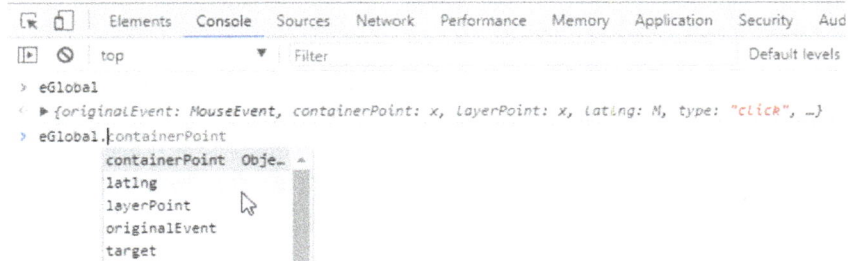

10.7   Getting Click Coordinates

Getting the latitude and longitude when clicking on the map is one of the most useful and most used functionalities in web mapping.

A click event exposes the MouseEvent event object, containing the property *latlng*, which holds an object. This object exposes two properties, *lat* and *lng*, which contain the latitude and longitude of the click (fig. 10.4).

Listing 10.5: Logging a click's coordinates

```
31    map.on('click', function(e) {
32
33        var lat = e.latlng.lat;
34        var lon = e.latlng.lng;
35
36        console.log('Clicked on:', lat, lon);
37
38    });
```

Figure 10.4: Click coordinates logged to the browser's console

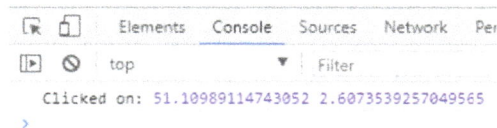

10.8   Adding Click Coordinates to an Element in the Page

Logging clicks to the browser console is useful as a developer, but for most users this is not very helpful. Often you need to show the click's coordinates in the web page. In the following example, two **<span>** elements are created. These elements will hold the coordinates after clicking:

Listing 10.6: Creating span elements

```
20    <h3>Click coordinates</h3>
21    <b>Lat</b>: <span id="latSpan"></span>
22    <br>
23    <b>Lon</b>: <span id="lonSpan"></span>
```

To display the coordinates, we register a click event and extract the latitude and longitude from the event object so they can be assigned to the **<span>** elements (fig. 10.5):

Listing 10.7: Adding click coordinates to span elements

```
36    map.on('click', function(e) {
37
38      var lat = e.latlng.lat;
39      var lon = e.latlng.lng;
40
41      document.getElementById('latSpan').innerHTML = lat.toFixed(5);
42      document.getElementById('lonSpan').innerHTML = lon.toFixed(5);
43
44    });
```

Click coordinates

Lat: 49.60926
Lon: 6.12937

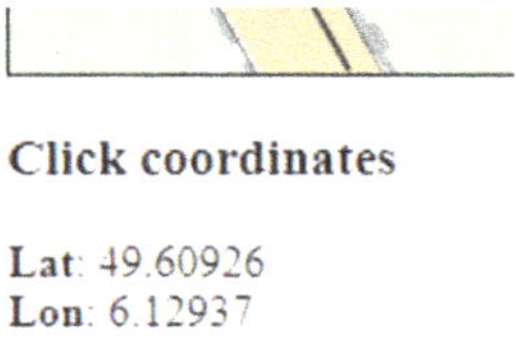

Figure 10.5: Adding coordinates to a span element

The coordinates are displayed in the **<span>** elements until they are replaced when the user clicks again.

If you do not want to replace the coordinates on each click but collect them in the page, you could create a list in your HTML and append a list element (**<li>**) on each click (fig. 10.6, on the following page):

Listing 10.8: Creating a list

```
25    <ul id="coordinatesList"></ul>
```

Listing 10.9: Adding click coordinates to the list

```
39    map.on('click', function(e) {
```

```
40
41          var lat = e.latlng.lat;
42          var lon = e.latlng.lng;
43
44          var li = document.createElement('li');
45
46          var liContent = document.createTextNode(lat.toFixed(5) + ', ' +
                lon.toFixed(5));
47
48          li.appendChild(liContent);
49
50          var ul = document.getElementById('coordinatesList');
51
52          ul.appendChild(li);
53
54      });
```

Figure 10.6: Adding coordinates to a list

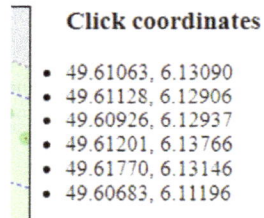

Click coordinates

- 49.61063, 6.13090
- 49.61128, 6.12906
- 49.60926, 6.12937
- 49.61201, 6.13766
- 49.61770, 6.13146
- 49.60683, 6.11196

10.9 Adding a Marker to a Clicked Location

Adding a marker to a clicked location is straightforward. Since the click event object reveals coordinates, all it takes is passing the coordinates to L.marker and adding the marker to the map:

Listing 10.10: Adding a marker to the clicked location

```
31      map.on('click', function(e) {
32
33          var lat = e.latlng.lat;
34          var lon = e.latlng.lng;
35
36          var marker = L.marker([lat, lon]);
37
38          marker.addTo(map);
39
40      });
```

Remember from Working with Coordinates in Leaflet, on page 44 that there are multiple ways to pass coordinates in Leaflet. Instead

of extracting the latitude and longitude from the event object's *latlng*
property, you could also send it directly to L.marker:

Listing 10.11: Adding a marker to the clicked location (short)

```
31    map.on('click', function(e) {
32
33      var marker = L.marker(e.latlng);
34
35      marker.addTo(map);
36
37    });
```

And if you wanted to shorten your code further you could also
achieve this by using a one-liner, as the variable is technically not
necessary:

Listing 10.12: Adding a marker to the clicked location (shortest)

```
31    map.on('click', function(e) {
32
33      L.marker(e.latlng).addTo(map);
34
35    });
```

You'll notice that in all of the examples above a marker is added
on each click using the addTo method. Perhaps you want to display
only one marker at a time, on each click removing the previously
added marker. There are multiple ways to do it.

One way would be to define the marker globally and on each click
set its location with the setLatLng method:

Listing 10.13: Changing a marker's position on click

```
31    var marker = L.marker();
32
33    map.on('click', function(e) {
34
35      marker.setLatLng(e.latlng);
36
37      marker.addTo(map);
38
39    });
```

Note that the addTo method is fired on each click, but since a layer
can only be added to the map once we do not have to worry about

this.

Instead of changing the marker's position, you could also check whether it exists and, if so, remove it. For this to work properly you have to define the marker's variable outside of the event handler:

Listing 10.14: Removing the marker if it exists

```
31    var marker;
32
33    map.on('click', function(e) {
34
35      if (marker) {
36
37        marker.remove();
38
39      }
40
41      marker = L.marker(e.latlng);
42
43      marker.addTo(map);
44
45    });
```

Yet another way to achieve the exact same goal would be using a feature group or a layer group. You can define a group solely for this purpose, add the group to the map, and on each click empty the group and add the new marker to it:

Listing 10.15: Using a layer group

```
31    var markerGroup = L.layerGroup();
32
33    markerGroup.addTo(map);
34
35    map.on('click', function(e) {
36
37      var marker = L.marker(e.latlng);
38
39      markerGroup.clearLayers();
40
41      marker.addTo(markerGroup);
42
43    });
```

10.10   Showing Mouse Coordinates on the Map

Many applications show the moving cursor's position. Whereas the coordinates could be shown in a separate div outside of the map, it is often more useful to show it inside the map.

Let's first create a new div that we append to the map div as a child. We change its position to absolute so we can adjust its z-index, which is essential to make the div show on top of the basemap:

Listing 10.16: Creating a div and adding it to the map

```
31    var div = document.createElement('div');
32    div.id = 'coordsDiv';
33    div.style.position = 'absolute';
34    div.style.bottom = '0';
35    div.style.left = '0';
36    div.style.zIndex = '999';
37    document.getElementById('map').appendChild(div);
```

We then register a mousemove event, which is fired each time the mouse moves. We extract the coordinates from the event object just like we extracted them from the click in the previous recipe. We then build a string that we add to the div:

Listing 10.17: Adding mouse coordinates to the div

```
39    map.on('mousemove', function(e) {
40
41      var lat = e.latlng.lat.toFixed(5);
42      var lon = e.latlng.lng.toFixed(5);
43
44      document.getElementById('coordsDiv').innerHTML = lat + ', ' +
             lon;
45
46    });
```

10.11   Accessing a Clicked Layer

Often you aren't interested in the information about the event (e.g. click, move, etc.) but about the element the event happened on. For example, when clicking on a layer, you might not want any information about the click, but you actually want information about the layer that was clicked. This can be extremely useful when reading attributes from a clicked layer or simply removing it (see the next recipe).

Accessing the element is simple. Each time you register an event on a layer or a feature, the event object includes a property called *target*. The target is the element involved in the event. In the following example a marker is created and a click event is registered on that marker. The target is then logged to the console (fig. 10.7).

Listing 10.18: Accessing and logging a clicked marker

```
35    var marker = L.marker([37.7769, -105.5672]).addTo(map);
36
37    marker.on('click', function(e) {
38
39      var clickedMarker = e.target;
40
41      console.log('You clicked:');
42      console.log(clickedMarker);
43
44    });
```

Figure 10.7: The clicked marker, logged to the console

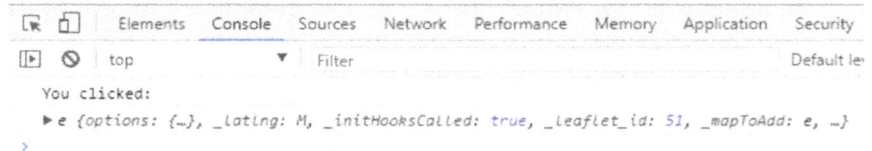

After logging the target you can explore it in the console. Remember that instead of logging it you could also explore it by assigning it to a global variable.

If you would like to double check that the target is the actual marker, you can log the marker variable separately. The log will return the exact same thing.

Note that his works for any layer (marker, polygon, GeoJSON, etc.).

Apart from a simple click you can also listen to the following events:

- dblclick
- mousedown

- mouseup
- mouseover
- mouseout
- contextmenu (right click)

You can find examples of these in the `recipe_10_11_2.html` file.

10.12   Removing a Marker When Clicked

There are multiple ways to approach removing a marker when it is clicked. You can attach a click handler to each marker you add to the map. Using the event object's target, the handler detects the clicked marker and then removes it using the `remove` method:

Listing 10.19: Removing a marker on click

```
33   L.marker([48.687, -113.771]).on('click', removeMarker).addTo(map);
34   L.marker([44.668, -110.621]).on('click', removeMarker).addTo(map);
35   L.marker([43.149, -113.543]).on('click', removeMarker).addTo(map);
36   L.marker([40.398, -105.677]).on('click', removeMarker).addTo(map);
37   L.marker([44.589, -104.714]).on('click', removeMarker).addTo(map);
38   L.marker([40.491, -108.959]).on('click', removeMarker).addTo(map);
39
40   function removeMarker(e) {
41
42     var clickedMarker = e.target;
43
44     clickedMarker.remove();
45
46     console.log(clickedMarker);
47
48   }
```

Adding a click handler to each marker, however, is cumbersome and can reduce the readability of your code. You could also iterate through the map's layers using `eachLayer` and on each iteration attach a handler (see recipe 10.18, on page 220).

Yet another approach is storing the markers in a group and then registering that event to the group, which propagates it to its members for us:

Listing 10.20: Removing a marker on click (group)

```
33       var group = L.featureGroup();
```

```
34
35       group.addTo(map);
36
37       L.marker([48.687, -113.771]).addTo(group);
38       L.marker([44.668, -110.621]).addTo(group);
39       L.marker([43.149, -113.543]).addTo(group);
40       L.marker([40.398, -105.677]).addTo(group);
41       L.marker([44.589, -104.714]).addTo(group);
42       L.marker([40.491, -108.959]).addTo(group);
43
44       group.on('click', function(e) {
45
46         var clickedLayer = e.layer;
47
48         group.removeLayer(clickedLayer);
49
50       });
```

Note that this approach only works for feature groups, and not for layer groups.

10.13   Getting the Map Center During and After a Move

The move event is used to repeatedly fire a function when the map is being moved. You can also detect when the map starts and stops moving, by registering movestart and moveend.

Since move is fired repeatedly while the map is moved, be careful. If the function you hook up to this event is complex, your browser might slow down or even crash. Most often, however, the event is hooked up to a rather simple function, such as returning the map's center, which you don't need to worry about.

To get the map's current center, you don't need to access an event object, but simply call the getCenter method:

Listing 10.21: Getting the map's center when moving the mouse and displaying it

```
33       map.on('move', function(e) {
34
35         var center = map.getCenter();
36
37         var lat = center.lat.toFixed(5);
38         var lon = center.lng.toFixed(5);
```

```
39
40          document.getElementById('mapCenter').innerHTML = 'The current
                map center is:<br><b>Lat</b>: ' + lat + '<br><b>Lon</b>: '
                + lon;
41
42      });
```

10.14   Getting a Moving/Moved Marker Position

Events are not limited to the map—you can also make other elements such as a markers listen to events.

When setting a marker's draggable option to true, you can use the movestart, moveend, and move events. Note that this time the coordinates are extracted from the event object and not from the map.

Listing 10.22: Getting a marker's position when moving it

```
33      var movingMarker = L.marker([0, 0], {draggable: true});
34
35      movingMarker.addTo(map);
36
37      movingMarker.on('move', function(e) {
38
39        var markerPosition = e.latlng;
40        var markerLat = markerPosition.lat.toFixed(5);
41        var markerLon = markerPosition.lng.toFixed(5);
42
43        document.getElementById('position').innerHTML = 'The marker is
                now at [' + markerLat + ', ' + markerLon + ']';
44
45      });
```

10.15   Panning and Zooming to a Mouse Click

To pan to a mouse click, you first have to read the click coordinates, then use the map's setView method:

```
map.setView([lat, lon]);
```

If you want to pan to a specific zoom level you can use the method's optional third parameter:

```
map.setView([lat, lon], 8);
```

Listing 10.23: Zooming to a clicked location

```
31    map.on('click', function(e) {
32
33      var lat = e.latlng.lat.toFixed(5);
34      var lon = e.latlng.lng.toFixed(5);
35
36      map.setView([lat, lon], 8);
37
38    });
```

10.16   Zooming to a Clicked Layer or Feature

The key to zooming to a clicked vector layer or feature is using the fitBounds method rather than the map's setView method. The fitBounds method zooms to a specified bounding box, instead of zooming to a single coordinate. Leaflet makes sure the entire bounding box fits within the map container.

When clicking on a point, it doesn't matter whether we use setView or fitBounds as we zoom to a single coordinate, which will always fit into the map container. However, polygons can have very different sizes and setting the view to the center of a polygon will, in many cases, not show the entire polygon.

When clicking on a vector you can get its bounds using the layer's getBounds method, which you then pass to the map's fitBounds method. In the following example, a GeoJSON layer holding some countries is loaded. Each geometry in the dataset is hooked up to a click event listener, reading the clicked geometry's bounds and then zooming to it.

Listing 10.24: Zooming to the bounds of a clicked vector

```
33    var some_countries_geojson = L.geoJSON(some_countries, {
34
35      onEachFeature: function(feature, layer) {
36
37        layer.on('click', zoomToClickedPolygon);
38
39      }
40
41    });
42
43    some_countries_geojson.addTo(map);
```

```
44
45        function zoomToClickedPolygon(e) {
46
47          var bounds = e.target.getBounds();
48
49          map.fitBounds(bounds);
50
51        }
```

Note that we registered the event multiple times, once for each feature. It is essential that we don't register it for the entire dataset or the map would zoom to the full dataset, regardless of which feature we click.

10.17   Highlighting a Polygon on Hover

To increase usability, many web maps highlight certain datasets when hovering the mouse over them. In this example we'll load some African countries. When the mouse is hovering over a country, we want it to be highlighted.

As you can see in the code example below, we register not one but two events.

To change the polygon's color we register the mouseover event. Once we move the mouse over the polygon its style is changed using the setStyle method.

However, this doesn't take care of what happens when the mouse leaves the polygon. In other words, every polygon the mouse touches would change and retain its highlighting, leading to every polygon being highlighted at some point. To avoid this, we also register a mouseout event so we can revert the polygon's style to what it looked like before the mouse hovered over it. Although we could use setStyle again, it is much more convenient to apply the resetStyle method, which switches the vector's style back to its original state.

Note that resetStyle is called on the entire GeoJSON layer and we pass the feature that should be reset.

Listing 10.25: Adding a GeoJSON layer and highlighting it on hover

```
32      var africa_subset_geojson = L.geoJSON(africa_subset, {
33        color: '#a8ba1f',
34        fillColor: '#4bb762',
35        weight: 1,
36        onEachFeature: function(feature, layer) {
37
38          layer.on('mouseover', highlightFeatureOnMouseOver);
39          layer.on('mouseout', resetFeatureStyle);
40
41        }
42      });
43
44      africa_subset_geojson.addTo(map);
45
46      function highlightFeatureOnMouseOver(e) {
47
48        e.target.setStyle({
49          color: 'red',
50          fillColor: '#4bb762',
51          weight: 3
52        });
53
54      }
55
56      function resetFeatureStyle(e) {
57
58        africa_subset_geojson.resetStyle(e.target);
59
60      }
```

This works fine, but if you have a closer look at adjacent polygons you see that their style might interfere with your highlighting. In the image below (fig. 10.8, on the facing page), you see that the border between Zimbabwe and Zambia looks unusual. This has to do with the fact that in the dataset, Zimbabwe is on top of Zambia, hence the highlighting of Zambia is showing below it.

Luckily, fixing this issue is very easy. In Leaflet you can bring any layer or feature to the top of all other overlays. Although this is often used to change the order of overlays, it can be especially helpful when working with highlighting. Add one more line of code using the bringToFront method and every highlighted feature will be brought to the front, fixing overlapping issues (fig. 10.9, on the next page):

Figure 10.8: Overlap effect

Listing 10.26: Fixing the overlap effect

```
46    function highlightFeatureOnMouseOver(e) {
47
48      e.target.setStyle({
49        color: 'red',
50        fillColor: '#4bb762',
51        weight: 3
52      });
53
54      e.target.bringToFront();
55
56    }
```

Figure 10.9: No overlap effect

Reminder: Registering Multiple Events

When registering multiple events you can pass an object to the on
method, instead of calling it multiple times:

```
36      onEachFeature: function(feature, layer) {
37        layer.on({
38          mouseover: highlightFeatureOnMouseOver,
39          mouseout: resetFeatureStyle
40        });
41      }
```

10.18 Adding an Event Listener to Each Element of a Specific Type

Sometimes it is necessary to add the same event listener to each element of a specific type. For example, you might want to add a click event to each marker on the map (to see this in action, have a look at recipe 10.12, on page 213).

To achieve this you can use the map's eachLayer method, which lets you execute a function for each layer in the map. The first parameter of that function always holds the current layer of an iteration. Then it is simply a matter of finding out whether the layer is an instance of what you are looking for. If you are looking to register an event listener to each marker you have to check whether the current layer is an instance of L.marker. You can check this by using JavaScript's instanceof operator.

Listing 10.27: Adding an event listener to each marker in the map

```
31      L.marker([48.68733, -113.77167]).addTo(map);
32      L.marker([44.66865, -110.62134]).addTo(map);
33      L.marker([43.14909, -113.54370]).addTo(map);
34      L.marker([40.39886, -105.67749]).addTo(map);
35      L.marker([44.58986, -104.71498]).addTo(map);
36      L.marker([40.49083, -108.95966]).addTo(map);
37
38      map.eachLayer(function(layer) {
39
40        if (layer instanceof L.Marker) {
41
42          layer.on('click', function() {
43
44            console.log('I am a marker and you clicked me!');
45
46          });
47
48        }
49
```

```
50        });
```

10.19   Showing Attributes on Hover

Knowing that the event object's target contains the element that was interacted with and knowing how to access a GeoJSON's attributes this is actually quite simple. All we have to do is register a function that extracts the feature's properties. In the example below we add a feature collection whose features contain African countries. Each feature has an attribute called NAME, such as:

Listing 10.28: Part of the dataset

```
{
 "type": "FeatureCollection",
 "name": "africa_subset",
 "crs": {"type": "name", "properties": {"name": "urn:ogc:..."
 "features": [
  {
   "type": "Feature",
   "properties": {"NAME": "Angola"},
```

Often you would like to display the attribute in the website, such as in a paragraph:

Listing 10.29: Creating a paragraph to display an attribute

```
21    <p id="countryName"></p>
```

You then register a mouseover event to each feature. Through the target, the event handler will access the feature and its attribute(s):

Listing 10.30: Reading an attribute and displaying it in the paragraph

```
34    var africa_subset_geojson = L.geoJSON(africa_subset, {
35
36      onEachFeature: function(feature, layer) {
37
38        layer.on('mouseover', showName);
39
40      }
41
42    });
43
44    africa_subset_geojson.addTo(map);
45
```

```
46    function showName(e) {
47
48      var name = e.target.feature.properties.NAME;
49
50      document.getElementById('countryName').innerHTML = "<b>Country
          </b>: " + name;
51
52    }
```

10.20   Highlighting a Clicked Polygon

Highlighting a polygon on click is very similar to highlighting a polygon on hover, the main difference being there is no mouseout event. Once a polygon is clicked it remains clicked. Therefore, we have to make sure that all polygons are reset to their original style before the clicked polygon is highlighted. This is easily achieved by iterating through the GeoJSON's features using eachLayer:

```
44    function highlightFeatureOnClick(e) {
45
46      africa_subset_geojson.eachLayer(function(e) {
47
48        africa_subset_geojson.resetStyle(e);
49
50      });
51
52      e.target.setStyle({
53        color: 'red',
54        fillColor: '#4bb762',
55        weight: 3
56      });
57
58      e.target.bringToFront();
59
60    }
```

10.21   Highlighting a Clicked Marker

Highlighting a marker is a little bit different from highlighting a polygon as we are not working with a style that is defined as a JavaScript object but with an image. Our only option is to change the icon when the event happens.

Let's write an example that switches a marker icon on click. All markers are grouped in a feature group, which enables us to easily hook up all markers with the same events.

We first create an icon for the highlighted marker, but we also define the original style again, since we need to revert back to it once another marker is clicked:

```
44      var highlightMarker = L.icon({
45        iconUrl: 'images/green-marker-icon.png',
46        shadowUrl: '../leaflet/images/marker-shadow.png'
47      });
48
49      var originalMarker = L.icon({
50        iconUrl: '../leaflet/images/marker-icon.png',
51        shadowUrl: '../leaflet/images/marker-shadow.png'
52      });
```

Since we want to avoid turning the map green marker by marker, we need to make sure the marker style is reset when another is clicked. To do that, we simply write a function that iterates through all markers in the group and sets their icon to the original Leaflet icon:

```
54      function resetMarkerIcons() {
55
56        markerGroup.eachLayer(function(layer) {
57
58          layer.setIcon(originalMarker);
59
60        });
61
62      }
```

Finally, we iterate through the group to hook each marker up to a click event. The event handler first calls the function that resets the original icon, then it assigns the new icon:

```
64      markerGroup.eachLayer(function(layer) {
65
66        layer.on('click', function(e) {
67
68          resetMarkerIcons();
69          e.target.setIcon(highlightMarker);
70
71        });
```

Optionally we can further expand this example by also resetting the icons when the map is clicked:

```
75    map.on('click', function() {
76
77        resetMarkerIcons();
78
79    });
```

11 *Geoprocessing and Analysis with Turf.js*

Contents

Sometimes you need to move beyond what Leaflet offers and add more advanced functionality to your application. In GIS, two topics are of major importance: analysis and geoprocessing. Historically, geoprocessing on the web was done server-side, using standards such as WPS (Web Processing Service). The browser sends a request to a server, the server runs the analysis, returns the resulting data which is then displayed on the map. This, however, makes a server-side architecture a necessity, often requiring heightened security as well as the installation of various software and databases.

In recent years, with advancement in browser efficiency and speed, a new kind of geoprocessing has emerged: geoprocessing that is run directly in the browser, requiring neither requests to a server, nor the maintenance of a server-side architecture.

This chapter introduces you to *Turf.js*, a JavaScript library that offers a multitude of geoprocessing and analysis functions.

In the data directory for this chapter you'll find numerous datasets to use when following along so you don't have to create or look for your own data. To get started as quickly as possible, all GeoJSONs are saved in a JavaScript file and have been assigned to a variable whose name is identical to the file name. All you have to do is include the file in your application. Also note that almost all datasets are stored as feature collections. If a Turf tool only accepts single features, we first have to access a single feature. If you use your own data you are free to use single features directly and are not required to work with feature collections.

11.1   A Brief Introduction to Turf.js

Turf.js is a JavaScript library that offers a good number of geospatial tools. Almost any standard functionality that makes up the core of a modern desktop GIS is included in Turf.js.

Turf.js doesn't offer any components for visualizing data—the library is solely used for analysis and processing, and visualization is up to the user. To some this might seem like a disadvantage at first, but it is actually one of the many benefits of using Turf.js. It means that the library can be hooked up to any existing application.

Turf.js works entirely with GeoJSON. With a few exceptions, all tools use GeoJSON geometries, features, or feature collections as input. This means that if you want to send spatial data to a Turf.js tool, you need to convert it to GeoJSON first. The returned data is most often GeoJSON, and sometimes a number or a boolean variable. If you are not familiar with GeoJSON yet, take a look back at Working with GeoJSON, on page 127.

From now on we will refer to Turf.js as simply Turf.

11.2   Downloading and Including Turf

Before we can use Turf we need to include it in an application, just like we included Leaflet in Chapter 2, on page 33.

Unlike Leaflet, Turf consists of a single JavaScript file. You don't need to load any CSS and Turf doesn't use any images internally.

Turf can be obtained on GitHub (`https://github.com/Turfjs/turf/`) or you can visit `http://turfjs.org` and have a look at the "Getting Started" section.

If you choose the latter option, you'll notice that Turf can be loaded through a CDN. You can go ahead and copy the entire code from that page and save it as a JavaScript file (e.g. `turf.js`) and then include it in your application:

```
<script src="turf.js"></script>
```

To test if Turf was included correctly, start your browser and open the console. Type `turf`. If no error is returned, Turf was included correctly (fig. 11.1):

Figure 11.1: Turf is available

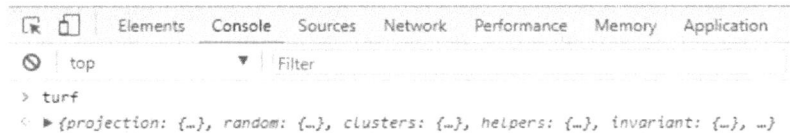

That's it—any method can now be called using the global variable `turf`.

Using npm

See https://www.npmjs.com/get-npm to install npm

You can also install Turf using `npm`:

```
npm install turf
```

To install a single tool, use:

```
npm install @turf/voronoi
```

11.3   Creating a Custom Build

You might have noticed that the Turf file is a bit large. If you're just getting to know Turf, this shouldn't be cause for concern. However, if you are including it in a public application and you are only using a handful of tools you might not want users to have to download the entire file. Luckily you can easily create your own build that includes only the tools you really need.

Browserify: `http://browserify.org/`

Before you can create your own build you need to install `npm`. Once you have `npm`, you need to install `browserify` and then you are ready to build.

First, install the Turf modules you want to use. For example, let's create a build that includes only `turf.explode` and `turf.voronoi`:

```
npm install @turf/explode @turf/voronoi
```

Once installed, we create a JavaScript file (`main.js`) that includes each tool as follows:

```
module.exports = {
  explode: require('@turf/explode'),
  voronoi: require('@turf/voronoi')
};
```

Finally, run the `browserify` command:

```
browserify main.js -s turf > ownBuildTurf.js
```

The resulting file, `ownBuildTurf.js`, is your personal Turf build and it includes only the `explode` and `voronoi` tools, as well as any tools and components that are needed to run them.

Note that the resulting file is not minified, so you can reduce the size even more by minifying it. To minify code you can use tools like UglifyJS or Google's Closure Compiler.

11.4   A Note About the Official Documentation

Just like Leaflet, Turf has great documentation and almost every tool is illustrated with an example: `http://turfjs.org/docs`

The only thing you have to be careful about is the input data. Whereas a lot of tools will accept a feature collection, not all of them do. Some require a single GeoJSON feature or a geometry, so it's important that you first access the feature or geometry or the tool will crash.

Let's look at the documentation for `turf.explode` (fig. 11.2, on the following page):

The input GeoJSON type is marked as GeoJSON. That means that you can pass any GeoJSON object to get this tool to run—geometries,

Figure 11.2: Input arguments for the
explode tool

explode

Takes a feature or set of features and returns all positions as points.

Arguments

Argument	Type	Description
geojson	GeoJSON	input features

features, and feature collections will work.

Now, let's look at another tool, turf.kinks (fig. 11.3):

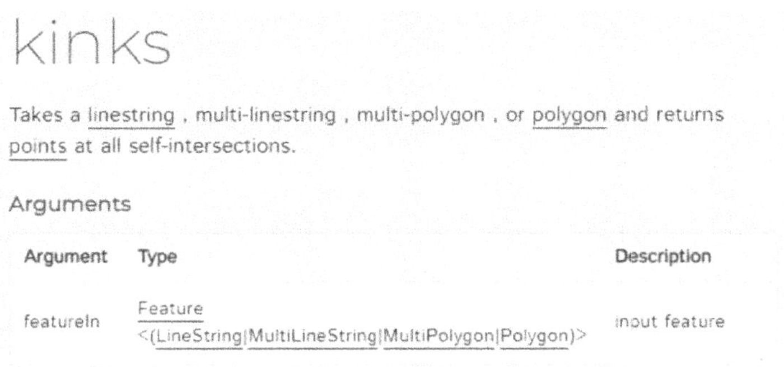

Figure 11.3: Input arguments for the
kinks tool

kinks

Takes a linestring , multi-linestring , multi-polygon , or polygon and returns
points at all self-intersections.

Arguments

Argument	Type	Description
featureIn	Feature <(LineString|MultiLineString|MultiPolygon|Polygon)>	input feature

This time you'll notice that only a feature is accepted. In this case a
feature collection would crash the tool. Often you end up crashing
tools because you assign a feature collection to them when a single
feature is required. Luckily the documentation is great and tells you
exactly what a tool accepts, so if your tool doesn't run through, just
double-check the documentation.

11.5   Meta Functions

Before we dive into analysis and processing tools, let's look at some
meta functions which can come in handy. If you are familiar with
the inner workings of GeoJSON these methods are straightforward.
Note that in some examples, the output has been shortened to fit on

the page.

Extracting the Type

The `turf.getType` function returns the type of an object as a string. Note that this always looks at the outermost element. For instance, if you have a feature collection containing polygons, then the returned type is FeatureCollection, not polygon.

```
turf.getType(poly1);
>>> FeatureCollection

turf.getType(poly1.features[0]);
>>> Polygon

turf.getType(points.features[0]);
>>> Point

turf.getType(line.features[0]);
>>> LineString
```

Extracting the Geometry

The `turf.getGeom` function returns the geometry object of a feature. This doesn't work for a feature collection, as it doesn't have a geometry.

```
turf.getGeom(points.features[0]);
>>> {"type":"Point","coordinates":[13.38994,52.51273]}

turf.getGeom(line.features[0]);
>>> {"type":"LineString","coordinates":[[13.3947, ...

turf.getGeom(poly1.features[0]);
>>> {"type":"Polygon","coordinates":[[[13.39348, ...
```

Extracting Coordinates

The `turf.coordAll` function returns a single array holding all coordinate pairs of a geometry, feature, or feature collection, taking into account multiple features and multigeometries. Note that for polygons, some coordinate pairs will appear twice, since a GeoJSON polygon requires the first and last vertex to be identical.

```
turf.coordAll(poly1);
>>> [[13.393, 52.514], [13.403, 52.513], ...]
```

The `turf.getCoords` function also returns an array containing coordinate pairs, but the pairs are wrapped in an additional array. This method only works for features and geometries.

```
turf.getCoords(poly1.features[0]);
>>> [[[13.393, 52.514], [13.403, 52.513], [13.402, 52.509], ...]]
```

The `turf.getCoord` function returns an array of a position and works only for point features and geometries.

```
turf.getCoord(points.features[0]);
>>> [13.38994, 52.51273]
```

Iterations

The `turf.featureEach` function iterates through each feature in a GeoJSON object. The feature as well as its index can be returned:

```
turf.featureEach(districts, function(currentFeature, fIdx) {
  console.log('Feature', fIdx, ':', currentFeature);
});
>>> Feature 0 : {"type":"Feature","properties":{"distr_name":"Mitte"
    },"geometry":{"type": ...
>>> Feature 1 : {"type":"Feature","properties":{"distr_name":"
    Friedrichshain-Kreuzberg"}, ...
...
```

The `turf.propEach` function iterates through each feature but only returns its properties:

```
turf.propEach(districts, function(currentProps, fIdx) {
  console.log('Feature', fIdx, ':', currentProps);
});
>>> Feature 0 : {distr_name: "Mitte"}
>>> Feature 1 : {distr_name: "Friedrichshain-Kreuzberg"}
>>> ...
```

The `coordEach` function iterates through each feature in a GeoJSON. It returns, in the following order, current coordinate pair, index of the pair, index of the feature, index of the multi feature, and index of the geometry.

```
turf.coordEach(poly1, function(currentCoord, cIdx, fIdx, mfIdx, gIdx)
    {
  console.log('Feature', fIdx, 'Geometry:', gIdx, 'Coor:', cIdx, '
      Coords:', currentCoord);
});
```

```
>>> Feature 0 Geometry: 0 Coor: 0 Coords: [13.3934, 52.5146]
>>> Feature 0 Geometry: 0 Coor: 1 Coords: [13.4034, 52.5139]
>>> Feature 0 Geometry: 0 Coor: 2 Coords: [13.4029, 52.5094]
>>> ...
```

The `turf.geomEach` function iterates through each feature in a GeoJSON and returns, in the following order, current geometry, index of the geometry, properties of the feature, bounding box, and feature ID.

```
turf.geomEach(districts, function(currentGeom, fIdx, props, bbox, fId
    ) {
 console.log('Feature', fIdx, 'Geom:', currentGeom, 'Props:', props,
     'BBOX:', bbox, fId);
});

>>> Feature 0 Geom: {type: "Polygon", ...} Props: {distr_name: "Mitte
    "} BBOX: undefined undefined
>>> Feature 1 Geom: {type: "Polygon", ...} Props: {distr_name: "
    Friedrichshain-Kreuzberg"} BBOX: undefined undefined
>>> ...
```

Note that in the above snippet the bounding box and feature ID are returned as `undefined`. The GeoJSON specification allows for each geometry, feature, or feature collection to have a *bbox* property. If a dataset includes unique identifiers, they shouldn't be stored in the properties object but rather as a property named *id*, directly in the feature.

The `turf.segmentEach` function iterates through each segment in a GeoJSON and returns, in the following order: current segment as a GeoJSON feature, index of the feature, index of the multi feature, index of the geometry, and index of the segment.

```
turf.segmentEach(poly1, function(currentSeg, fIdx, mfIdx, gIdx, sIdx)
    {
 console.log('Feature', fIdx, 'Geom:', gIdx, 'Segment:', sIdx,
     currentSeg);
});
>>> Feature 0 Geometry: 0 Segment: 1 Segment: {type: "Feature",
    properties: ...
>>> Feature 0 Geometry: 0 Segment: 2 Segment: {type: "Feature",
    properties: ...
>>> ...
```

11.6 Creating GeoJSON Data: Point, Line, and Polygon

In Chapter 6, Vector Layers, on page 93, you learned about converting vector datasets to the GeoJSON format and adding them to
Leaflet. But what if you want to create new data that doesn't exist in another format yet? Considering that writing GeoJSON from
scratch is time-consuming, error-prone, and most importantly, not
too much fun, it's important to look at what Turf's data creation
functions have to offer.

Turf has methods to create the following:

- feature (Point, LineString, Polygon, MultiPoint, MultiLineString,
  MultiPolygon)
- featureCollection
- geometryCollection

Listing 11.1: Creating GeoJSONs in Turf

```
33    var point = turf.point([6.12910, 49.61126]);
34
35    var line = turf.lineString([
36      [6.12604, 49.61225],
37      [6.13100, 49.61195]
38    ]);
39
40    var polygon = turf.polygon([
41      [
42        [6.12996, 49.61089],
43        [6.13161, 49.61099],
44        [6.13199, 49.61034],
45        [6.12994, 49.61028],
46        [6.12996, 49.61089]
47      ]
48    ]);
```

To see that this worked you can log the data to the console as shown
in figure 11.4, on the next page, or add it to the map (fig. 11.5, on
the facing page).

```
50    console.log(JSON.stringify(point));
51    console.log(JSON.stringify(line));
52    console.log(JSON.stringify(polygon));
53
54    L.geoJSON(point).addTo(map);
```

```
55      L.geoJSON(line).addTo(map);
56      L.geoJSON(polygon).addTo(map);
```

Figure 11.4: Logging data created with Turf

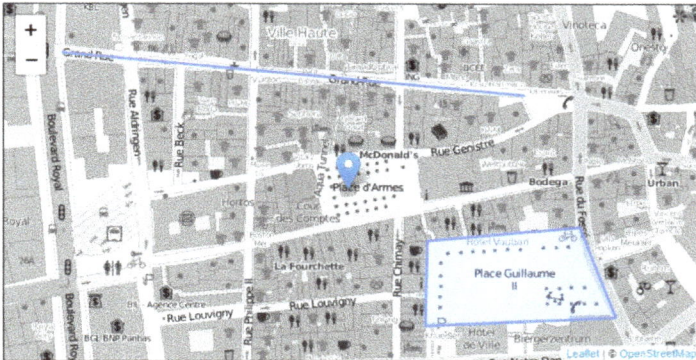

Figure 11.5: Data created with Turf

Creating Data with Attributes

A GeoJSON feature must be composed of a type, a geometry, and properties. If you don't define any properties, the *properties* object remains empty, as you see in Figure 11.4.

To add attributes to a feature, simply define an object after the coordinates, as in:

```
33      var point = turf.point([6.12910, 49.61126], {
34        name: 'Place d\'Armes',
35        city: 'Luxembourg',
36        type: 'square'
37      });
```

11.7   Creating Random Data

Turf can be used to create random data. This can be especially useful when you are in need of data to test something but you don't want to spend time looking for data or creating it from scratch. You can use the methods randomPoint, randomLineString, and randomPolygon to create random points, lines, and polygons. The only required parameter specifies the number of features to create.

Let's create ten random points, lines, and polygons, and add them to the map (fig. 11.6):

Listing 11.2: Creating random data

```
33      var randomPoints = turf.randomPoint(10);
34      var randomLines = turf.randomLineString(10);
35      var randomPolygons = turf.randomPolygon(10);
```

Figure 11.6: Random data created with Turf

You'll notice that lines and polygons can differ a lot, in both size and shape.

By default, the data is created in an entirely random location on the map, but often you want to create the data for a specific area. This is achieved by using the optional parameter *bbox*. This parameter takes a bounding box as an array of numbers in the following order: minX, minY, maxX, maxY. In other words: minimum longitude, minimum latitude, maximum longitude, maximum latitude.

Hint: To create random points that lie next to each other horizontally simply assign a bounding box with the same minimum and maximum latitude values. To have the points show up in a vertical line, assign the same minimum and maximum longitude.

Let's test this by creating an application that creates random data when we click on a button. The data should be generated only within the map's extent. Since Leaflet's getBounds method always returns the southwest and northeast corners of the bounds, our minimum longitude and latitude are found in the southwest corner and our maximum longitude and latitude are found in the northeast corner.

Listing 11.3: Creating a button

```
21    <input type="button" value="Create random data" id="btnRandomData">
```

Listing 11.4: Creating random data for a specific extent

```
35    function createRandomData() {
36
37        var bounds = map.getBounds();
38
39        var swLat = bounds._southWest.lat;
40        var swLon = bounds._southWest.lng;
41
42        var neLat = bounds._northEast.lat;
43        var neLon = bounds._northEast.lng;
44
45        var bbox = [swLon, swLat, neLon, neLat];
46
47        var randomPoints = turf.randomPoint(3, {bbox: bbox});
48        var randomLines = turf.randomLineString(3, {bbox: bbox});
49        var randomPolygons = turf.randomPolygon(3, {bbox: bbox});
50
51        L.geoJSON(randomPoints).addTo(map);
52        L.geoJSON(randomLines).addTo(map);
53        L.geoJSON(randomPolygons).addTo(map);
54
55    }
56
57    document.getElementById('btnRandomData').onclick =
             createRandomData;
```

Run this example a few times and you will notice that the points are always within the map. For lines and polygons, however, only their centroid is guaranteed to be within the specified bounds—the rest of the feature may fall outside. In the following image (fig. 11.7, on the next page) you can see that the polygon on the right exceeds the bounding box:

If you simply need a random pair of coordinates there is no need to first create a random point and then extract its coordinates. Instead use turf.randomPosition, which returns an array with a longitude and a latitude (fig. 11.8, on the following page):

Listing 11.5: Creating a random position

```
13    var randomPosition = turf.randomPosition();
```

Figure 11.7: Random data within a bounding box

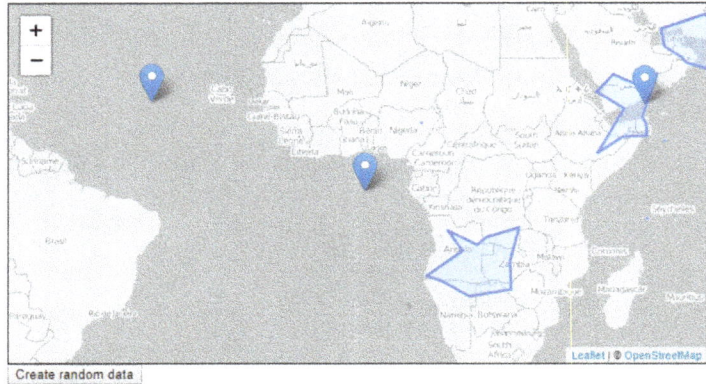

```
14        console.log(randomPosition);
```

Figure 11.8: A random position, returned as an array

This method also accepts a bounding box, but it doesn't have an option to return multiple coordinate pairs. If you need more than one random pair, simply use a loop.

Listing 11.6: Creating 15 random positions

```
17      for (var i = 0; i < 15; i++) {
18
19          var randomPosition = turf.randomPosition();
20          console.log(randomPosition);
21
22      }
```

If you need to run this code over and over with a different number of positions then it would be best to write a function. The following function accepts the number of positions to be created and returns an array containing them.

```
25      function returnRandomPositons(numberOfPositions) {
26
27          var randomPositions = [];
28
29          for (var i = 0; i < numberOfPositions; i++) {
```

```
30
31          var randomPosition = turf.randomPosition();
32
33          randomPositions.push(randomPosition);
34
35      }
36
37      return randomPositions;
38
39  }
```

11.8 Returning Samples

The turf.sample function lets you extract a given number of random features from a feature collection. The tool works for each geometry type, not just points as shown in the snippet below.

The only argument this method accepts is the number of features to be selected. Test the following snippet by refreshing your browser multiple times. You'll notice that each time, five different points are returned:

Listing 11.7: Returning a sample of 5 points from a feature collection
```
34      var pointsSample = turf.sample(randomPoints, 5);
```

There is no argument to provide a bounding box to further limit your sample, but as always you can combine multiple tools.

In the next snippet, we first create a bounding box by providing two diagonally opposite coordinate pairs. Then we use that bounding box to return all the points from the feature collection that are within it. And finally, we extract a sample from that subset. Note that displaying the bounding box is optional.

Listing 11.8: Returning a sample of 5 points within a bounding box
```
34      var bbox = turf.bboxPolygon([13.4255, 52.4881, 13.4282, 52.4894]);
35
36      L.geoJSON(bbox, {fill: false, color: 'green'}).addTo(map);
37
38      var pointsFilter = turf.pointsWithinPolygon(randomPoints, bbox);
39
40      var pointsSample = turf.sample(pointsFilter, 5);
41
```

```
42    L.geoJSON(pointsSample).addTo(map);
```

11.9   Line to Polygon, Polygon to Line

Any polygon can be turned into a line by calling `polygonToLine`
(fig. 11.9):

Listing 11.9: Generating a line from a polygon

```
34    var line = turf.polygonToLine(poly1.features[0]);
35
36    var lineGeoJSON = L.geoJSON(line, {color: 'green'});
```

Figure 11.9: A line created from a
polygon

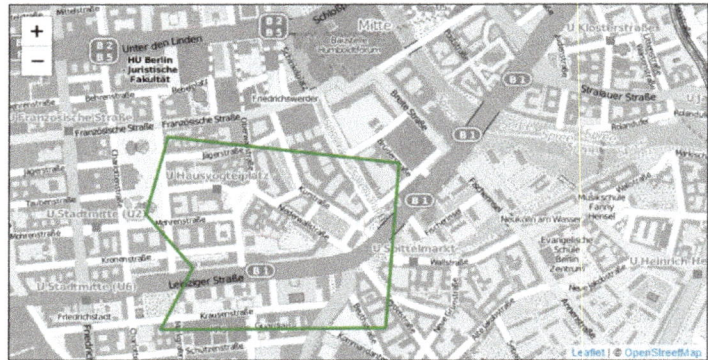

Lines can also be turned into polygons, but remember the first and
last position in a GeoJSON polygon must be identical. If the line's
first and last coordinate pair don't match, Turf will automatically
close the polygon, as you can see in the following example (See
Figures 11.10 and 11.11, on the facing page).

Listing 11.10: Generating a polygon from a line

```
34    var poly = turf.lineToPolygon(line.features[0]);
35
36    var polyGeoJSON = L.geoJSON(poly, {color: 'green'});
```

11.10   Cloning a GeoJSON Object

Sometimes it is necessary to clone a GeoJSON object.

Consider the line from the previous recipe. When adding the original line after running `turf.lineToPolygon`, the line appears with

Figure 11.10: The original line

Figure 11.11: A polygon created from the line

an extra segment between the first and last vertices (fig. 11.12):

```
34        var poly = turf.lineToPolygon(line.features[0]);
35
36        L.geoJSON(line,  {color: 'green'}).addTo(map);
```

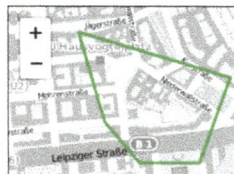

Figure 11.12: Line with an extra segment

Weird, isn't it? After all you never even touched the original feature.

If you don't need the original feature anymore, this is not a big issue, but if you need to work with it again, especially as input to other tools, it can lead to unexpected results.

To avoid this you can clone the GeoJSON. A cloned GeoJSON object is a copy that is completely detached from its original.

```
34        var clonedLine = turf.clone(line);
35
36        var poly = turf.lineToPolygon(line.features[0]);
37
38        L.geoJSON(clonedLine, {color: 'green'}).addTo(map);
```

11.11   Simplifying Geometries

Simplifying a geometry means reducing the number of vertices by a given amount.

Imagine you have a polygon showing Portugal (fig. 11.13):

Figure 11.13: The original Portugal GeoJSON

Let's simplify the Portugal polygon by using a tolerance of 0.1 (fig. 11.14):

```
38      var simplified = turf.simplify(portugal, {tolerance: 0.1});
```

Figure 11.14: The simplified Portugal GeoJSON

The higher the tolerance the more vertices will be removed by the algorithm. Depending on how detailed the dataset is, the same tolerance might have a different effect.

Although you can visualize the dataset to observe how much it has been simplified, you could also explode it to get a vertex count:

```
39      var exploded = turf.explode(simplified);
40      console.log(exploded.features.length);
41      L.geoJSON(simplified, {weight: 1}).addTo(map);
```

If you need to display a simplified version of your large dataset, it may be best to preprocess the data with Turf rather than loading it, then simplifying. This is especially true if Turf doesn't need to be part of your final application.

The algorithm behind the `simplify` method uses the Simplify.js library. You can find out more about it at `http://mourner.github.io/simplify-js/`

11.12   Removing Redundant Vertices

A common sign of improperly digitized geometries are multiple vertices that share the exact same coordinates. Although they might not be visible to the average user, they can be a nuisance when writing algorithms that look at each vertex individually. Using `turf.cleanCoords`, you can eliminate redundant vertices. In the following snippet we return a vertex count before and after cleaning the dataset (fig. 11.15, on the following page):

Listing 11.11: Removing redundant coordinates

```
36      var vNum = oceanDrive.features[0].geometry.coordinates.length;
37
38      console.log('Number of vertices (original):', vNum);
39
40      var cleaned = turf.cleanCoords(oceanDrive.features[0]);
41
42      vNum = cleaned.geometry.coordinates.length;
43
44      console.log('Number of vertices (cleaned):', vNum);
```

Figure 11.15: Returning the number of vertices

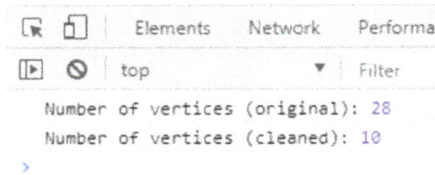

```
 ⌖  ⬚  │  Elements   Network    Performa

 ▶  ⊘  │  top              ▼  │  Filter

    Number of vertices (original): 28
    Number of vertices (cleaned): 10

  >
```

11.13   Adjusting Coordinate Precision

Many recipes in this book mention that Leaflet often returns a large number of decimal places, often more than are actually needed or would make a difference on the map. In other words, the dataset is larger for no justifiable reason. The same is true for GIS software—depending on where the GeoJSON was created, there is a chance that each coordinate may have too many decimal places. Most of the time we dealt with the large number of decimals by calling toFixed. This is perfectly fine when working with events that return a single position, but when working with larger GeoJSON datasets it would be painful to iterate through each coordinate pair and chop the decimals. You can get rid of these unnecessary decimals in GeoJSON by calling turf.truncate and specifying the number of places to remain.

In the following snippet we reduce the precision from 15 to 5 decimal places and log the result to the console:

Listing 11.12: Adjusting coordinate precision

```
37     var truncated = turf.truncate(portugal, {precision: 5});
38
39     console.log(JSON.stringify(truncated));
```

Copy the logged dataset into a text editor and save it as a .geojson file.

Figure 11.16: The original and truncated dataset

portugal.geojson	15.07.2018 13:46	GEOJSON-...	39 KB
portugal_truncated.geojson	15.07.2018 13:50	GEOJSON-...	18 KB

Notice the difference in size in figure 11.16? Yes, it's more than impressive, especially considering that we did not delete a single vertex. Add both datasets to the map and try to see how the original and the truncated datasets differ. You won't notice a difference as the precision provided by the decimals we chopped cannot be displayed in Leaflet.

If your application sharply grows in size with each GeoJSON object you add, remember you can most likely reduce the size by 50% using `turf.truncate`.

11.14   Flipping Latitude and Longitude

It's easy to confuse latitude and longitude. Not that this would ever happen to you, but it can happen when you are given data that is wrong from the beginning. Let's say you are given a dataset that has thousands of points and the latitude and longitude have been reversed for each one. It would be a daunting task to fix the dataset manually, and writing a script that fixes it might consume too much time as well. Fortunately, Turf can save the day with a method to fix your dataset: `flip`.

In the following example, Berlin is added to the map, but since its latitude and longitude were reversed, it ends up in the Indian Ocean. To fix it, we pass the feature to the `flip` method, and with one single line of code and without ever touching the original dataset, we get Berlin to show up in the correct place (fig. 11.17, on the following page):

Listing 11.13: Flipping latitude and longitude

```
33    // creating a GeJSON
34    var berlinWrong = turf.point([52.5134, 13.4017]);
35
36    L.geoJSON(berlinWrong).addTo(map);
37
38    // creating a new GeoJSON with flipped coordinates
39    var berlinCorrect = turf.flip(berlinWrong);
40
41    L.geoJSON(berlinCorrect, {
42
43      pointToLayer: function(feature, latlng) {
44
45        return L.circleMarker(latlng);
```

```
46
47          }
48
49      }).addTo(map);
```

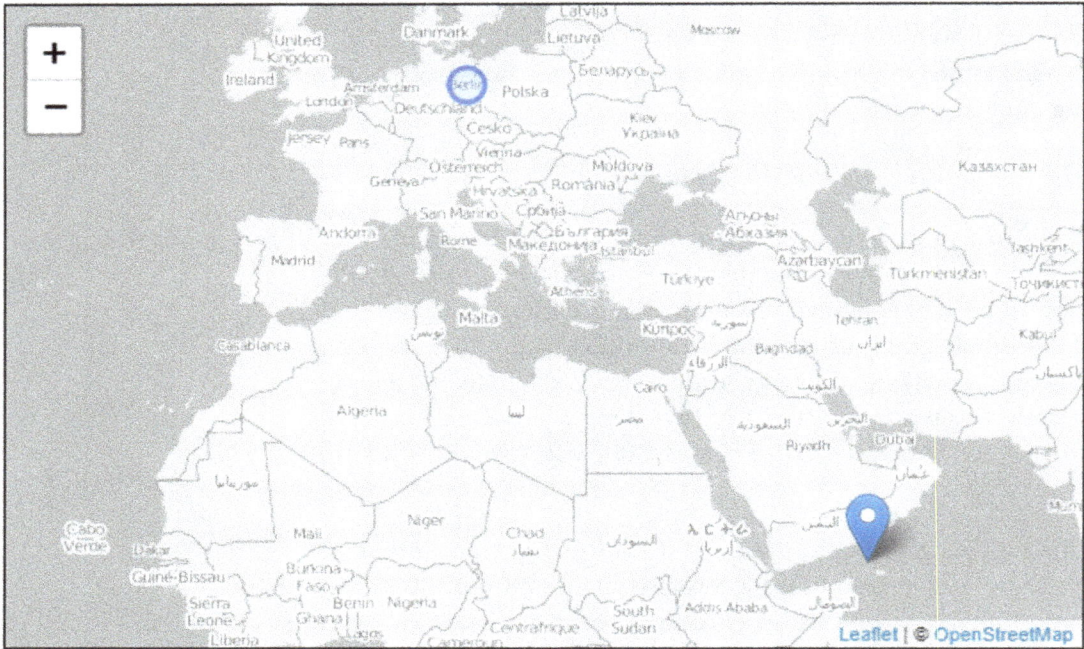

Figure 11.17: Berlin in the wrong location (marker) and the correct location (circle)

11.15   Calculating Distances

The `distance` method lets you calculate the distance between two point features:

Listing 11.14: Calculating the distance between two points

```
16    var point1 = turf.point([13.37771, 52.51627]);
17    var point2 = turf.point([13.40941, 52.52082]);
18
19    var distance = turf.distance(point1, point2, {units: 'kilometers'
         });
20
21    console.log('The distance between the two points is', distance, '
         kilometers.');
```

Although this looks similar to Leaflet's `distance` method, it differs in that this method takes GeoJSON point features as input—in Leaflet you simply have to provide coordinates. Also note that when creating a GeoJSON point feature with Turf, the longitude is provided before the latitude, so be careful when switching between Leaflet and Turf methods.

One considerable advantage when using this method is that you can optionally provide a unit and don't have to worry about converting the result yourself. Leaflet always returns distances in meters, but in Turf you can use the following units:

- meters
- kilometers
- miles
- degrees
- radians

11.16 Calculating Distances and Avoiding Obstacles

Normally, distances are calculated as the crow flies. But what if you would like to perform a calculation that takes into account obstacles? The method `shortestPath` lets you do exactly that (fig. 11.18, on the next page.

```
35      var point1 = turf.point([13.37771, 52.51627]);
36      var point2 = turf.point([13.40941, 52.52082]);
37
38      L.geoJSON(point1).addTo(map);
39      L.geoJSON(point2).addTo(map);
40
41      var shortestPath = turf.shortestPath(point1, point2, {
42        obstacles: obstaclePolygon
43      });
44
45      L.geoJSON(shortestPath, {color: 'red'}).addTo(map);
```

Note that `shortestPath` generates a line, and not a distance. If you are solely interested in the distance, not the geometry of the path, you need to also call the `length` method:

```
47      var distance = turf.length(shortestPath, {units: 'kilometers'});
```

Figure 11.18: The shortest path when ignoring an obstacle

```
48
49      console.log('The distance between the two points is', distance, '
            kilometers.');
```

Figure 11.19 shows a closeup of the shortest path.

Figure 11.19: Closeup of the shortest path

11.17   Calculating Areas and Lengths

You can calculate the length of a line using `turf.length`:

```
14      var length = turf.length(line);
15      console.log('The length of the line is:', length);
```

The optional parameter *units* lets you specify whether the result is in degrees, radians, miles, or the default, kilometers.

You can calculate the area of a polygon using `turf.area`:

```
17      var area = turf.area(poly1);
18      console.log('The area of the polygon is:', area);
```

The area is always returned in square meters. If you need a different unit, use the `convertArea` method.

Remember, if you display the results of these methods to users, think about using the `toFixed` method to reduce the number of decimal places.

11.18   Converting Areas and Lengths

You can convert lengths and areas by providing `turf.convertLength` and `turf.convertArea` with a number, the units that number is in, and the units you would like to get:

Listing 11.15: Converting lengths and areas

```
11   // Lengths
12   var kmToMi = turf.convertLength(1, 'kilometers', 'miles');
13   var miToKm = turf.convertLength(1, 'miles', 'kilometers');
14   var kmToM = turf.convertLength(1, 'kilometers', 'meters');
15   var mToFt = turf.convertLength(1, 'meters', 'feet');
16
17   console.log('1 kilometer is', kmToMi, 'miles.');
18   console.log('1 mile is', miToKm, 'kilometers.');
19   console.log('1 kilometer is', kmToM, 'meters.');
20   console.log('1 meter is', mToFt, 'feet.');
21
22   // Areas
23   var acToSqMi = turf.convertArea(500, 'acres', 'miles');
24   var sqMiToSqKm = turf.convertArea(200, 'miles', 'kilometers');
25
26   console.log('500 acres is', acToSqMi, 'square miles.');
27   console.log('200 square miles is', sqMiToSqKm, 'square kilometers.'
         );
```

The following units are available for both length and area conversion:

- kilometers, kilometre
- miles
- meters, metres
- yards
- feet
- inches
- centimeters, centimetres
- millimeters, millimetres

The following unit is only available for length conversion:

- nauticalmiles

The following unit is only available for area conversion:

* acres

Note that the units are always provided as a plural and that for units ending in 'meters' the American and British spelling is supported.

What if the unit you need is not included? Since these are all simple mathematical calculations instead of geographical computations it is rather simple to do the math and get whatever unit you need. Let's say you are developing an application for European farmers. In that case your most important units will most likely be *ares* and *hectares*. Knowing that an *are* is 100 square meters and that a hectare is 100 ares, you could use Turf to convert whatever number you have to meters, and then do the rest yourself:

Listing 11.16: Converting to ares and hectares

```
29    // Hectares
30    var sqKmToSqM = turf.convertArea(4, 'miles', 'meters');
31    var are = sqKmToSqM / 100;
32    var ha = are / 100;
33
34    console.log('4 square miles is', sqKmToSqM, 'square meters.');
35    console.log('4 square miles is', are, 'ares.');
36    console.log('4 square miles is', ha, 'hectares.');
```

If you need to do the conversion often you might as well write your own function:

Listing 11.17: Writing a function that returns hectares

```
38    function toHectares(area, inputUnit) {
39
40      var sqM = turf.convertArea(area, inputUnit, 'meters');
41
42      var ha = sqM / 10000;
43
44      return ha;
45
46    }
```

11.19   Working with Bounding Boxes

There are three methods to work with bounding boxes in Turf.

The `turf.bbox` method returns the bounding box of a GeoJSON as an array of coordinates:

```
38      var bbox = turf.bbox(poly1);
```

The `turf.envelope` method returns the bounding box of a GeoJSON as a feature:

```
41      var envelope = turf.envelope(poly1);
```

The `turf.bboxPolygon` method returns the bounding box of an array of coordinates as a feature:

```
44      var bboxPoly = turf.bboxPolygon([13.39255, 52.50936, 13.40343,
            52.51465]);
```

Note that by combining `turf.bboxPolygon` and `turf.bbox` you can achieve the same effect as simply creating an envelope:

```
47      bboxPoly = turf.bboxPolygon(turf.bbox(poly1));
```

11.20 Displaying Centroids of GeoJSON Polygons

You can get the centroid of a polygon using `turf.centroid`.

To get the centroids of every polygon feature in a dataset, you can combine Leaflet's `onEachFeature` with Turf's `centroid`:

```
35      L.geoJSON(districts, {
36
37        onEachFeature: function(feature, layer) {
38
39          var centroid = turf.centroid(feature);
40          L.geoJSON(centroid).addTo(map);
41
42        }
43
44      }).addTo(map);
```

Or you can use Turf only, by using the `featureEach` meta method:

```
35      turf.featureEach(districts, function(feature, index) {
36
37        var centroid = turf.centroid(feature);
38        L.geoJSON(centroid).addTo(map);
39
40      });
```

11.21   Detecting Whether a Geometry Lies Within Another Geometry

Let's add a polygon and two points to the map (fig. 11.20):

```
36    L.geoJSON(poly1, {color: 'green'}).addTo(map);
37    L.geoJSON(point1).addTo(map);
38    L.geoJSON(point2).addTo(map);
```

Figure 11.20: Point 1 (outside), point 2 (inside)

To check whether the points lie within the polygon you can use booleanWithin and log the result to the console (fig. 11.21):

```
40    var p1 = turf.booleanWithin(
41      point1.features[0],
42      poly1.features[0]
43    );
44
45    var p2 = turf.booleanWithin(
46      point2.features[0],
47      poly1.features[0]
48    );
49
50    console.log('Point 1 is within the polygon:', p1);
51    console.log('Point 2 is within the polygon:', p2);
```

Figure 11.21: Logging point in polygon checks

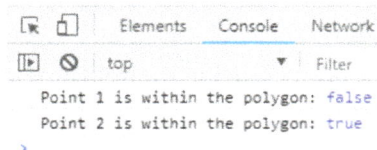

Note that this works for more than just points. You can also check if a line or a polygon lies within a polygon. You can even check whether a point lies 'within' a line (i.e. if its coordinates correspond to a vertex).

You can also test the exact opposite by running `booleanContains`:

```
40    var p1 = turf.booleanContains(
41      poly1.features[0],
42      point1.features[0]
43    );
44
45    var p2 = turf.booleanContains(
46      poly1.features[0],
47      point2.features[0]
48    );
```

As mentioned above, `booleanWithin` works for all geometries. If you know from the beginning that you are solely doing point in polygon checks, then you can also use `booleanPointInPolygon`:

```
40    var p1 = turf.booleanPointInPolygon(
41      point1.features[0],
42      poly1.features[0]
43    );
44
45    var p2 = turf.booleanPointInPolygon(
46      point2.features[0],
47      poly1.features[0]
48    );
```

11.22   Detecting Whether a Click Lies Within a Polygon

To check whether a click lies within a polygon you can generate a point feature on every click and then use `booleanWithin`:

```
36    map.on('click', function(e) {
37
38      var lat = e.latlng.lat;
39      var lon = e.latlng.lng;
40
41      var clickedPoint = turf.point([lon, lat]);
42
43      var inside = turf.booleanWithin(
44        clickedPoint,
45        poly1.features[0]
46      );
47
48      console.log('Click is inside polygon?', inside);
49
```

```
50        });
```

11.23   Detecting Points Within Polygons

Instead of checking whether individual points reside within a polygon you can also check an entire feature collection against a polygon. The result is a new feature collection that contains only points within the polygon:

```
37        var pointsWihthinPolygon = turf.pointsWithinPolygon(
38          points,
39          poly1
40        );
```

11.24   Finding Line Intersections

Intersections can be returned as a point feature collection using turf.lineIntersect. In the following example we find where the line intersects the polygon (fig. 11.22):

```
38        var intersections = turf.lineIntersect(line, poly2);
```

Both inputs can be lines or polygons.

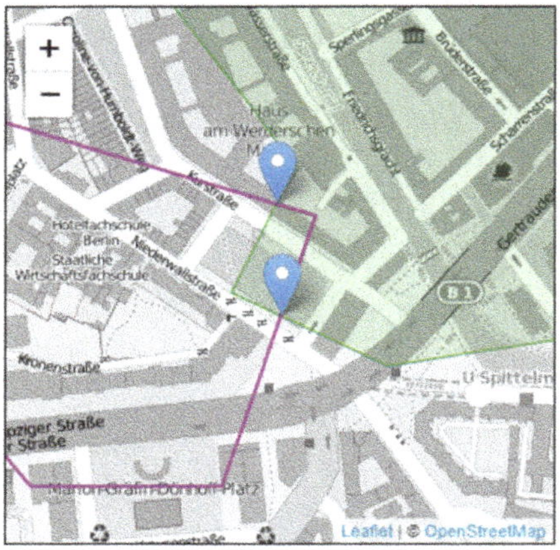

Figure 11.22: Finding intersections

11.25   Detecting and Fixing Self-Intersections

Self-intersections, in Turf named kinks, can be a source of dramatic errors when running geoprocessing tools. Ideally, polygons shouldn't contain self-intersections. Turf not only lets you check whether a polygon has self-intersections, but it also lets you fix them.

Consider the polygon dataset in figure 11.23.

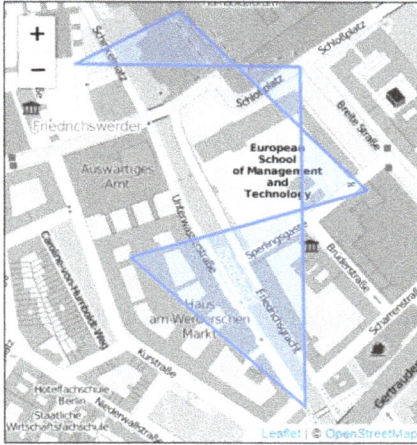

Figure 11.23: A polygon with self-intersections

What at first looks like four distinct features is in reality a single feature with three self-intersections.

You can run turf.kinks to detect self-intersections in a polygon. If self-intersections exist, they are returned as a point feature collection as shown in Figure 11.24, on the next page:

```
36      var kinks = turf.kinks(polyWithKinks.features[0]);
```

To get rid of the self-intersections, run turf.unkink:

```
34      var unkinked = turf.unkinkPolygon(polyWithKinks);
```

Again, you might not be able to tell whether a polygon has self-intersections or not, and the unkinked polygon might look exactly like the one including kinks. To check that it worked, return the number of features in the feature collection, which in our case now amounts to four:

```
console.log('Number of features:', unkinked.features.length);
```

Figure 11.24:   Pointing out self-
intersections

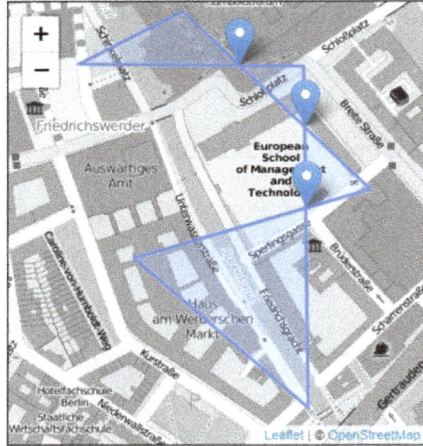

11.26   Extracting Vertices from Polygons

Sometimes it's useful to get each vertex from a polygon.

You can use the `explode` method to blow a polygon to smithereens,
the smithereens being its vertices, which are returned as a feature
collection (fig. 11.25):

Listing 11.18: Exploding a polygon

```
36      var explode = turf.explode(poly1.features[0]);
```

Figure 11.25: The original polygon
and its vertices

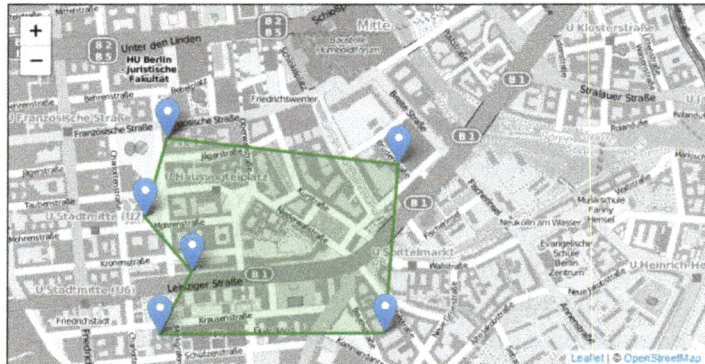

If you are not interested in receiving a feature collection but would just like to extract the coordinate pairs as arrays, you can use `coordAll`, as described in the recipe Meta functions, on page 230.

Note that both `explode` and `coordAll` return one more point than you actually see on the map. Remember that in a GeoJSON polygon, the first and last coordinate pair have to be identical. Although you count six markers on the map, there are actually seven. If you want to get rid of the last coordinate pair, simply remove the last element from the array:

Listing 11.19: Removing the last element from the coordinate array
```
coordsArray.pop();
```

11.27   Generating a Buffer

Creating a buffer in Turf is rather simple, as long as you remember that the input is not a coordinate pair but a geometry, feature, or feature collection. In the following snippet we create a point feature and then generate a 500 meter buffer around it:

```
33    var point = turf.point([13.4008, 52.5146]);
34    var buffer = turf.buffer(point, 500, {units: 'meters'});
```

Note that you can buffer points, lines, and polygons, but the more complex the geometry the longer the calculations take.

For polygons you can also generate inner buffers by assigning a negative buffer distance (fig. 11.26, on the following page):

```
37    var buffer = turf.buffer(poly1, -100, {units: 'meters'});
38    L.geoJSON(buffer, {color: 'purple'}).addTo(map);
```

11.28   Merging and Intersections

Have a look at the overlapping polygons in Figure 11.27, on the next page.

You can merge them to generate one contiguous polygon using `turf.union` (fig. 11.28, on the following page):

Listing 11.20: Merging two polygons
```
35    var union = turf.union(poly1.features[0], poly2.features[0]);
```

Figure 11.26: An inner buffer (purple)

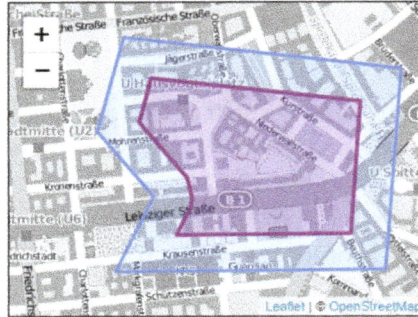

Figure 11.27: Two polygons before merging

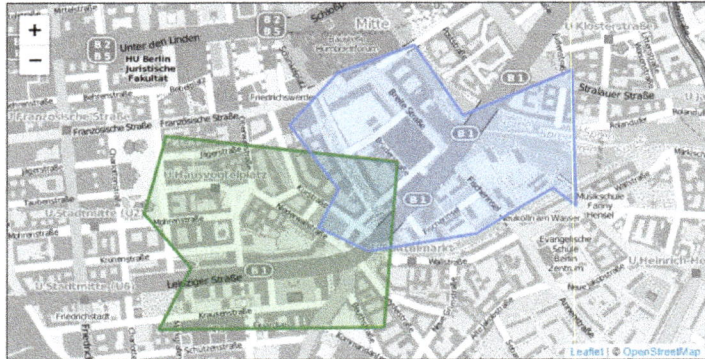

Figure 11.28: Merged polygons

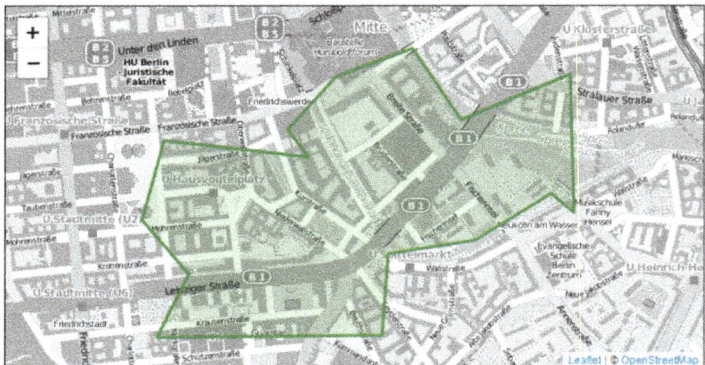

You can also find their intersection using `intersect` (fig. 11.29, on the next page):

Listing 11.21: Getting the intersection of two polygons
```
35  var intersect = turf.intersect(poly1.features[0], poly2.features[0]);
```

Figure 11.29: The intersection of two polygons

If you are not immediately interested in returning an intersection and only want to check whether an intersection exists you can run the booleanDisjoint method which returns true if features are disjoint, i.e. are not overlapping:

```
turf.booleanDisjoint(poly2.features[0], poly1.features[0]);
```

Or simply run booleanOverlap, which returns true if polygons overlap.

```
turf.booleanOverlap(poly2.features[0], poly1.features[0]);
```

11.29 Erasing from Polygons

Using turf.difference, you can erase one polygon from another. The method accepts two polygon features. The area from the second polygon that is shared with the area from the first polygon is subtracted from the first. See figures 11.30 through 11.32, on the following page.

Listing 11.22: Erasing from polygons
```
39  var erasePoly1From2 = turf.difference(
40    polyErase1.features[0],
41    polyErase2.features[0]
42  );
43
44  var erasePoly2From1 = turf.difference(
```

```
45          polyErase2.features[0],
46          polyErase1.features[0]
47      );
```

Figure 11.30: Polygon 1 (blue), polygon 2 (green)

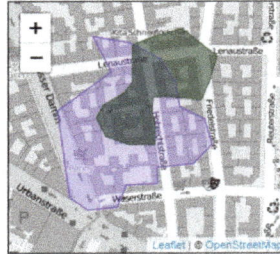

Figure 11.31: Polygon 2 erased from polygon 1

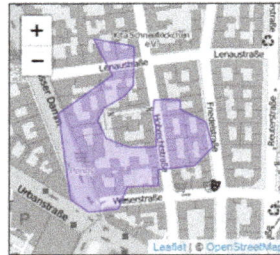

Figure 11.32: Polygon 1 erased from polygon 2

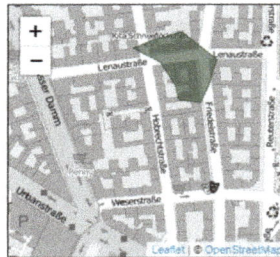

11.30   Lines Versus Great Circles

The difference between a normal line and a great circle is that the normal line simply connects each vertex by drawing a straight line in between them. Although this is the shortest way to connect points on a map, it is not necessarily the shortest distance on the Earth's surface. A great circle is a line too, but it follows the curvature of the Earth. Not only is this the correct way to display a line but it also looks more realistic.

Let's create a normal line (dashed) and a great circle (fig. 11.33):

```
33    L.marker([45.486, -122.678]).addTo(map);
34    L.marker([25.781, -80.223]).addTo(map);
35
36    var l = turf.lineString([
37      [-122.678, 45.486],
38      [-80.22354, 25.781]
39    ]);
40
41    var gc = turf.greatCircle(
42      [-122.678, 45.486],
43      [-80.22354, 25.781]
44    );
45
46    L.geoJSON(l, {dashArray: '10, 10'}).addTo(map);
47    L.geoJSON(gc).addTo(map);
```

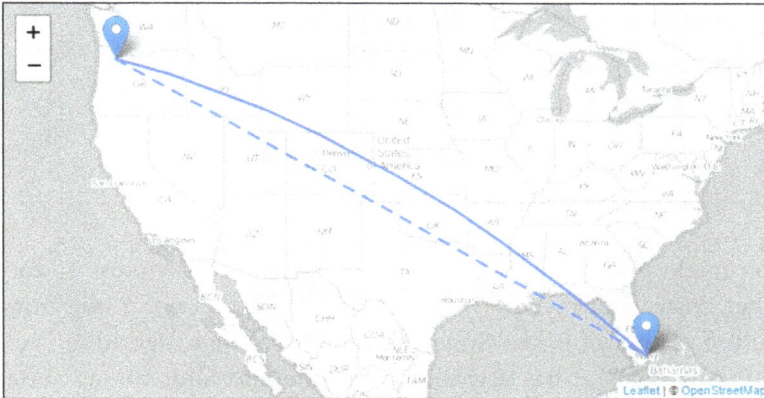

Figure 11.33: Normal line (dashed) vs. a great circle

11.31   Segmentizing a Line into Equal Parts

There are quite a few Stack Exchange questions dedicated to converting a line into equally distanced points. In Turf it's pretty easy. You can chop a line into chunks of the same length using turf.lineChunk:

```
34    var segmented = turf.lineChunk(
35      spreeRiver,
36      300,
37      {units: 'meters'}
38    );
```

At first glance this might not look like it did anything. No surprise, how would you detect a few extra vertices on a line anyway? Let's prove that it worked by running `turf.explode` to return each of the line's vertices (fig. 11.34):

```
42        var explode = turf.explode(segmented);
```

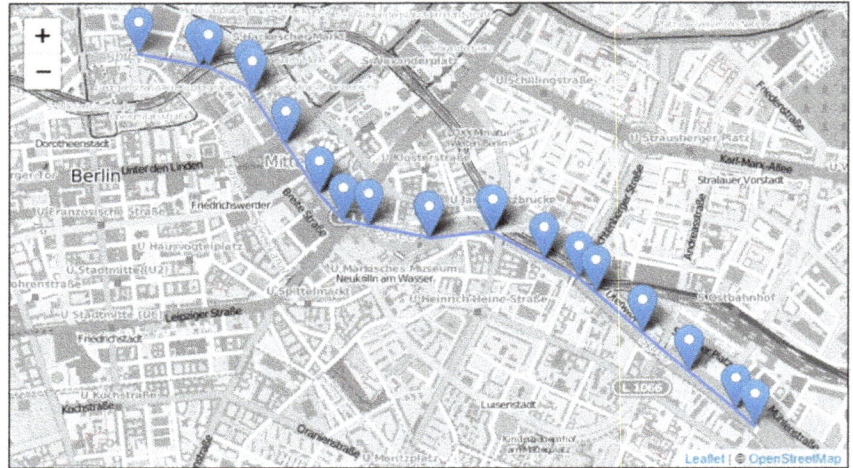

Figure 11.34: The vertices of the chunked dataset

You might notice that some vertices are suspiciously close to each other, instead of being 300 meters apart. This is not a bug but a feature. Think of it like this: when the lineChunk algorithm is executed it starts at the beginning of a line and adds a new vertex every so many meters, but it doesn't touch the original vertices. If the algorithm deleted or moved the original vertices, the line could end up looking quite different!

To show this more clearly, point out the original vertices by exploding the input line and visualizing the points as a circle marker (fig. 11.35, on the next page):

```
34        var vertices = turf.explode(spreeRiver);
35
36        L.geoJSON(vertices, {
37          pointToLayer: function(feature, latlng) {
38            return L.circleMarker(latlng, {color: 'red', weight: 3});
39          }
40        }).addTo(map);
```

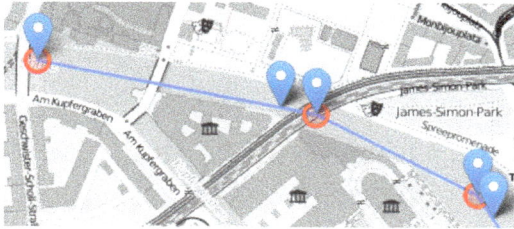

Figure 11.35: Pointing out the original vertices

11.32   Extracting a Part of a Line

The turf.lineSlice function lets you extract part of a line by providing point features to mark the beginning and the end of the extraction. The provided points don't need to be vertices of the line feature, nor do they need to reside exactly on the line (fig. 11.36).

```
39      var beginSlice = turf.point([13.40, 52.5132]);
40      var endSlice = turf.point([13.3977, 52.5103]);
41      var sliced = turf.lineSlice(
42        beginSlice,
43        endSlice,
44        line.features[0]
45      );
```

Figure 11.36: Slicing a line

11.33   Generating a Bezier Curve

A bezier curve lets you smooth out a line. This comes in handy when you have lines that don't contain a lot of vertices, giving them a rough appearance. Have a look at the following image of the Spree, one of Berlin's rivers (fig. 11.37, on the next page):

Figure 11.37: A roughly digitized
sketch of the Spree

Notice that it looks very rough. Maybe it was hastily digitized or maybe it was digitized at a smaller scale. Whatever the reason for the line's number of vertices, it doesn't look too great on the map.

The `bezierSpline` method lets you fix this within seconds (fig. 11.38):

Listing 11.23: Generating a bezier curve

```
34    var bezier = turf.bezierSpline(spreeRiver.features[0]);
```

Figure 11.38: A smoothed out sketch
of the Spree

You can further influence how the curve is generated by using the options *sharpness* and *resolution*. The sharpness (default: 0.85) defines how curvy the output is in between splines, and the resolution can strongly influence how many vertices are created, i.e. how smooth the line ends up being. The resolution is defined as the time in milliseconds between vertices, and its default is 10,000. Generally, the higher the resolution the more vertices will be created. Play with this option to observe its effect but be aware that the browser might struggle at some point.

To display the vertices that make up the curve, run the `explode` method:

```
var exploded = turf.explode(bezier);
L.geoJSON(exploded).addTo(map);
```

11.34   Creating Voronoi Polygons

You can create Voronoi polygons based on a point feature class. The only parameter is an optional bounding box, which clips the output polygons. It is recommended to use the bounding box. Try to omit it in the following snippet and you will see why. The bounding box can be easily generated by running turf.bbox (fig. 11.39):

```
36      var bbox = turf.bbox(points);
37      var voronoiPoly = turf.voronoi(points, {bbox: bbox});
```

Figure 11.39: Voronoi polygons

If you want the clipping box to be slightly larger than the original bounding box, then no need to do complex math. Simply build a polygon from the bounding box, generate an enlarged polygon using turf.transformScale, and then get the new polygon's bounding box:

```
36      var envelope = turf.envelope(points);
37      var enlared = turf.transformScale(envelope, 1.5);
38      var bbox = turf.bbox(enlared);
39      var voronoiPoly = turf.voronoi(points, {bbox: bbox});
```

11.35   Finding the Closest Marker to a Click

The `turf.nearestPoint` function takes a point and a point feature collection as inputs and returns the feature from the feature collection that is closest to the input point.

In the following example, we extract the nearest point's latitude and longitude to build a circle marker. We use a feature group, which we keep clearing, so only one circle is ever visible (fig. 11.40).

```
36    var group = L.featureGroup();
37    group.addTo(map);
38
39    map.on('click', function(e) {
40
41      var lat = e.latlng.lat;
42      var lon = e.latlng.lng;
43      var clickedPoint = turf.point([lon, lat]);
44
45      var nearestPoint = turf.nearestPoint(
46        clickedPoint,
47        restaurants
48      );
49
50      var nearestPointLat = nearestPoint.geometry.coordinates[1];
51      var nearestPointLon = nearestPoint.geometry.coordinates[0];
52
53      group.clearLayers();
54
55      L.circleMarker([nearestPointLat, nearestPointLon], {
56        color: 'purple'
57      }).addTo(group);
58
59    });
```

Figure 11.40: Highlighting the nearest marker to a click

11.36   Finding the Closest Vertex to a Click

Since `turf.nearestPoint` only works with a point feature collection and not polygons, you can simply explode the polygon into its individual vertices and then use the resulting feature class as input (fig. 11.41):

```
39      var explode = turf.explode(poly1);
40
41      map.on('click', function(e) {
42
43        var lat = e.latlng.lat;
44        var lon = e.latlng.lng;
45        var clickedPoint = turf.point([lon, lat]);
46
47        var nearestPoint = turf.nearestPoint(clickedPoint, explode);
48        ...
```

Figure 11.41: Highlighting the nearest vertex to a click

11.37   Finding all Markers in a Specified Distance of a Click

Finding all markers within a specified distance of a click can be solved by creating a buffer on click and then extracting all points within the buffer using the `pointsWithinPolygon` method. In the following snippet we find all markers within 500 meters of a click (fig. 11.42, on the following page).

```
36      var group = L.featureGroup();
37      group.addTo(map);
38
39      map.on('click', function(e) {
40
```

```
41        var lat = e.latlng.lat;
42        var lon = e.latlng.lng;
43        var clickedPoint = turf.point([lon, lat]);
44
45        var buffer = turf.buffer(clickedPoint, 0.5); // default unit is
               kilometers
46        group.clearLayers();
47        L.geoJSON(buffer, {color: 'green', weight: 1}).addTo(group);
48
49        var withinBuffer = turf.pointsWithinPolygon(
50          restaurants,
51          buffer
52        );
53
54        L.geoJSON(withinBuffer, {
55
56          pointToLayer: function(feature, latlng) {
57
58            return L.circleMarker(latlng, {color: 'purple'});
59
60          }
61
62        }).addTo(group);
63
64      });
```

Figure 11.42: Highlighting all markers within 500 meters of a click

Note that displaying the buffer is optional.

11.38   Showing Polygons That Are Larger Than a Given Area

To only show polygon features that are larger than a specified area you can use the L.GeoJSON's `filter` function and on each iteration get the area of the current feature. Then it comes down to using a simple `if` statement to only return a feature if it fulfills the criterion.

The following snippet iterates through Berlin's districts and only returns a district if it has an area larger than 100 square kilometers:

```
35    L.geoJSON(districts, {
36
37      filter: function(feature) {
38
39        var area = turf.area(feature);
40
41        if (area > 100000000) { // 100000000 sqm = 100 sqkm
42
43          return true;
44
45        }
46
47      }
48
49    }).addTo(map);
```

11.39   Converting WGS 84 and Web Mercator Coordinates

Remember that any coordinate you ever have to deal with in Leaflet is in WGS 84, so this recipe might not be relevant to you. If you are using a different web mapping library, such as OpenLayers, converting between WGS 84 and Web Mercator can be an essential part in getting your application to work. Turf has methods to do exactly that: `toMercator` and `toWgs84`. Both methods accept a point feature as input, not simple coordinates, and they both also return a point feature.

Let's write a click handler that logs each click in WGS84 and Web Mercator:

Listing 11.24: Logging a click as WGS and Web Mercator

```
33    map.on('click', function(e) {
34
```

```
35          var lat = e.latlng.lat;
36          var lon = e.latlng.lng;
37
38          var point = turf.point([lon, lat]);
39
40          var webMercator = turf.toMercator(point);
41
42          var x = webMercator.geometry.coordinates[0].toFixed(0);
43          var y = webMercator.geometry.coordinates[1].toFixed(0);
44
45          console.log(lon, lat);
46          console.log(x, y);
47
48      });
```

12 *Mobile Development and Geolocation*

Contents

This chapter treats two topics that are more than relevant these days: geolocation and mobile development. Millions of people use smartphones to accomplish minor to complex tasks on a daily basis, and dynamic interactive maps are playing an important role in this—from looking for a restaurant to finding your way to a meeting. What would smartphones be without maps and GPS?

In this chapter we will first look at geolocation, or in other words: how one can acquire the location of a device. Then we'll create an Android app using Cordova. With just a few simple commands any web application can be turned into an app that can be installed on a smartphone.

12.1 Detecting the User's Browser

You can detect the user's browser using `L.Browser`.

The command returns an object with about 30 keys, each having a true or a false value.

In addition to telling you what browser is being used, it also contains useful information such as whether the browser runs on a mobile device, whether the browser allows touch events, or whether the device has a high-resolution screen.

As your application grows you might notice limitations or bugs in certain browsers and this way you can target these devices with custom fixes. Or, think about differentiating between desktop and mobile devices. Imagine your application contains a side panel holding various tools. On desktop devices the panel should be shown when the page loads. On mobile devices, because the available width is limited, the panel should be collapsed when the page loads:

Listing 12.1: Targeting mobile devices

```
12    var userBrowser = L.Browser;
13
14    if (userBrowser.mobile === true) {
15      // collapse side panel
16    }
```

12.2   Getting the User's Position

Getting the user's position is achieved by using the map's `locate` method.

Note that modern browsers block geolocation requests from insecure origins, meaning that geolocation only works on pages hosted via HTTPS, not on pages hosted via HTTP. This doesn't require the entire website to be secure, but only those pages that actually use geolocation. When using a testing or development environment such as XAMPP this constraint usually does not apply.

```
map.locate();
```

Let's test this by first creating a button:

Listing 12.2: Creating a location button

```
20    <input type="button" value="Find me!" id="btnLocation">
```

and then writing a function that calls the `locate` method, hooking it up to the button's `onclick` event:

Listing 12.3: Calling the locate method

```
49    function getLocation() {
50
51      map.locate();
52
53    }
54
55    document.getElementById('btnLocation').onclick = getLocation;
```

When clicking the button you will first be asked if you want to share your position (fig. 12.1):

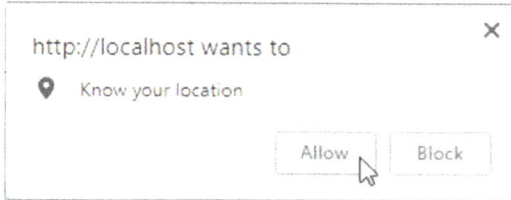

Figure 12.1: The browser wants to access your location

When testing this you might think that nothing really happens. This is not entirely true. In fact, the `locate` method did indeed get the user's location. When the map acquires the user position, a `locationfound` event is fired and we can extract interesting and useful information from the event object. The `locationfound` event object holds the following information:

- location (latitude and longitude)
- accuracy of the location (meters)
- altitude (meters above the WGS84 ellipsoid)
- accuracy of the altitude (meters)
- heading (degrees, clockwise from North)
- speed (meters per second)
- time

Let's try to extract that information and add it to our web page.

First, create the HTML:

Listing 12.4: Preparing HTML input fields

```
22  <p>
23    <b>Location</b>: <span id="lat"></span>, <span id="lon"></span>
24    <br>
25    <b>Location accuracy</b>: <span id="locationAccuracy"></span>
26    <br>
27    <b>Altitude</b>: <span id="altitude"></span>
28    <br>
29    <b>Altitude accuracy</b>: <span id="altitudeAccuracy"></span>
30    <br>
31    <b>Heading</b>: <span id="heading"></span>
32    <br>
```

```
33      <b>Speed</b>: <span id="speed"></span>
34      <br>
35      <b>Time</b>: <span id="time"></span>
36    </p>
```

And then register the locationfound event on the map and write the extracted information to the page's elements (fig. 12.2):

Listing 12.5: Registering the locationfound event

```
57    map.on('locationfound', function(e) {
58
59        console.log('Location found!');
60
61        var lat = e.latlng.lat;
62        var lon = e.latlng.lng;
63        var locationAccuracy = e.accuracy;
64        var altitude = e.altitude;
65        var altitudeAccuracy = e.altitudeAccuracy;
66        var heading = e.heading;
67        var speed = e.speed;
68        var time = e.timestamp;
69
70        document.getElementById('lat').innerHTML = lat;
71        document.getElementById('lon').innerHTML = lon;
72        document.getElementById('locationAccuracy').innerHTML =
                locationAccuracy;
73        document.getElementById('altitude').innerHTML = altitude;
74        document.getElementById('altitudeAccuracy').innerHTML =
                altitudeAccuracy;
75        document.getElementById('heading').innerHTML = heading;
76        document.getElementById('speed').innerHTML = speed;
77        document.getElementById('time').innerHTML = time;
78
79    });
```

Figure 12.2: Information returned by geolocation (desktop)

Location: 52.4909261, 13.416140599999999
Location accuracy: 8825
Altitude: undefined
Altitude accuracy: undefined
Heading: undefined
Speed: undefined
Time: 1536504065311

You notice that some of the information we extracted simply says undefined. Depending on the device you use, not every piece of information mentioned in the list above is available, some being only available on mobile devices.

12.3   Zooming to the User's Position

Zooming to the user's position is achieved by passing the *setView* option to the `locate` method. The option does exactly what the map's `setView` method does, but instead of you having to provide the coordinates, the `locate` method does it for you.

```
map.locate({setView: true});
```

The option also changes the zoom level, so if you want to avoid this you can use another option, *maxZoom*, which won't let the map zoom beyond a certain level. In the following snippet, once the location is found, the map zooms to the location but it stays at zoom level 5:

```
map.locate({setView: true, maxZoom: 5});
```

Alternatively you could set the view yourself by reading the coordinates revealed by the event object and calling the `setView` method on the map:

```
map.on('locationfound', function(e) {

  var lat = e.latlng.lat;
  var lon = e.latlng.lng;

  map.setView([lat, lon]);

});
```

This can be useful if you do not always want the map to move. For example, maybe you would like to keep the map from moving if the position has only shifted a little bit. In that case you would calculate the distance between the newly acquired position and the last position, and if the distance doesn't exceed a given threshold the map view is not changed.

12.4   Watching the User's Position

By default, the location is acquired only once. In the previous recipes the location was acquired when clicking on a button and each time you need an updated location you have to click the button again.

You can change this behavior by using the *watch* option:

```
map.locate({watch: true});
```

When using the *watch* option the `locate` method is fired repeatedly and each time the position changes the `locationfound` event is fired. Test this by simply logging to the console (fig. 12.3):

Listing 12.6: Watching the position

```
33    function getLocation() {
34
35      map.locate({watch: true});
36
37    }
38
39    document.getElementById('btnLocation').onclick = getLocation;
40
41    map.on('locationfound', function(e) {
42
43      console.log('Location found!');
44
45    });
```

Figure 12.3: Watching the location

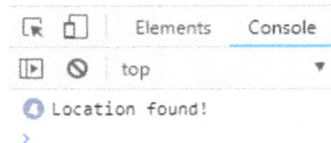

Once started, the device will keep watching the location indefinitely, but you can stop the watch process at any time using:

```
map.stopLocate();
```

12.5   Location Errors

Unfortunately, getting the location doesn't always work—what if the user denies sharing their location? That's when the `locationerror` event comes in. It is registered just like the `locationfound` event and its event object provides you with a code and a message (fig. 12.4, on the facing page):

Listing 12.7: Logging location errors

```
47    map.on('locationerror', function(e) {
48
49      console.log('Location error!');
50
51      console.log('Error code:', e.code, ' --- Message:', e.message);
52
53    });
```

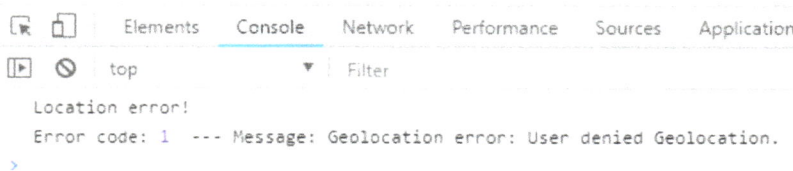

Figure 12.4: Error because the user denied geolocation

If geolocation is an essential component of your application it is crucial to detect errors and possibly warn users.

There are four error codes:

```
Error 1: PERMISSION_DENIED
  Permission was denied by the user
Error 2: POSITION_UNAVAILABLE
  Geolocation is unavailable
Error 3: TIMEOUT
  The device wasn't able to acquire the position after a given amount of time has passed
Error 4: UNKNOWN_ERROR
  Geolocation failed but the error is unknown
```

Error 3 can possibly be fixed by increasing the timeout. By default, the device tries to acquire a location for 10 seconds before aborting the process. You can override this default by using the *timeout* option. Note that the time is always specified in milliseconds. The following snippet increases the timeout to 15 seconds:

```
map.locate({timeout: 15000});
```

12.6   Using Geolocation Without Leaflet

In the previous recipe you learned how to acquire the user's position through the map. Although this is very useful, it's not always an option, such as when your application doesn't include a map, or maybe it includes a map, but on a different page. In that case use the Geolocation API. Setting it up is a little more work, but the result is exactly the same:

https://w3.org/TR/geolocation-API/

Listing 12.8: Getting a position without Leaflet

```
13   function startGeolocation() {
14
15     if (navigator.geolocation) {
16
17       navigator.geolocation.getCurrentPosition(success);
18
19     } else {
20
21       alert('Your browser does not support geolocation!');
22
23     }
24
25   }
26
27   function success(location) {
28
29     var lat = location.coords.latitude;
30     var lon = location.coords.longitude;
31
32     console.log(lat, lon);
33
34   }
```

Optionally, you can pass an error callback to getCurrentPosition:

```
navigator.geolocation.getCurrentPosition(success, error);

...

function error(e) {

  console.log('Error:', e.code);

}
```

The error codes that are returned are identical to those in the previous recipe.

12.7   *Setting the Initial Scale and Device Width*

When developing for mobile devices, which includes applications on websites that might be opened on a mobile device, it is crucial that you add the following meta tag to your page's **<head>**:

```
<meta name="viewport" content="width=device-width, initial-scale=1">
```

This tag allows the page width to adjust to the device and sets the page zoom level to 1.

Have a look at the following image (fig. 12.5). On the left is the map that doesn't include the viewport meta tag, on the right, the one that does does. It isn't hard decide which one looks better.

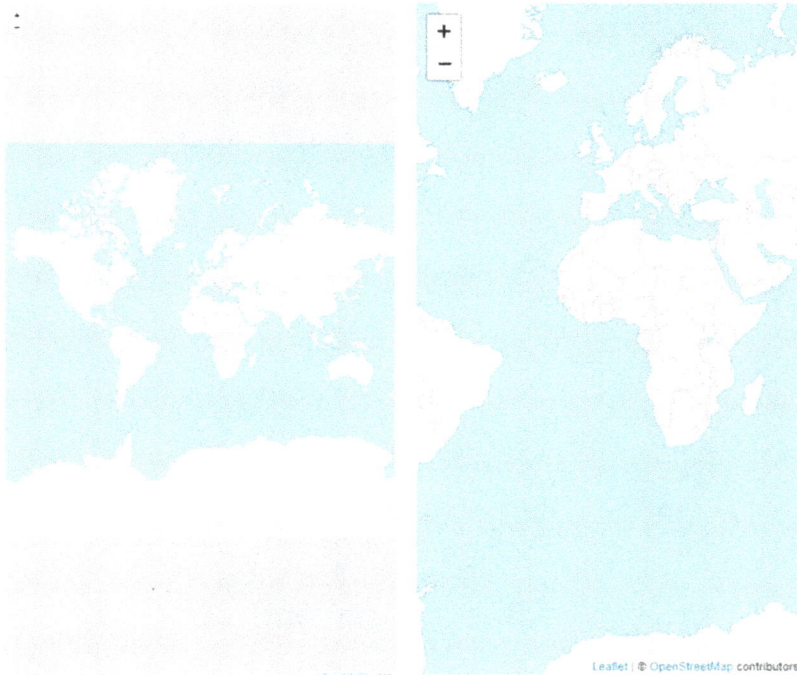

Figure 12.5: Default width and initial scale versus adjusted

12.8   Setting up Android Studio and Cordova

To create an Android application you first of all need to install Android Studio on your computer:

`https://developer.android.com/studio/`

Once installed, start Android Studio and go to *Configure* to open the SDK Manager (fig. 12.6):

Figure 12.6: Android SDK Manager

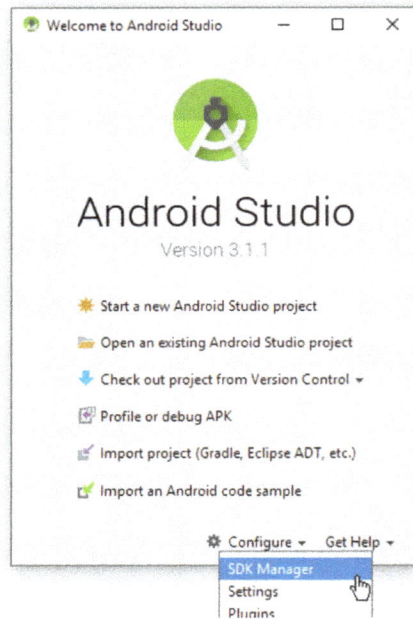

Under Android SDK you can check which Android versions have been installed. If the one you need is missing you can simply install it (see figure 12.7, on the next page).

That's it, Android Studio is ready to go. In order to create an app, we also need to install Cordova. We'll install Cordova using npm, so it is important that you install npm if you do not have it already.

npm website: https://www.npmjs.com/

Then start your preferred IDE and open its terminal to install Cor-

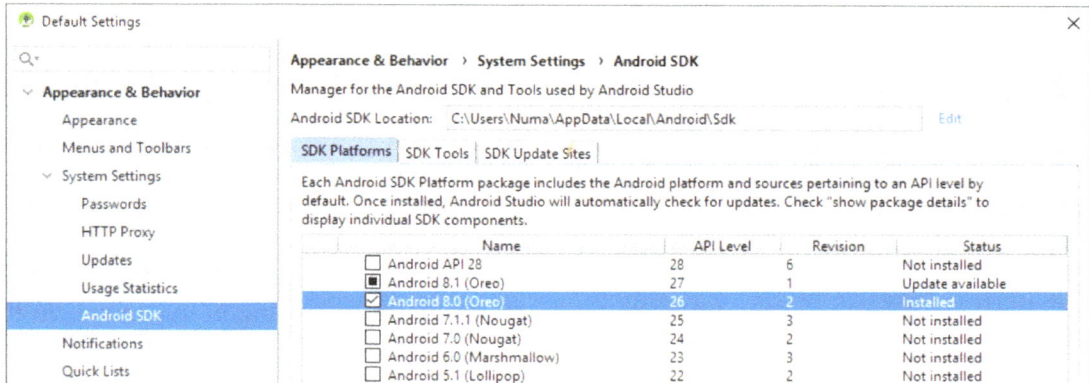

Figure 12.7: Installed Android versions

dova:

```
npm install -g cordova
```

12.9   Creating a Mobile Application with Cordova

Choose a location on your computer and create a new folder for this recipe.

In the command line (e.g. your IDE's terminal), run the following:

```
cordova create leafletCookbookApp com.leaflet.cookbook LeafletApp
```

This creates a directory called leafletCookbookApp. The directory holds a few folders, including www, which includes the source code of our application. You should not make any changes to this directory structure.

Every app needs a unique identifier. We named it com.leaflet.cookbook. The naming doesn't matter, but it must be unique, so be careful when copying from one application to another. LeafletApp is simply the name of our app, as it will appear on the smartphone.

So far our app is generic and it doesn't know yet that it will be an Android app. To actually create an Android app we need to install the Android platform in our application folder.

With your terminal, change to the main folder, i.e. `leafletCookbookApp`, and run the following:

You only need to run this the very first time you create an app!

```
cordova platform add android
```

Now navigate to www. This is the folder that will hold your actual application. By default, the folder contains a test app. Since we want our own app, we can delete everything in this folder. In this folder you can now develop a Leaflet application or you can just copy and paste some code that has been prepared for you. From the data folder for the chapter, copy everything inside `mobileApp`: a folder called `leaflet` and a file named `index.html`. The former contains the Leaflet source code and the latter contains our application's functionality. The application is very simple: it lets you set points on a map and you can then drag these points.

Once this has been accomplished we can create the app by building it:

```
cordova build
```

That's it, you just created your first Android app.

You can find the app under:

```
leafletCookbookApp/platforms/android/app/build/outputs/apk/debug
```

The file is called `app-debug.apk`. APK stands for Android Package and the Android operating system uses it to install apps. Transfer this file to your phone and install it to test the app.

Hint: Debugging

Transferring an app to the device takes a little time and can become very unpleasant when you constantly change something, especially minor things that need to be tested after only a few lines of code.

Luckily we can avoid this. On your device, navigate to *Settings |*

About Phone. The developer options can be unlocked by tapping *Build number* 7 times. In the developer options, allow USB debugging.

Now connect your smartphone to your computer and in your IDE run:

```
cordova run android
```

Cordova will now send the app straight to the phone and install it. This saves an incredible amount of time, and it even allows you to debug the application.

If you are a Chrome user, open:

chrome://inspect/#devices

At the bottom under WebView look for com.leaflet.cookbook and click it. This opens a console, which lets you communicate directly with the app. Try to set a marker on the smartphone and move it—you'll see it move in the browser as well. This also means you can develop this way, benefit from features like console logging or the debugger, and you do not have to build a new app for each minor change.

12.10   Installing Cordova Plugins

A number of plugins can be installed when working with Cordova. Plugins let you do a variety of things, such as accessing the device's internal or external storage, accessing contacts, using geolocation, scanning a QR code, and so on.

Almost any time you need to do something that cannot be done with pure HTML, CSS and JavaScript or requires you to access the device, you have to install a plugin.

Have a look at the plugin repository: https://cordova.apache.org/plugins/

To install a plugin, use:

```
cordova plugin add repo-name
```

To show installed plugins, run:

```
cordova plugin ls
```

13 *Databases*

Contents

So far the examples in this book have been mostly static. Datasets were created directly in the code or they were loaded from files that were saved in a folder. Once the complexity of an application grows it can become cumbersome to near impossible to work with local datasets. Often a database, installed on a server and separate from the web application, is used to store the data the application consumes.

In this chapter we'll learn how to send data from a web application to a database and vice versa. The crucial difference between other examples in the book is that we cannot solely rely on JavaScript anymore, and need to look into another programming language. Because of security reasons, JavaScript in your browser cannot directly communicate with a server. We will use an AJAX request to send parameters to a file stored on a server and that file will do the work for us, communicating with the database. Although any server-side language would work to accomplish this, we are going to use PHP because it is preinstalled on almost any web server and in addition, it is fairly easy to use.

Since Python is becoming increasingly important in GIS, the end of this chapter teaches you how to use Python to accomplish the same tasks we did in PHP. For a database, we are going to use Post-greSQL. PostgreSQL is one of the most widely used open source database management systems and is especially popular in GIS and web mapping because of its PostGIS extension. PostGIS adds spatial data types to a PostgreSQL database and extends it with hundreds of spatial functions.

http://postresql.org

http://postgis.net

This chapter will only explain what is necessary to get started with PostgreSQL, PostGIS, PHP, and Python. Anything more would go beyond the scope of this book. If you want to learn more about these topics, don't worry—entire books have been written about them. To keep the main text from being interrupted too often, most explanations that point out PHP syntax and concepts are mentioned in margin notes.

If you are new to PostgreSQL and PostGIS you should first visit:

```
https://www.postgresql.org/download/
```

and install PostgreSQL. Make sure to also install PostGIS. If working on Windows, it is easiest if you get an installer that already includes PostGIS.

The examples in this chapter will not work by simply double-clicking files. It is important that the files are stored on a server. If you don't have access to a server you should have a look at XAMPP, which is mentioned in the first chapter. XAMPP will get you up and running with a server-like infrastructure within minutes.

13.1   Setting up a PostgreSQL Database

This recipe covers the absolute basics to get started with PostgreSQL. If you are a PostgreSQL / PostGIS user already and want to learn how to hook up a PostgreSQL database to a Leaflet application, then skip to the next recipes.

The PostgreSQL installation includes pgAdmin, a graphical user interface that lets you connect to PostgreSQL servers and databases. We are now going to use pgAdmin to create our first database.

In pgAdmin click the plug button, which lets you establish a connection to a PostgreSQL server (fig. 13.1):

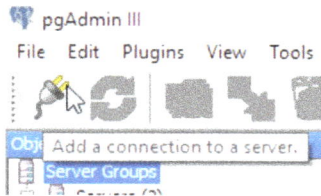

Figure 13.1: Connecting to a server

Now enter a name for your connection (e.g. localhost), the host (localhost), the port (5432), a username (postgres) and a password (postgres). What you enter here depends on your installation. If you are new to PostgreSQL you most likely went with the defaults (fig. 13.2, on the next page). The host tells pgAdmin where your databases reside. In most projects the host is an external server that can be reached using an IP address—in that case you would enter the server's IP address. If you installed PostgreSQL on the same computer you are using for this cookbook, use localhost. By default, PostgreSQL uses postgres as the username and the password. It is highly recommended that you change this if you use your database for anything other than testing or getting to know PostgreSQL.

Once you have connected to your local PostgreSQL, go ahead and create a new database by right-clicking *Databases*, as seen in Figure 13.3, on the following page.

Assign a name to the database (e.g. leaflet_cookbook) and set its owner to postgres (fig. 13.4, on the next page).

Once the database has been created you can add a new table, which will hold our data (fig. 13.5, on page 289).

Figure 13.2: Connecting to a server

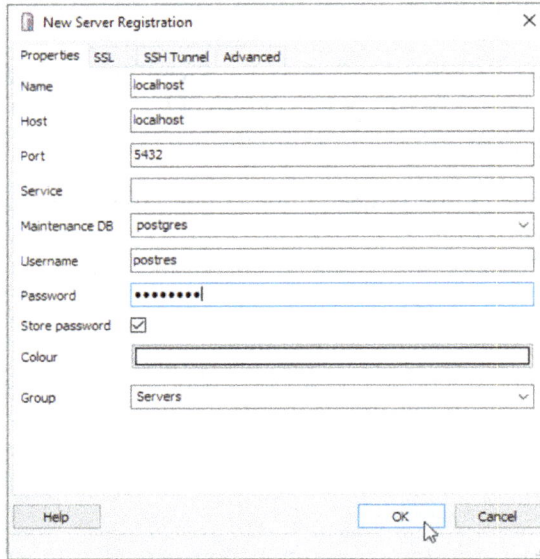

Figure 13.3: Creating a new database

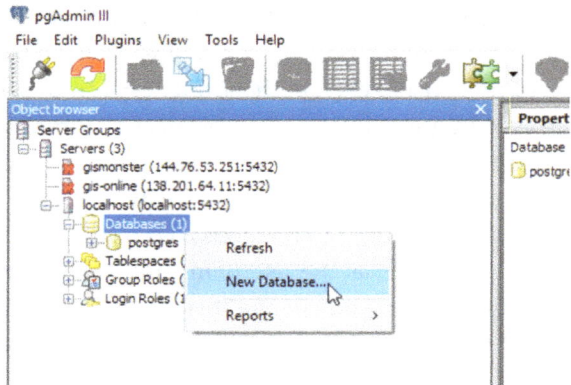

Figure 13.4: Assigning a name and owner to the database

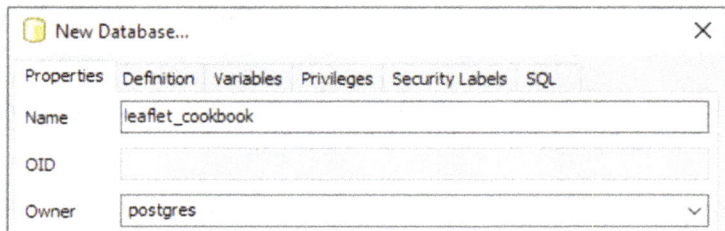

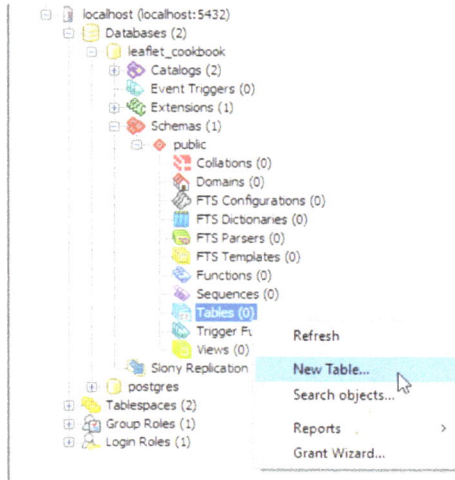

Figure 13.5: Creating a new table

Under Properties name the table cities and set its owner to postgres (fig. 13.6).

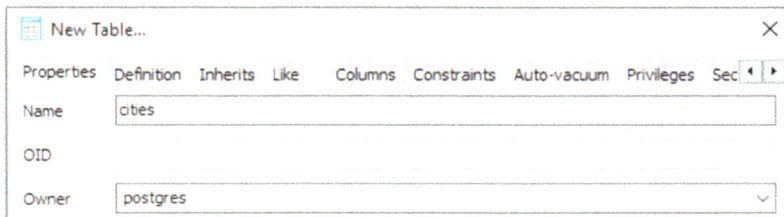

Figure 13.6: Assigning a name and owner to the table

Under *Columns* click the *Add* button and add columns with the following names and data types:

- Name: gid, data type: serial
- Name: name, data type: character varying
- Name: lat, data type: numeric
- Name: lon, data type: numeric

Click OK so the table is created, then open the properties again, switch to the *Constraints* tab, and add a Primary Key. Under *Properties* name it gid_pk and under Columns assign the gid column to it and click OK.

Your table is now ready. You can have a look at it by opening it using the table button in the upper toolbar (fig. 13.7):

Figure 13.7: The SQL and table buttons

You can now manually populate the table with cities of your choice, or you can use a sample dataset by clicking on the SQL button and running the following set of queries:

```sql
INSERT INTO cities (name, lat, lon) VALUES ('Providence', 41.8315,
    -71.4105);
INSERT INTO cities (name, lat, lon) VALUES ('Luxembourg', 49.6083,
    6.1308);
INSERT INTO cities (name, lat, lon) VALUES ('Siena', 43.3241,
    11.3276);
INSERT INTO cities (name, lat, lon) VALUES ('Ottawa', 45.2804,
    -75.8124);
INSERT INTO cities (name, lat, lon) VALUES ('Cheyenne', 41.1233,
    -104.8402);
```

13.2   Getting Data from a PHP File

Before we can do anything truly interesting, we need to make sure PHP actually works. In this recipe we are going to request a PHP file and get a simple string from it.

To keep complexity at a minimum we can use jQuery. So far we have used pure JavaScript in this book instead of using a framework. Writing requests with pure JavaScript is cumbersome, however, and therefore we are using jQuery to assist us.

Download it at `https://jquery.com/` and include it in the page's **<head>**:

```
6      <script src="../jquery/jquery-3.3.1.min.js"></script>
```

echo is used in PHP to output a string from a file.

Create a new subdirectory called php and create a new PHP file: `readFromPhpFile.php`. Let's keep the file simple and just echo a string:

Listing 13.1: Echoing a string

```
1    <?php
```

```
2   echo 'A message from a PHP file!';
3   ?>
```

Note that the contents of a PHP file are always between the opening `<?php` and closing `?>` tag.

Now, switch to the HTML file's script tag and write an AJAX request using jQuery:

```
12      $.post('php/readFromPhpFile.php',
13
14        function(data) {
15
16          console.log(data);
17
18        }
19
20      );
```

This request calls our PHP file. If the request succeeds, the first parameter of the callback function contains whatever the PHP file returns, in this case a string.

13.3 Reading Data from a PostgreSQL Database

Now that we set up the communication between a web application and a server, let's use a PHP file that doesn't simply return a string but actual geographic data, which resides in a PostgreSQL database.

> You need to make sure that your PHP is allowed to connect to a PostgreSQL database. A default installation might comment out specific, but in our case important, lines in the PHP configuration file, `php.ini`. To uncomment these lines just remove the leading semicolon. On Windows, uncomment `extension=php_pgsql.dll` and on Linux, `extension=pgsql.so`.

To get data from a PostgreSQL database using PHP we need to connect to the database, similar to what we manually did in pgAdmin. Although not required, the connection parameters are often stored in their own file, instead of each file that connects to the database. This is especially convenient when the parameters change—for instance when the password changes. Instead of individually editing multiple files you only have to modify one file.

Let's create a file for this purpose and name it `config.php`.

An associative array in PHP works like an object in JavaScript. You define keys and values and later on you can access a value by its key.

In it, we create and return an associative array that holds the database's connection parameters:

Listing 13.2: An array holding database credentials

```php
1  <?php
2  return array(
3    "server" => "localhost",
4    "username" => "postgres",
5    "password" => "postgres",
6    "database" => "leaflet_cookbook",
7    "port" => "5432"
8  );
9  ?>
```

Next, we'll create the file that will be called from our JavaScript and populate it with the logic that connects to the database, sends a query to the cities table, and then processes the result of the query to return it to the browser.

We'll name the file readPointsFromDb.php. Have a look at the entire code first, and then skip to the explanation:

You may have noticed that in line 3 of the script we have used error_reporting(0). This "turns off" the default PHP error messages. While helpful when debugging, we don't need them since we are providing our own error messages and PHP error messages can get a bit long.

```php
1  <?php
2
3  error_reporting(0);
4
5  $config = include('config.php');
6
7  $server = $config['server'];
8  $username = $config['username'];
9  $password = $config['password'];
10 $database = $config['database'];
11 $port = $config['port'];
12
13 $dbconn = pg_connect("host=$server dbname=$database user=$username
14 password=$password port=$port") or die('connection error');
15
16 $query = "SELECT name, lat, lon FROM cities";
17
18 $result = pg_query($dbconn, $query) or die('query error');
19
20 $city = array();
21
22 $citiesArray = array();
23
24 while ($row = pg_fetch_row($result)) {
25   $city["name"] = $row[0];
26   $city["lat"] = $row[1];
```

```
27    $city["lon"] =  $row[2];
28    array_push($citiesArray, $city);
29  }
30
31  echo json_encode($citiesArray, JSON_UNESCAPED_UNICODE);
32
33  pg_close($dbconn);
34
35  ?>
```

Lines 5-14: We include `config.php` and store its contents in variables, followed by the `pg_connect` function, which requires a single string holding all connection parameters. Note the `or die(...)` after the database connection. The `die` function simply exits a script and returns a string while doing so, in our case `connection error`. The `or` operator makes sure that the `die` function is only executed if the previous function returns `false`, which only happens when the database connection fails.

In PHP variables always begin with the $ sign. Variables can also be used in a string. You don't have to break up a string to concatenate it with variables.

Lines 16-18 We define a simple select query as a string and store it in a variable, which we then send to the database by calling `pg_query`. Note that `pg_query` first receives the database connection and then the query. Here again we call the `die` function—if the query fails the script exits, otherwise it continues.

Lines 20-29: If the database finds records it returns them as one or more rows, which we can individually access using `pg_fetch_row`. Because we assume that the result contains multiple rows we use a while loop to iterate through the set of rows. In each iteration we create an associative array, `$city`, holding the returned information and push it into the `$citiesArray` array that we created before the loop.

Line 31 We then get a JSON representation of the array by calling `json_encode` and echo it. Remember that echo is used to return a string from a PHP file. Echoing the array we just created would simply return a string holding the word Array, but we want much more than that, which is why we convert the array to a string that can be parsed by JavaScript.

Line 33 Finally, it is important that we close the connection to the database by passing our connection to `pg_close`. Just like you shut the fridge after grabbing a cold drink, you close a database connection after fetching the values.

Now that our PHP is ready, we can write an AJAX request that calls the file. Before we add the data to the map, let's log it first, so we can check that our request works (fig. 13.8):

```
38      $.post('php/readPointsFromDb.php',
39
40        function(data) {
41
42          console.log(data);
43
44        }
45
46      );
```

Figure 13.8: The result from the AJAX request

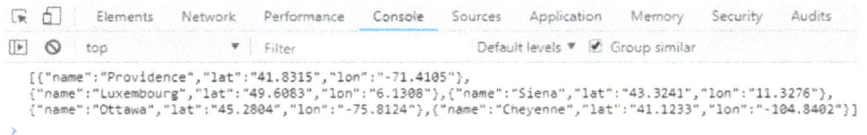

There we go! The log shows exactly what we built in PHP—an array holding associative arrays (i.e. JavaScript objects).

Since both the database connection and the query can fail and since we used the `die` function to inform us about errors, it is wise to first check if either error is returned, instead of creating markers right away.

```
38      $.post('php/readPointsFromDb.php',
39
40        function(data) {
41
42          if (data === 'connection error') {
43
44            console.log('Error connecting to the database!');
45
46          } else if (data === 'query error') {
47
48            console.log('Error querying the database!');
49
```

```
50              }
51
52          }
53
54       );
```

Once the error handling has been taken care of we can expand the previous example by adding an `else` statement, since we know that only if there are no errors do we actually have the data to create markers.

Since the data was transmitted as a string containing a JSON, we first need to parse that string, which we can do using `JSON.parse`. Once parsed, we are left with an array that contains an object for each returned city. Now, it comes down to a matter of iterating through the array and in each iteration extracting the coordinates to create a marker that we can add to the map. Since our database also includes names, we can use these to create popups:

```
50          } else {
51
52              data = JSON.parse(data);
53
54              for (var i = 0; i < data.length; i++) {
55
56                  var name = data[i]['name'];
57                  var lat = data[i]['lat'];
58                  var lon = data[i]['lon'];
59
60                  var marker = L.marker([lat, lon]);
61
62                  marker.bindPopup(name);
63
64                  marker.addTo(map);
65
66              }
67
68          }
```

You'll notice that the markers are now loaded, but the map view isn't changed. Let's alter the example slightly so the map view is adjusted to the extent of all markers. A quick way to accomplish this is by using a feature group, whose bounds we can request after it has been populated. Create a feature group before the loop and instead of adding the markers to the map, add them to the feature group. After the loop, get the group bounds and call the fitBounds method:

```
51          } else {
52
53            data = JSON.parse(data);
54
55            var group = L.featureGroup();
56
57            for (var i = 0; i < data.length; i++) {
58
59              var name = data[i]['name'];
60              var lat = data[i]['lat'];
61              var lon = data[i]['lon'];
62
63              var marker = L.marker([lat, lon]);
64
65              marker.bindPopup(name);
66
67              marker.addTo(group);
68
69            }
70
71            group.addTo(map);
72
73            var bbox = group.getBounds();
74
75            map.fitBounds(bbox);
76
77          }
```

13.4   Writing Data to a PostgreSQL Database

Let's create an application that lets you set a marker that can be saved to the cities table in our database.

First, create an input mask that includes three text inputs, a button, and an empty paragraph to display a status (fig. 13.9, on the facing page):

```
37    <div id="inputDiv">
38      <b>Lat</b>: <br>
39      <input type="text" id="latInput"> <br>
40      <b>Lon</b>: <br>
41      <input type="text" id="lonInput"> <br>
42      <b>Name</b>: <br>
43      <input type="text" id="nameInput"> <br> <br>
```

```
44        <input type="button" value="Save to Database" id="btnSave">
45        <p id="status"></p>
46     </div>
```

To keep the mask from being displayed under the map we use some CSS to place it in the top-right corner of the map. Be careful to assign a high z-index to the input container or it will appear behind the map:

```
22     #inputDiv {
23        background-color: white;
24        padding: 15px;
25        position: fixed;
26        top: 0px;
27        right: 0px;
28        z-index: 999;
29     }
```

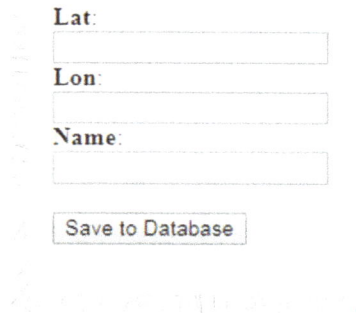

Figure 13.9: The input mask

In the following snippet we add a marker to the map and register a click event on the map. On each click the coordinates are extracted and the marker position is changed before writing the coordinates into the text input:

```
59     var marker = L.marker([0, 0]).addTo(map);
60
61     map.on('click', function(e) {
62
63        var lat = e.latlng.lat.toFixed(5);
64        var lon = e.latlng.lng.toFixed(5);
65
66        marker.setLatLng([lat, lon]);
67
68        document.getElementById('latInput').value = lat;
69        document.getElementById('lonInput').value = lon;
```

```
70
71          document.getElementById('nameInput').value = '';
72          document.getElementById('status').innerHTML = '';
73
74      });
```

Now we can write a function that is called when clicking the *Save to Database* button. In the function body we first read the coordinates and the name from the text inputs and then we form an AJAX request, which communicates with the file `writePointsToDb.php` (the file doesn't exist yet).

When communicating with a PHP file we can add a JavaScript object whose data is added to the request. The transmitted data can then be read by the PHP script. In *lines 83-87*, we form an object that holds three properties: *lat, lon,* and *name*.

The callback function remains rather simple this time—either the save was successful and we clear the input mask and show a success message or the save failed and we notify user of the error.

```
76      function saveToDb() {
77
78          var latInput = document.getElementById('latInput').value;
79          var lonInput = document.getElementById('lonInput').value;
80          var nameInput = document.getElementById('nameInput').value;
81
82          $.post('php/writePointsToDb.php',
83            {
84              lat: latInput,
85              lon: lonInput,
86              name: nameInput
87            },
88            function(data) {
89
90              if (data === 'success') {
91
92                  document.getElementById('latInput').value = '';
93                  document.getElementById('lonInput').value = '';
94
95                  document.getElementById('nameInput').value = '';
96                  document.getElementById('status').innerHTML = 'Saving
                        successful!';
97
98              } else {
99
```

```
100                document.getElementById('status').innerHTML = 'Error!';
101
102            }
103        }
104      );
105
106    }
107
108    document.getElementById('btnSave').onclick = saveToDb;
```

Finally, we need to create writePointsToDb.php and populate it with logic. After reading the connection parameters from the config file we extract the data that was transmitted along with the request. The JavaScript object that was transmitted is turned into an associative array in PHP and is automatically stored in a variable called $_POST.

In *lines 11-13* below, we read the values that have been transmitted. Note that the keys we request correspond to the ones we defined in the JavaScript object.

This time too, we form an SQL statement in a string and send it to the database. Note that we form this string in a slightly different manner and use the pg_query_params function instead of pg_query. When using values that are supplied by users you should always use pg_query_params because it deals with strings containing quotes, and most importantly, it protects against SQL injection attacks.

pg_query_params assigns elements in an array to placeholders in a string. These placeholders are always composed of the $ sign and a number which corresponds to an element in the array.

```
1   <?php
2
3   $config = include('config.php');
4
5   $server = $config['server'];
6   $username = $config['username'];
7   $password = $config['password'];
8   $database = $config['database'];
9   $port = $config['port'];
10
11  $lat = $_POST['lat'];
12  $lon = $_POST['lon'];
13  $name = $_POST['name'];
14
15  $dbconn = pg_connect("host=$server dbname=$database user=$username
16  password=$password port=$port") or die('error');
17
```

```
18   $query = "INSERT INTO cities (name, lat, lon) VALUES ($1, $2, $3)";
19   $params = array($name, $lat, $lon);
20   $result = pg_query_params($dbconn, $query, $params) or die("error");
21
22   echo "success";
23
24   pg_free_result($result);
25
26   pg_close($dbconn);
27
28   ?>
```

Go ahead and refresh the application we created in the previous recipe and notice that the newly added point is available. Feel free to combine both examples into a single application.

13.5 Enabling PostGIS and Setting up a Spatial Table

So far we haven't worked with actual geometries. The point coordinates were stored as numbers in a column and we used these coordinates to create a layer in Leaflet, but the database doesn't know this—to the database the coordinates remain simple numbers. Now we'd like to work with true geometries.

A PostgreSQL database isn't spatial by default, even if you installed PostGIS. PostGIS needs to be individually enabled for each database.

To add PostGIS to your database, click the SQL button in pgAdmin and run the following query:

```
CREATE EXTENSION postgis;
```

After a few seconds your database should be spatially enabled.

How can we tell? Let's look at some details.

In PostGIS, coordinate systems are referred to as SRS (spatial reference system). Other software might use the CRS (coordinate reference system) abbreviation. Both refer to the same thing.

In pgAdmin You'll notice that postgis now shows up under Extensions—the database now has a lot of spatial functions and an extra table holding coordinate system definitions was added to the database (figures 13.10 through 13.12, on the next page).

Figure 13.10: The newly added Post-GIS extension

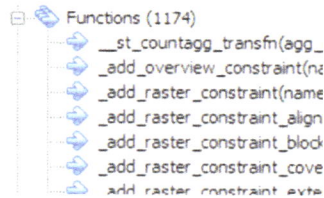

Figure 13.11: Spatial functions

Figure 13.12: The table holding coordinate system information

Now that our database is spatially enabled we can import a geographic dataset. In the data folder for this chapter you'll find the dataset africa.shp. Adding a shapefile to a PostGIS database could not be easier—just click the Plugin button and select *The Shapefile and DBF Loader* (fig. 13.13):

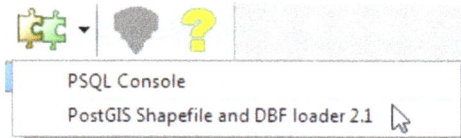

Figure 13.13: Shapefile and DBF Loader

The plugin will open as a popup and you can search your computer by clicking *Add File* (fig. 13.14, on the next page). The imported shapefile will be stored as a table. In the interface, specify the table name (by default it takes the shapefile name) and make sure to enter the correct SRID. The spatial reference ID is always an EPSG code and it is essential that you enter the correct code or the geometry will not end up in the right spot. The Africa dataset uses EPSG:4326, so we enter 4326.

In PostGIS, both geometries and attributes are stored in the same table. The geometry column is usually called geom. If you stumble upon older examples or tutorials, the column is often named the_geom. In the end, it doesn't matter what you name this column, as it really is just a name, but for consistency it is recommended to call it geom.

Click Import and you should see the new table (fig. 13.15, on the following page).

Figure 13.14: Adding a shapefile

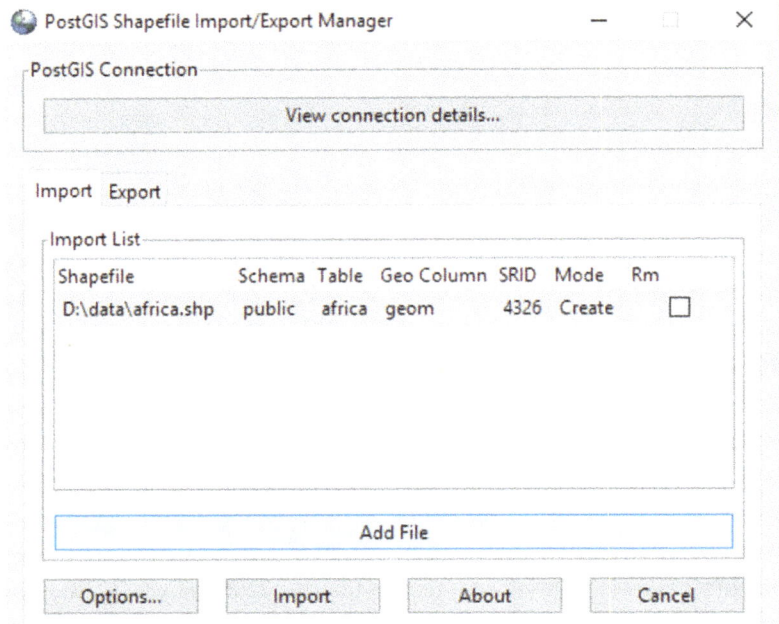

Figure 13.15: The newly imported table

Let's proceed to the next recipe and add this table to Leaflet.

> You can also import data into your database from the command line using shp2pgsql which comes with PostGIS, and ogr2ogr, one of the GDAL/OGR utilities (see https://gdal.org/ogr2ogr.html).

13.6   Building a GeoJSON from a PostGIS Table

Adding the Africa layer to a Leaflet map can be accomplished by first turning it into GeoJSON in PHP and then sending it to the browser. First create a PHP file that has the same setup as the previous ones. The only thing we change is the query and how the result of the query is treated.

Lines 16-23 in the following code select all features from the `africa` table and return them as a GeoJSON feature collection. Setting up the query is a little more work and explaining it line by line is beyond the scope of this book. If you aren't a regular PostGIS user then know that you can easily reuse this query by changing the table name (africa), its alias (a), and the columns you want to return (admin, pop_est, iso_a3).

In *lines 27-31* we loop through the result line by line and turn each line into a JSON.

```
16   $query = "SELECT row_to_json(fc)
17   FROM (
18     SELECT 'FeatureCollection' As type, array_to_json(array_agg(f)) As
            features
19     FROM (SELECT 'Feature' As type,
20     ST_AsGeoJSON(a.geom, 4)::json As geometry,
21     row_to_json((SELECT l FROM (SELECT admin, pop_est, iso_a3) As l))
            As properties
22       FROM africa As a ) As f
23   ) As fc;";
24
25   $result = pg_query($query) or die('query error');
26
27   while ($line = pg_fetch_array($result, null, PGSQL_ASSOC)) {
28     foreach ($line as $col_value) {
29       echo json_encode($col_value);
30     }
31   }
```

Now in the JavaScript part of your application, write a post request to call the PHP file and get the result. Note that we are dealing with a JSON in a JSON so we need to run `JSON.parse` twice.

```
39       $.post('php/createGeoJsonFromDb.php', function(response) {
40
41         var geojson = JSON.parse(JSON.parse(response));
42
43         L.geoJSON(geojson, {
44
45           onEachFeature: function(feature, layer) {
46             var props = feature.properties;
47             var name = props.admin;
48             var pop = props.pop_est;
49             var iso = props.iso_a3;
50
51             layer.bindPopup(
```

```
52                    '<b>Name</b>: ' + name + '<br>'
53               +  '<b>Population</b>: ' + pop + '<br>'
54               +  '<b>ISO Code</b>: ' + iso + '<br>'
55            );
56        }
57
58      }).addTo(map);
59
60    }
61
62    );
```

13.7   Building a GeoJSON from a Nonspatial Table

You can also manually build an entire GeoJSON without using Post-GIS functions, such as ST_AsGeoJSON. This comes in handy when your database doesn't support spatial data types (i.e. PostGIS isn't installed or enabled), when you are working with a database management system for which spatial extensions don't exist, or when your coordinates are stored as numbers, instead of actual geometries.

Let's select all entries from the cities table and iterate through the result to build a feature collection:

```
16   $query = "SELECT * FROM cities";
17
18   $result = pg_query($query) or die('query error');
19
20   $geojson = array(
21     'type'      => 'FeatureCollection',
22     'features'  => array()
23   );
24
25   while ($line = pg_fetch_array($result, null, PGSQL_ASSOC)) {
26     $feature = array(
27       'type' => 'Feature',
28       'geometry' => array(
29         'type' => 'Point',
30         'coordinates' => array(
31           (float)$line['lon'],
32           (float)$line['lat']
33         )
34       ),
35       'properties' => $line
36     );
```

```
37    array_push($geojson['features'], $feature);
38  }
39
40  echo json_encode($geojson);
```

The JavaScript is straightforward as always. Request the file and turn the result into a GeoJSON layer:

```
38      $.post('php/geoJsonFromNonspatialTable.php', function(data) {
39
40        var geojson = JSON.parse(data);
41
42        L.geoJSON(geojson, {
43
44          onEachFeature: function(feature, layer) {
45
46            layer.bindPopup(feature.properties.name);
47
48          }
49
50        }).addTo(map);
51
52      });
```

13.8   Running Spatial Functions

If you looked at the Turf chapter you know that a lot of geoprocessing can be done in the browser without a server-side infrastructure. Once the data becomes large, however, you might notice that your browser isn't handling the algorithms too well. Often, you might simply want to use data that is stored somewhere else, not at the client.

In this recipe we will click on the map and send the click coordinate to PostGIS, where we are going to generate a buffer that is then returned to the browser. For functionality like this we could use Turf, but let's use a simple example as a proof of concept.

First we write a click handler that sends the latitude and longitude of each click to a PHP file and, after getting a response, builds a GeoJSON layer:

```
38      map.on('click', function(e) {
39
40        var lat = e.latlng.lat;
```

```
41          var lon = e.latlng.lng;
42
43          $.post('php/buffer.php', {
44              clickLat: lat,
45              clickLon: lon
46          }, function(data) {
47
48              var geojson = JSON.parse(JSON.parse(data));
49
50              L.geoJSON(geojson, {color: 'green', weight: 2}).addTo(map);
51
52          });
53
54      });
```

In the PHP file we then build a PostGIS query that returns a 200 meter buffer around a point. The point is dynamically created based on the parameters the file receives.

```
32  $lat = $_POST['clickLat'];
33  $lon = $_POST['clickLon'];
34
35  $dbconn = pg_connect("host=$server dbname=$database user=$username
36  password=$password port=$port") or die('connection error');
37
38  $query = "SELECT ST_AsGeoJSON(ST_Buffer(ST_GeomFromText(
39          'POINT($lon $lat)', 4326)::geography, 250), 5);";
40
41  $result = pg_query($query) or die('query error');
42
43  while ($line = pg_fetch_array($result, null, PGSQL_ASSOC)) {
44    foreach ($line as $col_value) {
45      echo json_encode($col_value);
46    }
47  }
48
49  pg_free_result($result);
50
51  pg_close($dbconn);
```

Note that this example neither reads nor writes to a table but nevertheless uses PostGIS functions.

13.9   Getting Data from a Python File

If you prefer Python to PHP, the above examples can also be achieved using Python. Since Python has become one of the most used languages in GIS development for automating tasks and writing plugins, there is a chance that you have some scripts that you'd like to connect to a web application. This can be done fairly easily.

Unlike PHP, Python isn't installed on most web servers, so make sure to install it first.

Second, once it has been installed, a script has to be saved in a directory that allows CGI. If you are using XAMPP you need to place your Python files in the `cgi-bin` directory. If you are using any other setup, make sure to first find your CGI folder. If you cannot find it, there is no need to worry, as technically any folder can be adjusted in a server's configuration to make it a CGI folder.

Let's place a Python file in the `cgi-bin` folder. Name the file:

```
readFromPythonFile.py:
```

```
1   #!/Python27/python
2   print("Content-type: application/text")
3   print('')
4   print('A message from a Python file!')
```

The only thing this script does is print a message. While PHP uses echo, in Python you use `print`. Notice the blank line we're printing. HTTP requests require the header and the body (the actual content we are transmitting) to be separated by a blank line.

Once the Python file is ready we can hook it up to an AJAX request:

```
12      $.post('../../cgi-bin/readFromPythonFile.py', function(data) {
13
14        console.log(data);
15
16      });
```

Load the application and see that the message from the Python file is logged.

13.10   Reading Data from a PostgreSQL Database with Python

Let's use Python to do what we did in recipe 13.3, Reading Data from a PostgreSQL Database, on page 291.

In *lines 2-3* below, we import two modules: json and psycopg2. The json module is a built-in module that we'll use to format the result of the query as a JSON. The psycopg2 module is an external module that needs to be installed first. It is used to connect to a PostgreSQL database and send queries to it.

Using psycopg2 is easy. You first connect to a database (*lines 5-6*) and then create a cursor. The cursor is the element that lets you communicate with a database and executes queries, as well as fetch the query result.

In *lines 10-14* we define a select query as a string, just like we did in PHP, and then we use the cursor to execute the query and fetch its results.

Finally, we iterate through the result, each iteration containing one row from the table. The indices of the columns correspond to the order of the columns in the select statement. In each iteration we build a dictionary named city that holds the name, latitude, and longitude. We then add the dictionary to the response list that we created before the loop.

We proceed to close the connection (*line 26*) and then print the result. Since we are returning a JSON we define a JSON header. The request body simply contains the response list, which we encode as a JSON, so it can be transmitted.

```
1    #!/Python27/python
2    import json
3    import psycopg2
4
5    connection = psycopg2.connect(host="localhost", port="5432",
6    user="postgres", password="postgres",database="leaflet_cookbook")
7
8    cursor = connection.cursor()
9
```

```
10   query = "SELECT gid, name, lat, lon FROM cities;"
11
12   cursor.execute(query)
13
14   rows = cursor.fetchall()
15
16   response = []
17
18   for row in rows:
19       gid = row[0]
20       name = row[1]
21       lat = float(row[2])
22       lon = float(row[3])
23       city = {'name': name, 'lat': lat, 'lon': lon}
24       response.append(city)
25
26   connection.close()
27
28   print("Content-type: application/json")
29   print('')
30   print(json.JSONEncoder().encode(response))
```

Finally, we write an AJAX request that requests the Python file and builds markers from its result:

```
38       $.post('../../cgi-bin/readPointsFromDb.py', function(data) {
39
40         var group = L.featureGroup().addTo(map);
41
42         for (var i = 0; i < data.length; i++) {
43
44           var name = data[i]['name'];
45           var lat = data[i]['lat'];
46           var lon = data[i]['lon'];
47
48           L.marker([lat, lon])
49           .bindPopup(name)
50           .addTo(group);
51
52         }
53
54         map.fitBounds(group.getBounds());
55
56       });
```

13.11   Writing Data to a PostgreSQL Database with Python

The JavaScript in this recipe is identical to that in the PHP recipe:

```
76      function saveToDb() {
77
78        var latInput = document.getElementById('latInput').value;
79        var lonInput = document.getElementById('lonInput').value;
80        var nameInput = document.getElementById('nameInput').value;
81
82        $.post('../../cgi-bin/writePointsToDb.py',
83          {
84            lat: latInput,
85            lon: lonInput,
86            name: nameInput
87          },
88          function(data) {
89            console.log(data)
90          }
91        );
92
93      }
```

What differs in this recipe is that the Python file receives data from
the browser. In the AJAX request we send lat, lon, and name to the
Python file. Since we'd like to write these to the database, we need
to extract them from the request, similar to what we did in PHP.
To do this we import the built-in cgi module (*line 2*), and call the
FieldStorage method. From the field storage, which we assign to
the variable data, we then extract parameters using the getValue
method. Note that we convert the coordinates to a float.

Next we connect to the database, write an insert query, and execute
it. When using psycopg2 to change something in a database (e.g.
add columns, write values) it is important that we call the commit
method before closing the connection or the changes will not be
saved.

Since we don't return any data from the database, we simply return
a success message.

```
1  #!/Python27/python
2  import cgi
3  import psycopg2
4
5  data = cgi.FieldStorage()
6  lat = float(data.getvalue("lat", "error"))
7  lon = float(data.getvalue("lon", "error"))
8  name = data.getvalue("name", "error")
```

```
 9
10   connection = psycopg2.connect(host="localhost", port="5432",
11   user="postgres", password="postgres", database="leaflet_cookbook")
12
13   cursor = connection.cursor()
14
15   query = """
16         INSERT INTO cities (name, lat, lon)
17         VALUES ('{0}', {1}, {2});
18         """.format(name, lat, lon)
19
20   cursor.execute(query)
21
22   connection.commit()
23
24   connection.close()
25
26   print("Content-type: application/text")
27   print('')
28   print('success')
```

14 *Advanced Topics*

Contents

In this chapter we'll have a look at some recipes that don't directly fit in any other chapter or that are using functionalities that go beyond using Leaflet by itself. We'll also take a look at three Leaflet plugins.

Whenever you are looking for functionality that isn't mentioned in the documentation, there is a good chance there is a plugin that does exactly what you need. There is a plugin for practically everything, from measuring and digitizing to searching addresses and calculating routes. Therefore, before writing a lot of code, have a look at the official plugin repository:

```
https://leafletjs.com/plugins.html
```

Since plugins extend Leaflet it is important that you include them in the application after including Leaflet.

14.1 *Dragging and Dropping Data to the Map*

Let's create an application that allows us to drag and drop GeoJSON files on the map.

First we create a file reader, which is used to read the dropped file and convert it to a GeoJSON layer. In *lines 39-53* we assign a function to the file reader's *onload* property. This function is executed once the reader obtains a file, which from then on is stored in the reader's *result* property. In our case we know this is going to be a GeoJSON file, stored as text, so we parse the content before creating a layer and adding it to the map. We also request the layer's bounding box, so the map zooms to it right after adding it.

```
37      fileReader = new FileReader();
38
39      fileReader.onload = function() {
40
41        var fileContent = fileReader.result;
42
43        var geojson = JSON.parse(fileContent);
44
45        var layer = L.geoJSON(geojson);
46
47        layer.addTo(map);
48
49        var bounds = layer.getBounds();
50
51        map.fitBounds(bounds);
52
53      }
```

But when is the file read? Before the file can be read we need to handle what happens when users both drag the file over the map and drop it. For both cases we define a function.

The function that handles the drag event simply blocks all default browser behavior and makes sure the file is copied once the user drops it:

```
55      function onFileDragOver(e) {
56
57        e.stopPropagation();
58        e.preventDefault();
59        e.dataTransfer.dropEffect = 'copy';
60
61      }
```

The function that handles the dropping event also first takes care of ignoring defaults and then reads the dropped files from the event object. Since multiple files can be dropped at once we are given an array. Assuming that users only drop a single file at a time we access the array's first element, which we then pass to the file reader's `readAsText` method. This method triggers the function we assigned to the *onload* property.

```
63      function onFileDrop(e) {
64
65         e.stopPropagation();
66         e.preventDefault();
67
68         var files = e.dataTransfer.files;
69         var uploadedFile = files[0];
70         fileReader.readAsText(uploadedFile);
71
72      }
```

Finally, we need to define which element files are allowed to be dropped to so we can hook the `onFileDragOver` and `onFileDrop` functions up to this element. In our case that element is the map.

```
74      var dropDiv = document.getElementById('map');
75      dropDiv.addEventListener('dragover', onFileDragOver, false);
76      dropDiv.addEventListener('drop', onFileDrop, false);
```

14.2   Adding a .txt or .csv File to the Map

This recipe needs to be run on a server.

Let's save the following data as a `.txt` or a `.csv` file and store it in a folder called `data`:

```
31.227,121.492,Shanghai
-46.85,-125.283,R'lyeh
18.0131,-76.791,Kingston
35.704,139.735,Tokyo
```

You cannot directly read the files but you can form a request and then read their content. This is easily done using jQuery. In the following snippet we read the file's content into a string and then use the `split` method to create an array that holds each individual line. Then we simply loop through the array, and since each line is now stored as a string, we split each line again, but this time according to the delimiter that separates the latitude, longitude and name:

```
37      $.get('data/cities.txt', function(data) {
```

```
38
39          var lines = data.split('\n');
40
41          for (var i = 0; i < lines.length; i++) {
42
43            var singleLine = lines[i].split(',');
44            var lat = parseFloat(singleLine[0]);
45            var lon = parseFloat(singleLine[1]);
46            var name = singleLine[2];
47            L.marker([lat, lon]).bindPopup(name).addTo(map);
48
49          }
50
51        });
```

Note that we convert the coordinates to a float as they are stored as a string.

This recipe needs to be run on a server.

14.3   Adding More File Formats (KML, GPX, WKT, etc.)

Sometimes you need to move beyond using GeoJSON, or you simply don't want to spend the time transforming your existing data into a GeoJSON. That's where the *omnivore* plugin comes in. It lets you load the following file formats:

- CSV (.csv)
- GeoJSON (.geojson)
- GPX (.gpx)
- KML (.kml)
- WKT (.wkt)
- TopoJSON (.topojson)

Using the plugin could not be easier:

```
38        omnivore.kml('data/test.kml').addTo(map);
```

14.4   Loading a .geojson File

Loading a GeoJSON saved in a JavaScript file has the advantage that it can be directly added to your page's head and doesn't require further requests. Loading a .geojson file directly is possible too, but you need to write an AJAX call to request it. Using pure JavaScript to write such a call requires a few lines of code, so you are better off using a framework or library that simplifies AJAX requests. With jQuery this is so easy the following snippet doesn't need further explanation:

```
36        $.getJSON('data/africaPoints.geojson', function(geojson) {
37
38          L.geoJSON(geojson).addTo(map);
39
40        });
```

14.5   Saving Datasets to a File

You can write files directly in the browser, without ever having to communicate with a server. Although writing files should work by default, the implementation sometimes differs. To get this running as quickly as possible we are going to use a library called `FileSaver.js`, which takes care of cross-browser issues.

In this example we are going to click on the map to create markers and then export them to a GeoJSON file.

First download `FileSaver.js` and add it to your application's head: `https://github.com/eligrey/FileSaver.js/`

If you get an error message that an unexpected token *export* is encountered and you are not familiar with how to fix this, then use the `FileSaver.js` file that you can find under the code files for this chapter.

Let's first create an export button and an input field that lets users specify the name of the file that is going to be exported:

```
21        <input type='button' value='Export to file' id='btnExport'>
22        <input type='text' id='txtFileName'>.geojson
```

Now, let's register a click event on the map and create a marker on each click. We collect the markers in a feature group so we can easily bundle them to a GeoJSON feature collection. This is more convenient than having to iterate through the map's layers and create the feature collection manually.

```
37        var group = L.featureGroup();
38
39        group.addTo(map);
40
41        map.on('click', function(e) {
42
43          var marker = L.marker([e.latlng.lat, e.latlng.lng]);
44
45          marker.addTo(group);
46
47        });
```

In our export function we read the text input value so we can use it as a file name. In case it is empty we'll assign it a default name (export). Then we use the toGeoJSON method to export the entire group to a GeoJSON feature collection, which we then transform to a string so we can easily write it to a file. Writing the file comes down to only two lines of code, which consist of defining the file's content as a Blob and then calling the saveAs function, which is exposed by *FileSaver.js*. The saveAs function receives the content we'd like to write as well as the file name and its ending:

```
49        function exportToFile() {
50
51          var fileName = document.getElementById('txtFileName').value;
52
53          if (fileName.length === 0) {
54
55            fileName = 'export'
56
57          }
58
59          var markersGeoJson = group.toGeoJSON();
60
61          var markersGeoJsonString = JSON.stringify(markersGeoJson);
62
63          var fileContent = new Blob([markersGeoJsonString], { type: "
                text/plain;charset=utf-8" });
64
65          saveAs(fileContent, fileName + '.geojson');
66
67        }
68
69        document.getElementById('btnExport').onclick = exportToFile;
```

14.6 Transforming Coordinates into Different Coordinate Systems

The Proj4.js library lets you transform data between almost every known coordinate system. Should your application require coordinate transformations, Proj4 is your best bet.

Using `proj4.defs` you define a coordinate system name and parameters. To find the parameters you should have a look at `http://spatialreference.org/` or `http://epsg.io` to find projection parameters for practically any coordinate system.

Once defined, you call the `proj4` function and pass three parameters: the original coordinate system, the one you want to transform to, and an array holing an x and y value to be transformed.

The following example extracts coordinates on mouse move, transforms them to Web Mercator, and then displays them in a div.

```
49    proj4.defs("EPSG:4326", "+proj=longlat +ellps=WGS84 +datum=
         WGS84 +no_defs");
50    proj4.defs("EPSG:3857", "+proj=merc +a=6378137 +b=6378137\
51    +lat_ts=0.0 +lon_0=0.0 +x_0=0.0 +y_0=0 +k=1.0 +units=m +
         nadgrids=@null +wktext  +no_defs");
52
53    map.on('mousemove', function(e) {
54
55      var lat = e.latlng.lat;
56      var lon = e.latlng.lng;
57
58      var trans = proj4(proj4('EPSG:4326'), proj4('EPSG:3857'), [
           lon, lat]);
59
60      var x = trans[0].toFixed(0);
61      var y = trans[1].toFixed(0);
62
63      document.getElementById('coordDiv').innerHTML = x + ', ' + y;
64
65    });
```

Note that Proj4 defines EPSG:4326 and EPSG:3857 by default, so no need to actually define them; we only did so for the example.

14.7 Clustering Markers

This is a common scenario: your map includes so many markers that they overlap and you can barely distinguish them (fig. 14.1). Fixing this problem could be approached by using a smaller customized icon or by using circles and circle markers. But sometimes even that won't work. The Leaflet.markercluster plugin intelligently clusters nearby markers into groups and expands these groups when zooming in to them.

You create a cluster by instantiating L.markerClusterGroup() whose usage resembles working with layer and feature groups. First you create the group and then you add data to the group. Don't forget to add the actual group to the map (fig. 14.2, on the next page).

```
40    var points = L.geoJSON(africaPoints);
41
42    var markerCluster = L.markerClusterGroup();
43
44    points.addTo(markerCluster);
45
46    markerCluster.addTo(map);
```

Figure 14.1: Before clustering

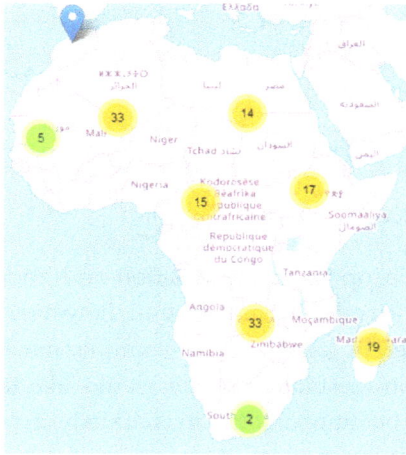

Figure 14.2: After clustering

14.8 Grouping Layers in a Layer Control

Once your map includes a larger number of layers, the layer switcher can become hard to deal with. The groupedlayercontrol plugin lets you define groups in the layer control so you can classify data. This greatly helps with readability, as you see in the image below (fig. 14.3). Using it is very simple. Instead of passing an object with key-value pairs to the layer control you create a wrapper object whose keys are the group names that will be displayed, and its values are objects holding layers.

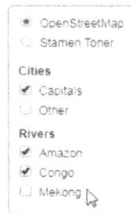

Figure 14.3: Grouped layer in a layer control

```
80    var groups = {
81      'Cities': {
82        'Capitals': capitals,
83        'Other': other
84      },
85      'Rivers': {
86        'Amazon': amazonRiver,
```

```
87              'Congo': congoRiver,
88              'Mekong': mekongRiver
89          }
90      };
91
92      L.control.groupedLayers(basemaps, groups).addTo(map);
```

14.9   Persistence

Normally the map opens at the position and zoom level that has been defined in the code. It can be useful, however, to let users open the map at a different location. For example, maybe you found an interesting spot on the map and you would like to share it with a friend. It would be cumbersome to manually explain to someone how to get to that exact spot—it would be much more convenient to share a link that includes the position and the zoom level.

The pound sign can be used to append to the base URL of a web page, for example:

```
application.html#52.50452,13.40607,10
```

When navigating to the web page in a browser you still find the right page, but anything past the pound sign is extra information and can influence what happens right after the page is loaded. Often this information includes an HTML element's ID , for instance, and the web page then jumps to a specific part of the website. In our case we'd like to add the latitude, longitude, and zoom level.

To get or set the part of the URL that starts with the hash you can simply call `document.location.hash`.

Let's first write a function that sets the hash to a comma delimited string, including the latitude and longitude of the map center, as well as its zoom level. The function should be called anytime the user moves the map or zooms:

```
33      function updateUrl() {
34
35          var center = map.getCenter();
36          var lat = center.lat.toFixed(5);
```

```
37            var lon = center.lng.toFixed(5);
38
39            var zoom = map.getZoom();
40
41            var view = lat + ',' + lon + ',' + zoom;
42
43            document.location.hash = view;
44
45        }
46
47        map.on('move', updateUrl);
48        map.on('zoom', updateUrl);
```

After moving and zooming you now see that the hash of the URL is constantly updated.

The only thing left to do is take care of the hash when the page is loaded.

The following function reads the hash and checks whether it is empty or not. If it is empty there is no need to keep going, if it isn't empty, we assume that it contains the information we need. Should you include this in a stable application, you would add further checks, such as if the hash fits a specific pattern, etc.

Once we have access to the hash, we split it into an array, using a comma as the delimiter. Note that the first element in the array includes the pound sign, so we call substring to return a subset of the string that starts at the second character. We then pass these pieces of information to the setView method:

We call the function right after defining it so it is executed when the page loads.

```
50        function setViewFromUrl() {
51
52          var hash = document.location.hash;
53
54          if (hash.length !== 0) {
55
56            var splitHash = hash.split(',');
57
58            var lat = splitHash[0].substring(1);
59            var lon = splitHash[1];
```

```
60              var zoom = splitHash[2];
61
62              map.setView([lat, lon], zoom);
63
64          }
65
66      }
67
68      setViewFromUrl();
```

This is only a simple example that includes the map view, but you can add much more to the page hash, such as the current basemap or which layers are checked in the layer control.

15 Index

Books from Locate Press

QGIS Map Design - 2nd Edition

LEARN HOW TO USE QGIS 3 TO TAKE YOUR CARTOGRAPHIC PRODUCTS TO THE HIGHEST LEVEL.

QGIS 3.4 opens up exciting new possibilities for creating beautiful and compelling maps!

Building on the first edition, the authors take you step-by-step through the process of using the latest map design tools and techniques in QGIS 3. With numerous new map designs and completely overhauled workflows, this second edition brings you up to speed with current cartographic technology and trends.

See how QGIS continues to surpass the cartographic capabilities of other geoware available today with its data-driven overrides, flexible expression functions, multitudinous color tools, blend modes, and atlasing capabilities. A prior familiarity with basic QGIS capabilities is assumed. All example data and project files are included.

Get ready to launch into the next generation of map design!

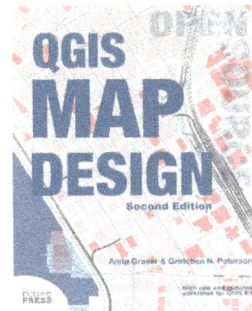

The PyQGIS Programmer's Guide

WELCOME TO THE WORLD OF PYQGIS, THE BLENDING OF QUANTUM GIS AND PYTHON TO EXTEND AND ENHANCE YOUR OPEN SOURCE GIS TOOLBOX.

With PyQGIS you can write scripts and plugins to implement new features and perform automated tasks.

This book is updated to work with the next generation of QGIS—version 3.x. After a brief introduction to Python 3, you'll learn how to understand the QGIS Application Programmer Interface (API), write scripts, and build a plugin.

The book is designed to allow you to work through the examples as you go along. At the end of each chapter you will find a set of exercises you can do to enhance your learning experience.

The PyQGIS Programmer's Guide is compatible with the version 3.0 API released with QGIS 3.x and will work for the entire 3.x series of releases.

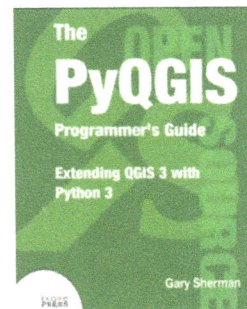

pgRouting: A Practical Guide

WHAT IS PGROUTING?

It's a PostgreSQL extension for developing network routing applications and doing graph analysis.

Interested in pgRouting? If so, chances are you already use PostGIS, the spatial extender for the PostgreSQL database management system.

So when you've got PostGIS, why do you need pgRouting? PostGIS is a great tool for molding geometries and doing proximity analysis, however it falls short when your proximity analysis involves constrained paths such as driving along a road or biking along defined paths.

This book will both get you started with pgRouting and guide you into routing, data fixing and costs, as well as using with QGIS and web applications.

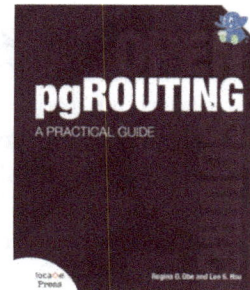

Geospatial Power Tools

EVERYONE LOVES POWER TOOLS!

The GDAL and OGR apps are the power tools of the GIS world—best of all, they're free.

The utilities include tools for examining, converting, transforming, building, and analysing data. This book is a collection of the GDAL and OGR documentation, but also includes new content designed to help guide you in using the utilities to solve your current data problems.

Inside you'll find a quick reference for looking up the right syntax and example usage quickly. The book is divided into three parts: *Workflows and examples*, *GDAL raster utilities*, and *OGR vector utilities*.

Once you get a taste of the power the GDAL/OGR suite provides, you'll wonder how you ever got along without them.

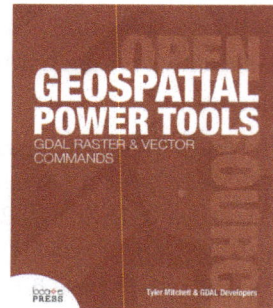

Discover QGIS

GET MAPPING WITH DISCOVER QGIS!

Get your hands on the award winning GeoAcademy exercises in a convenient workbook format.

The GeoAcademy is the first ever GIS curriculum based on a national standard—the U.S. Department of Labor's Geospatial Competency Model—a hierarchical model of the knowledge, skills, and abilities needed to work as a GIS professional in today's marketplace.

The GeoAcademy material in this workbook has been updated for use with QGIS v2.14, Inkscape v0.91, and GRASS GIS v7.0.3. This is the most up-to-date version of the GeoAcademy curriculum. To aid in learning, all exercise data includes solution files.

The workbook is edited by one of the lead GeoAcademy authors, Kurt Menke, a highly experienced FOSS4G educator.

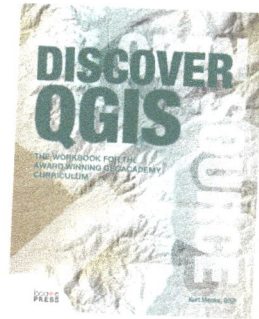

See these books and more at http://locatepress.com